THE FEW

THE BATTLE OF BRITAIN started on 10 July 1940, ending 16 weeks later on 31 October 1940. The Luftwaffe's intention was to destroy Fighter Command, domination of the skies being crucial to Hitler's invasion plan. During that fateful summer, young RAF fighter pilots, flying Spitfires and Hurricanes, were scrambled time and time again to face insuperable odds – and the Luftwaffe was, until that point, unbeaten. The enemy fighter pilots, in their brightly painted Messerschmitt 109s, were the most experienced in the world. But somehow the RAF pilots, fighting desperately in a spider's web of intricate vapour trails, and with sudden and violent death an ever present companion, prevailed. Afterwards, Churchill paid homage to them all: 'Never in the field of human conflict has so much been owed by so many to so few'. A legend had been born.

Dilip Sarkar has been fascinated by the Battle of Britain since childhood and began seriously researching the subject in the 1970s. He wrote thousands of letters and travelled extensively over the UK interviewing the fabled 'Few'. Over the last 30 years he has interviewed more Battle of Britain survivors than any other author and his archive is a unique collection of veterans' 'voices'. In this new book Dilip Sarkar chronicles the Battle of Britain from start to finish drawing extensively from his interviews with pilots.

ABOUT THE AUTHOR

DILIP SARKAR has written over twenty books on the Battle of Britain, including the only biographical works formally endorsed by the families of both Group Captain Sir Douglas Bader and Air Vice-Marshal Johnnie Johnson. In 2003, Dilip was made an MBE for services to aviation history, and in 2006 he was elected to the Fellowship of the Royal Historical Society. He lives in Worcester.

THE FEW

The Story of the Battle of Britain
in the Words of the Pilots

DILIP SARKAR
MBE FRHistS

AMBERLEY

For my wife, Karen

This edition first published 2010

Amberley Publishing Plc
Cirencester Road, Chalford,
Stroud, Gloucestershire, GL6 8PE

www.amberley-books.com

ISBN 978 1 4456 0050 5

Typesetting and Origination by Fonthill
Printed in Great Britain

CONTENTS

ALSO BY DILIP SARKAR

FOREWORD BY LADY BADER

I have known Dilip Sarkar for many years now, his diligent and tenacious research into the flying career of my late husband, Group Captain Sir Douglas Bader, and his pilots enormously and immediately impressed me. The Battle of Britain story, I know, Dilip finds greatly inspirational, and over the last thirty years he has sought out and interviewed or corresponded with numerous survivors worldwide. Many of these were not famous combatants like Douglas, but those who formed the unsung backbone of Fighter Command in 1940. Without Dilip's patient recording and collation of their memories, many of these survivors would not have left behind a permanent record of their experiences. That fact alone justifies Dilip's dedication to his chosen quest.

The Few represents an important benchmark in the written record of the Battle of Britain, crammed as it is with first-hand accounts which provide an insight into the summer of 1940 as experienced by those who survived: sometimes moving, always dramatic. My late husband once wrote that for him the Battle of Britain was a 'kaleidoscope of memories', which, effectively, is what this book is. Marking as it does the Battle of Britain's 70th anniversary year, this book makes compelling reading and I hope it achieves the success that the effort put into its creation deserves.

Lady Bader OBE

AUTHOR'S NOTE

The aviation minded reader will notice that I have referred to German Messerschmitt fighters by the abbreviation 'Me' (not 'Bf', which is also correct), or simply by their numeric designation, such as '109' or '110'. This not only reads better but is authentic; during the Battle of Britain, Keith Lawrence, a New Zealander, flew Spitfires and once said to me, 'To us they were just 109s or 110s, simple.'

In another attempt to preserve accuracy, I have also used the original German, wherever possible, regarding terms associated with the Luftwaffe, such as:-

Eichenlaub The Oak Leaves, essentially being a bar to the *Ritterkreuz*

Erprobungsgruppe Experimental group, in the case of *Erprobungsgruppe* 210 skilled precision bombing unit

Expert A fighter 'ace'. Ace status, on both sides, was achieved by destroying five enemy aircraft

Fliegerkorps Airfleet Division

Freie hunt A fighter sweep

Gefechstand Operations headquarters

Gefreiter Aircraftman

Geschwader The whole group, usually of three *gruppen*

Geschwaderkommodore The group leader

Gruppe A wing, usually of three squadrons

Gruppenkeil A wedge formation of bombers, usually made up of vics of three

Gruppenkommandeur The wing commander

Jagdbomber A fighter-bomber, or *Jabo*

Jagdflieger Fighter pilot

Jagdgeschwader Fighter group, abbreviated JG

Jagdwaffe The fighter force

Kampffleiger Bomber aircrew

Kampfgeschwader Bomber group, abbreviated KG

Katchmarek Wingman

Lehrgeschwader Literally a training group, but actually a precision bombing unit, abbreviated LG

Luftflotte Air Fleet

Obergefreiter Leading Aircraftman

Oberkannone The 'Top Gun'

Oberkommando der Wehrmacht (OKW) The German armed forces high command

Ritterkreuz The Knight's Cross of the Iron Cross

Rotte A pair of fighters, comprising leader and wingman, into which the *Schwarm* broke once battle was joined

Schwarm A section of four fighters

Seenotmaschine Air Sea Rescue Aircraft

Stab The staff flight

Staffel A squadron

Staffelkapitän The squadron leader

Störflug Harrassing attacks, usually by lone Ju 88s

Stuka The Ju 87 dive-bomber

Sturkampfgeschwader Dive-bomber group, abbreviated StG

Valhalla Large Formation of Bombers

Vermisst Missing

Zerstörer Literally 'destroyer', the term used for the Me 110

Zerstörergeschwader Destroyer group, abbreviated ZG

Each *geschwader* generally comprised three *gruppen*, each of three *staffeln*. Each *gruppe* is designated by Roman numerals, i.e. III/JG 26 refers to the third *gruppe* of Fighter Group 26. *Staffeln* are identified by numbers, so 7/JG 26 is the 7th *staffel* and belongs to III/JG 26.

Rank comparisons may also be useful:

Unteroffizier Corporal, no aircrew equivalent in Fighter Command

Feldwebel Sergeant

Oberfeldwebel Flight Sergeant

Leutnant Pilot Officer

Oberleutnant Flight Lieutenant

Hauptmann Squadron Leader

Major Wing Commander

Oberst Group Captain.

Many of the survivors whose accounts are included in this book ultimately retired from the RAF with senior, even Air, rank. In this narrative, however, I have used their ranks as per 1940.

This book concentrates on the day fighting, although there was another, separate, battle being fought by night. Forced to operate at night due to such heavy daytime losses, as Britain's nocturnal defences were in their infancy however, the enemy bombers were able to operate at night with impunity. That, though, is another story, as is Bomber Command's early efforts throughout this time, mounting night raids on Germany.

Some 200 years before the Battle of Britain, the poet Thomas Gray composed some lines which were astonishingly prophetic, and which, I think, leads perfectly into this book.

The time will come when thou shall lift up thine eyes
To watch a long-drawn battle in the skies;
While aged peasants, too amazed for words,
Stare at the flying fleets of wondrous birds.
England, so long the mistress of the sea,
Where wind and waves confess her sovereignty;
Her ancient triumphs yet on high shall bear
And reign, the sovereign of the conquered air.

Dilip Sarkar MBE FRHistS

PROLOGUE

The guns fell silent, at last, on 11 November 1918, thus ending the 'Great War' which had consumed the world in flames for four long and miserable years. Afterwards the victorious Allies vowed to make this the 'War to end all wars', and determined to ensure that Germany would never again represent a military threat. At the subsequent Treaty of Versailles in 1919, Germany was, among other things, denied an air force, tanks and submarines, allowed an extremely limited army and navy, deprived of various territories and, having been made to accept full responsibility for causing the war, forced to pay vast sums in reparations. Moreover, the old jingoistic Imperial Germany was removed from the world stage forever, replaced by the Weimar Republic which was naturally seen as merely a liberal puppet controlled by the Allies. German national pride was absolutely shattered, the Versailles *Diktat* hated; far from ensuring a lasting peace, therefore, the Allies actually paved the way for the growth of fascism in Germany and, indeed, had started the countdown to an even greater conflagration: the Second World War of 1939–45.

After Versailles, Britain and France set about disarming, massively reducing the strength of their armed forces, and spending little or nothing on the research into and development of new weapons. Nonetheless, the French, on whose soil much of the First World War had been fought, constructed the 'impregnable' Maginot Line of concrete defences, planned to extend from the Channel coast to beyond the Franco-German border, behind which France would be completely safe from any further German belligerence. America, which in spite of arriving fairly late in the day still suffered immense casualties fighting for the Allied cause, withdrew from events in Europe, pursuing a policy of isolationism. In short each power looked to its own, licking wounds and making good the devastation suffered during intense fighting on land, at sea and, to a degree, in the air.

Air power was, of course, in its infancy: across the Atlantic, the Wright Brothers had only made the first powered flight, at Kittyhawk, on 17 December 1903. During the Great War, aircraft – biplanes – had at first been used in army co-operation roles, largely reconnaissance, fighters being used to protect these scouts; German gas-filled zeppelins, however, bombed British cities and in so doing made clear that air power was to be feared, especially by civilian populations. On 1 April 1918, the British Royal Air Force was born, and in 1921, the 'Father' of this junior service, Marshal of the RAF Sir Hugh Trenchard, stated that:

> It is not necessary for an air force, in order to defeat the enemy nation, to defeat its armed forces first. Air power can dispense with that immediate step, can pass over the enemy navies and armies, and penetrate the air defences and attack direct the centre of production, transportation and communication from which the enemy war effort is maintained. It is on the destruction of enemy industries and above all, in the lowering of morale of enemy nationals caused by bombing that the ultimate victory lies.

'Boom' Trenchard added that: 'The aeroplane is the most offensive weapon that has ever been invented. It is a shockingly bad weapon for defence.' Indeed, Trenchard considered defensive aeroplanes – fighters – necessary only 'to have some defence to keep up the morale of your own people'. This was, however, the man who, when a Major-General in France during the Great War, forbade his aircrew to wear parachutes, believing the life-saving silk umbrellas to be 'bad for morale'.

The British politician Stanley Baldwin, in 1932, said:

> I think it well for the man in the street to realize that there is no power on earth that can protect him from being bombed. Whatever people may tell him, the bomber will always get through. The only defence is offence, which means that you have to kill more women and children more quickly than the enemy, if you want to save yourselves. I just mention that, so that people may realize what is waiting for them when the next war comes.

It is incredible to think that this really was what people in positions of responsibility and power believed at the time: Baldwin talked not of using fighters and other defences to destroy enemy bombers before reaching their target, but instead using bombers to cause greater execution and terror among the enemy's civilian population. With this underpinning mindset that 'the bomber will always get through', even in a climate of precious little spending on armament generally, the bomber force was given priority. One man, however, disagreed, and the free world will forever be in his debt.

Air Marshal Sir Hugh Dowding, Air Member for Research & Development, did not endorse the view that 'the bomber will always get through', or that investing in the bomber force should be a priority. On the contrary, he considered that although the fighter force should not be expanded at the bomber's expense, a powerful bomber force was actually useless unless the fighter force was strong enough to ensure that its commander did not lose a decisive battle before the bomber force commander had the opportunity and time to fight one. According to Dowding, 'Trenchard had forgotten that security of base is an essential prerequisite.' It was fortunate indeed for his country that Dowding not only took this view, but was also prepared to fight anyone, regardless of rank or position, who opposed his single-minded and dedicated efforts to prepare a sound defence for these islands.

During the Great War, Dowding had seen action as first a squadron then wing commander in the Royal Flying Corps, serving under Trenchard. In 1915, Dowding complained to his boss that his squadron had been delivered the wrong size propellers, but Trenchard merely ordered that he must fit and use said airscrews regardless. Subsequently Dowding proved their unsuitability with a test flight in which he was almost killed. Trenchard later wrote that the incident emphasized Dowding's 'self-righteous stubbornness'. Dowding considered the matter 'typical of Trenchard's technical stupidity'. Intellectual, somewhat austere and a spiritualist, Dowding's exterior hid a nerve of steel, a great technical brain, and a single-mindedness of purpose: in the 1930s there could not possibly have been anyone better suited to be Air Member for Research & Development.

In 1933, Adolf Hitler and the Nazis came to power in Germany. Hitler soon denounced Versailles and set about re-arming, at first secretly then in open defiance of the Diktat. As time went on it became increasingly clear that the Führer was on course to restore Germany as a dominant military power. In October 1935, production of Professor Willy Messerschmitt's new single-engined monoplane fighter, the Me 109, was ordered. This fast and highly manoeuverable little aircraft completely outclassed the wood and fabric biplanes in service with the world's air forces and set a new benchmark in performance.

Back in 1930, the Air Ministry had issued a specification for a monoplane fighter to replace the crusty old biplanes with which its squadrons were equipped. This new design had to be capable of being both a day and night-fighter, which could be flown by the average pilot. The requirement was also for a greater speed, an enclosed cockpit and eight machine-guns. Among the British designers working on this project was Supermarine's Reginald Joseph Mitchell, whose sleek, bullet-like, racing seaplanes had already won the coveted Schneider Trophy, a matter of intense national pride. Hawker's Sydney Camm also produced a design, which, like Supermarine's submission, was built around the Rolls-Royce Merlin engine: called the Hurricane, it first flew in November 1935, and was immediately ordered by the Air Ministry. Ominously, however, the Hawker Hurricane was already obsolete: the Me 109 was 30mph faster.

Mitchell's first attempt at producing a Supermarine fighter was an ugly gull-winged monoplane that he knew was not up to Germany's challenge. Although living beneath the shadow of rectal cancer, Mitchell returned to the drawing board and created a revolutionary design: the fuselage was of three sections, the wing's main spar comprised girders of different lengths, the thickest part being at the wing root where most strength was required. The wing leading edges were covered in heavy gauge aluminium, the trailing edges in a lighter covering.

The wings were elliptical, and this forward-thinking construction provided an unparalleled combination of strength and lightness. On 5 March 1936, Mitchell's new fighter – called 'Spitfire' – flew from Eastleigh airfield, near Southampton. Supermarine's chief test pilot, 'Mutt' Summers, made a short but successful flight, after which he told excited onlookers that he did not want any of the aircraft's controls altered in any way. Some interpreted this as Summers meaning that the Spitfire was perfect right from the off, which is clearly ridiculous, but nonetheless from that maiden flight Mitchell's fighter became legendary.

The Hawker Hurricane reached the squadrons in January 1938, production being much easier than the Spitfire, which required new construction techniques and skilled engineers. Camm relied upon a tried and tested construction, leading to the Air Ministry ordering 600 Hurricanes against 300 Spitfires. Although the Hurricane was inferior to the Me 109, at least it was superior to the biplanes which would otherwise have supported the Spitfire force when the time came. Had that scenario come to pass, the RAF pilots' courage would not have been found wanting, but the Me 109 would have swept biplane fighters from the sky with little ado. Dowding, as Air Member for Research & Development, had much to do with commissioning the new designs, and his technical mind was also considering a newfangled science: radar, a defensive weapon every bit as crucial as fighter aircraft.

The RAF air exercises in August 1934, had shown the weakness of the 'early warning system', which depended largely upon the Observer Corps and meant that enemy aircraft could only be detected if they ventured within sight and earshot. Even when practising with the ancient Vickers Virginia, which plodded through the sky at just 80mph at 7,000 feet, the warning provided was inadequate. Acoustic locators had proved of little use, and the Chandler-Adcock system of radio-direction, which allowed aircraft to be plotted and controlled from the ground, relied upon the 'target' aircraft sending regular transmissions – hostile aircraft, however, were unlikely to be so obliging! A more general means of detection was therefore required, but had yet to be discovered, and this became of increasing concern: Mr A.P. Rowe, the Air Ministry's assistant director of scientific research, reported to his chief, Harry Wimperis, that 'unless science finds a new method of assisting air defence, any war within 10 years will be lost'. In 1932, work by the Post Office indicated that aircraft reflected radio signals, this prompting further research by Robert Watson-Watt who, in 1935, submitted his report on the subject. This inspired memorandum identified three areas of research: the re-radiation of aircraft waves (to detect aircraft), radio-telephone communications between fighters and ground controller, and a means of transmitting coded signals from aircraft (so as to identify friend from foe). Immediately recognizing the significance of this detailed study, Wimperis requested £10,000 for further experimental work. Dowding advised caution and requested a practical demonstration: 'Let us first see if the system works,' he said. A month later the scientists sufficiently impressed Dowding and the research went ahead, in great secrecy, on the Suffolk coast. This new technology, together with the new eight-gun monoplane fighters, would soon form the cornerstone of the radar-based system of early warning, interception and control. This was one crucial respect in which Britain was far ahead of Germany's scientists, and for which no accolade is too great for the 'boffins' involved. Radar, in fact, concluded any chance whatsoever that the 'bomber will always get through'.

For more than a decade, all functions of air defence had been overseen by the Air Defence of Great Britain (ADGB), although the Commander-in-Chief of which was responsible for both fighter and bomber forces, a matter which Dowding felt 'ponderous'. With Germany clearly re-arming, the British expansion programme of 1936, saw the creation of five separate commands: Fighter, Bomber, Coastal, Training and Maintenance. Dowding's personal first-hand experience as a fighter pilot during the Great War, together with his involvement in commissioning the Spitfire and Hurricane, and with radar, marked him as the perfect choice for RAF Fighter Command's first Commander-in-Chief. Now he could really get to grips with his vision to ensure 'security of base'. Air Marshal Dowding was fifty-four when he took up his new appointment on 14 July 1936. The new Fighter Command's headquarters was located at Bentley Priory, a large country house situated to the north of London, at Stanmore. There the new Commander-in-Chief discovered some 'lamentable deficiencies to be made good', his immediate task being to create the 'ideal Air Defence System', and his experience to date uniquely equipped him to do so.

Upon formation, Fighter Command comprised two groups, 11 and 12, and for administrative purposes, 22 Army Co-operation Group and the civilian Observer Corps. Formed in June 1936, the primary function of 11 Group, commanded by Air Marshal Leslie Gossage, was the defence of London and the south-east, while 12 Group was created in May 1937, to protect eastern England. It is important to understand that at this time any air attacks made by Germany were expected to approach from the east, across the North Sea, and, due to the range involved such raids, were not expected to involve a fighter escort. At that time, therefore, 12 Group, defending the industrial Midlands and the north, represented a crucial responsibility. On 14 December 1937, Air Commodore Trafford Leigh-Mallory became 12 Group's Air Officer Commanding. A Cambridge graduate, during the Great War Leigh-Mallory had first served in France with the King's Liverpool Regiment before becoming a scout pilot with the RFC. His subsequent leadership of 8 Squadron led to Major Leigh-Mallory receiving the Distinguished Service Order (DSO), and his extensive experience of army co-operation laid the foundations for his subsequent RAF career. Groomed for high office, 'LM' attended the Imperial Defence College, the most senior of all service staff colleges, before taking command of 12 Group at Hucknall in Nottinghamshire. Interestingly, although now entrusted with a vital command, Leigh-Mallory had absolutely no personal experience of fighters whatsoever.

It was impractical, however, for Britain to be covered by two such large and unwieldy groups, and so 13 Group was created with responsibility for the north of England and Northern Ireland. In due course, 10 Group would be created to protect the West Country and South Wales (although 10 Group did not become operational until 8 July 1940, just two days before the Battle of Britain officially began). Each group was sub-divided into sectors, the main fighter station in each being known as the 'sector station'. Radar had made great progress, and RDF stations were constructed around southern England: by the summer of 1940, there would be twenty-two 'Chain Home' stations supplemented by thirty 'Chain Home Low' stations. Each was positioned, in theory at least, to ensure that every aircraft approaching Britain from the east or south would be detected by a minimum of two stations. The Germans, of course, knew about the RDF stations, with their 350 foot lattice masts, but believed that the operators of this equipment, in times of stress, would be unable to distinguish between large and small formations, and that the whole system would break down if large numbers of aircraft approached simultaneously. In due course the enemy would find itself much mistaken, and likewise that the greatest value of RDF was to direct fighters against specific attacks as they developed, rather than dissipate effort in flying constant standing patrols awaiting the enemy. RDF now became the keystone of Dowding's system of air defence, into which he also absorbed Observer Corps posts and centres, sector operations rooms, radio-telephony transmitters, landlines and ancillary devices.

The 'system' was, in fact, as perfect as technology and resources permitted. At Stanmore's underground filter room, RDF information was sifted by filterers and filter officers, displayed on a gridded map and passed by tellers through closed speech circuits to both the adjacent Command Operations Room and to the appropriate groups and sectors. It took just four minutes between an RDF operator identifying a plot to this information appearing in the operations rooms. The Sector Controller would then guide his fighters by radio telephone to intercept the enemy. Dowding believed that tactical control, especially during periods of hectic action, should not be exercised by either Fighter Command or group, but by the sector controllers themselves.

After incoming aircraft had crossed the coast, the Observer Corps was responsible for tracking their progress. Observer posts reported to observer centres, which were connected by landline to the Command Operations Room. From the latter, instructions were issued to local authorities as to when sirens should be sounded, warning the local populace of impending attack. The gun operations room tied anti-aircraft guns into the system, making a cohesive whole.

In each group operations room there was always at least one controller on duty. He scrutinized the large gridded map of his group area. Aircraft approaching or passing over were represented by coloured plaques, manipulated by WAAFs, armed with magnetized wands and headphones linked to a teller at an observer centre or filter room. Facing the controller was a 'totalisator', showing the location and readiness state of squadrons available. The group controller's job was to decide how to meet each threat: his responsibility was clearly a heavy one.

Sector operations rooms were places where great drama would be played out before too long. Linked by landlines and loudspeakers directly to the aircraft dispersal points, where pilots and aircraft waited to fly, it was also linked to one or more radio-telephony transmitters, placed far enough away to ensure that intercepted transmissions did not reveal its whereabouts. The sector controller brought his squadrons to 'readiness', or sent them off to intercept in accordance with orders received from Group. Once the squadrons were airborne, he was responsible for giving them orders and information with the express intention of placing them in a favourable position to attack the enemy. Controllers and formation leaders used a special code: 'scramble' meant take off urgently; 'pancake' was the order to land; 'angels' corresponded to height measured in thousands of feet, and while 'bandits' were definitely hostile aircraft, 'bogeys' were as yet unidentified plots. Pilots were directed by the provision of a compass heading, or 'vector', expressed in degrees, or by reference to landmarks given codenames. 'Buster' was the instruction for fighters to travel at top speed, and 'liner' was to do so at cruising speed. When the formation leader cried 'tally ho', the controller knew that the formation leader had sighted the enemy and was about to attack. After that, tactical control was passed to the formation leader in the air, while those in control rooms anxiously awaited the combat's outcome.

Having established this system of aerial defence, Dowding believed more than ever that 'security of base' was paramount, indeed that it 'overrides all considerations'. The bomber remained the greatest fear, but still those in power believed that 'the bomber would always get through', no matter what. Indeed, the Germans gave the world a shocking demonstration of the destructive power of their modern bombers during the Spanish Civil War when the Basque town of Guernica was badly hit. Still Dowding fought for the system, obstinately insisting that his demands be met, and winning no friends in high places during the process. Indeed, he found himself in almost constant dispute with the air staff, where, he later wrote, his name 'stank'. One such issue concerned the Boulton Paul Defiant fighter, which was foisted upon Dowding by the Assistant Chief of the Air Staff (ACAS), Air Vice-Marshal Sholto Douglas. During the Great War, Douglas had flown the Bristol Fighter, an inline two-seater in which a gunner occupied the rear seat and a type which did tremendous service. Douglas therefore believed that there was a place for a similar monoplane, and supported Boulton Paul's design for a Merlin powered fighter featuring a gunner in a power operated rear turret. This was, of course, the same power-plant that propelled Spitfires and Hurricanes, but because of the turret and extra crewman, the Defiant was much heavier than these single-seater types. This, of course, considerably reduced performance, but catastrophically the Defiant, unlike the Bristol Fighter, had no forward firing armament whatsoever. The pilot and gunner, therefore, had to work together, but Douglas was missing the crucial point: modern fighters travelled in excess of 300mph, infinitely faster than his old Bristol Fighter, and immediate eye-to-hand co-ordination was therefore required. Nonetheless, in June 1938, Douglas informed Dowding that he must form fifteen squadrons of Defiants for day-fighting. Dowding immediately recognized the Air Staff's incompetence, and was understandably angry that such an important decision had been made without his consultation. His arguments held some sway, as the number of Defiant squadrons was reduced to nine, and, in the event, only two were formed in time for action in 1940; sadly, as we shall see, only the virtual annihilation of these units would prove Dowding absolutely right.

This was, however, a period of expansion, the danger from Germany at last recognized and reacted to, albeit at eleventh hour, and the RAF began increasing in size accordingly. Indeed, in 1936, the RAF Volunteer Reserve (VR) was created, providing a pool of trained pilots who could be called up for full time service in the event of war. Volunteers all, aged between eighteen and twenty-five, these men – who may not otherwise have had the opportunity to fly – were trained at weekends and even paid a retainer of £25 per annum for the privilege. Many were former grammar school boys, employed full-time and learning to fly in their spare time. By 1937, 800 reservists were undergoing flying training, and by 1939, 310 reservists were fully trained pilots serving in Fighter Command (200 of which saw action during the Battle of Britain). Indeed, at the war's end in 1945, it was not a professional airman who was officially the RAF's top scoring fighter pilot, but James Edgar 'Johnnie' Johnson – a reservist from Leicestershire. These VR pilots were clearly a vital resource, as, indeed, was the Auxiliary Air Force (AAF). While the volunteer reservists wore a brass 'VR' on their uniform lapels, the auxiliaries wore a simple 'A', although they were more commonly known as the 'Millionaire Mob', wealthy young men who could afford to fly for pleasure at weekends and who were absorbed into locally formed squadrons. Before joining the VR, Johnnie Johnson had applied for the AAF:

I went along for this interview and the senior officer there, knowing I was from Leicestershire, asked, 'With whom do you hunt, Johnson?'

I said, 'Hunt, Sir?'

He said, 'Yes Johnson, hunt; with whom do you hunt?'

I said, 'Well I don't hunt, Sir, I shoot.'

He said, 'Oh, well thank you, Johnson, that will be all!'

Clearly the fact that I could shoot game on the wing impressed him not one bit. Had I been socially acceptable, however, hunting with Lord so-and-so, things would have been different, but, back then, this is what the auxiliaries were like. Do not forget that many of these young men were of independent means, which I certainly wasn't!

Nonetheless, by the time the Battle of Britain was fought, twelve of Dowding's forty-two fighter squadrons were auxiliary units, more than a quarter of his strength and all would do sterling service that fateful summer.

In July 1938, as Hitler moved the world ever closer to war, Dowding received a new Senior Air Staff Officer (SASO) at Bentley Priory, a tough New Zealander and a Great War fighter 'ace': Air Commodore Keith Park. Dowding and Park would become a brilliant team, and Dowding at last had loyal and unfailing support in the perfect right-hand man.

Keith Park was an officer of great experience, having received a Military Cross (MC) and bar for his Great War service as a fighter pilot. Interestingly, Park had insisted in maintaining his own machine-guns and sights, and took a great technical interest in both his aircraft and engine. In 1919, together with a Captain Stewart, he made what was only the second non-stop flight around Britain's coastline, for which he was awarded the Distinguished Flying Cross (DFC). By the time of his posting to Dowding's staff, Park had, in addition to various staff appointments, commanded a fighter squadron and two frontline fighter stations. His experience with both fighters and the system was therefore current, and he fully understood Fighter Command's intended method of operating. Fortunately for Britain, Dowding and Park knew as much about fighter warfare as anyone else in the world at that time. Unfortunately, Park, like Dowding, found it difficult to tolerate incompetent interference by both the Air Ministry and Air Staff, and likewise made himself unpopular in high places as he supported Dowding to the hilt.

On 1 January 1938, 111 (F) Squadron at Northolt took delivery of the first Hurricanes. Eight months later, on 4 August, Supermarine test pilot Jeffrey Quill delivered the first production Spitfire to 19 (F) Squadron at Duxford. Those lucky squadrons had been chosen to re-equip with the new monoplanes, and busied themselves with learning how to operate and fly the Hurricane and Spitfire. Slowly, over the next year, virtually all of Fighter Command's squadrons would exchange their Gladiator and Gauntlet biplanes for the new, fast, monoplanes, which was just as well: just one month after 19 Squadron received that first Spitfire, the world was again on the brink of war. By this time, Hitler had re-occupied the Rhineland and unified Germany and Austria, both prohibited by Versailles. The extent of Germany's contempt for the *Diktat* was no longer clandestine but flaunted in demonstrations of national military pride. Still, many sympathized with Germany and believed that Hitler's demands for the restoration of former German territories were reasonable, and not worth making much of a fuss over. The British Prime Minister, Neville Chamberlain, pursued a policy of appeasing Hitler by agreeing to his demands, and hoped that this would lay the foundations of a lasting peace – as Versailles had not. In September 1938, Hitler demanded that the German-speaking Sudetenland of Czechoslovakia be incorporated into the Third Reich. Hitler actually expected, and was prepared for, confrontation with the Allies over this issue, but Britain and

Flying Officer Barry Sutton, Flight Lieutenant Gus Holden and Pilot Officer Peter Down of 56 Squadron at North Weald. Down sports white pre-war flying overalls emblazoned with the Squadron's badge. On 28 August 1940, Sutton was shot down, possibly by a Spitfire in an incident of 'friendly fire', and badly burned; he survived the war, as did both Holden and Down.

France betrayed the Czechs and failed to make a stand. Although Chamberlain famously returned to Heston airport clutching his piece of paper, bearing Hitler's signature alongside his own and proclaiming 'peace for our time', all this policy of appeasement did was encourage the Nazi dictator to brinkmanship. Confident that the leaders of Britain and France were too weak to oppose him, in March 1939, Hitler occupied the remainder of Czechoslovakia – land to which Germany had absolutely no legal claim on whatsoever and a clear indication that Hitler's territorial ambitions were far more sinister than the doves had hoped and prayed for; the time for hawks was fast approaching.

In the Far East too another territorially ambitious and jingoistic nation, Japan, looked to expand its territories. In 1936, Japan had been condemned by the League of Nations for invading Manchuria; Japan simply resigned its membership and instead became a party to the Anti-Comintern Pact with Germany and Italy. On 23 August 1939, the Russians, astonishingly, signed a non-aggression pact with Hitler, a secret clause of which divided up Poland between them. In the wake of having sold out Czechoslovakia, Britain and France pledged support to Poland in the event of German belligerence, although in reality neither power was geographically situated to offer any direct military

'B' Flight of 56 Squadron at North Weald, 3 September 1939; from left: P/Os L. Freminsky & P.D.M. Down, F/L I. Soden, F/O J. Coghlan, P/Os P. Illingworth & F. Rose; seated, from left: unknown, F/O John Hulton-Harrop. Coghlan and Down went on to fight in the Battle of Britain; Down survived the war but Coghlan was killed with a parachute training unit in August 1940.

assistance. On 1 September 1939, German forces invaded Poland, unleashing the new and paralyzing blitzkrieg – 'lightning war' – in which fast moving tanks, supported by motorized infantry and aircraft, completely overran the Poles, who fought back bravely but hopelessly using obsolete aircraft and even mounted cavalry against the panzers. Britain and France delivered Hitler an ultimatum to withdraw from Poland or suffer the consequences; unsurprisingly this was ignored. On 3 September 1939, therefore, left with no other alternative, Britain and France declared war on Nazi Germany.

After Poland fell, in just three weeks, Britain and France braced themselves and prepared for Hitler's onslaught against the west. The British Expeditionary Force (BEF), comprising largely territorials and reservists, was immediately dispatched to France. The King of the Belgians was determined to remain neutral, however, and refused to allow the BEF to fortify his border with Germany. The British and French, therefore, dug in along the Franco-Belgique and Franco-German borders and there awaited events. Although the RAF contributed the Advanced Air Striking Force (AASF) to the BEF, Dowding, fully appreciating the Spitfire's superiority of performance, if not yet numbers, only sent Hurricanes to France. The Spitfire, he knew, was far too precious to waste, being desperately required for the defence of Britain itself. Moreover, without wishing to detract at all from the invaluable Hurricane and the pilots who went to war in her, the Spitfire already had a charisma and charm all of its own. In April 1940, for example, Pilot Officer Hubert 'Dizzy' Allen reported to fly Spitfires with 66 'Clickety-Click' Squadron at Duxford:

> I didn't know where Duxford was and nor was I aware of what aircraft 66 Squadron had – they could have been Hurricanes, which did not appeal to me in any way. On the other hand they might be Spitfires, which appealed to me very much. I had seen a Spitfire in flight, had seen many pictures of it, to me it was the very pink of perfection (which, with experience, proved to be the case). When I arrived at Duxford's hangars I could see nothing but Spitfires littering the airfield – not a Hurricane in sight. Whatever Heaven is, St Peter opened the doors to it that day I arrived at Duxford!

Bob Morris was posted to 'Clickety-Click' a month later:

> In May 1940, I passed out of the RAF Technical School at Halton as an aeronautical engineer, and was posted to 66 Squadron at Coltishall. I knew not where Coltishall was, or what aircraft 'Clickety-Click' had. My first glimpse of Coltishall airfield in Norfolk, and of 66 Squadron, was from the bus, which travelled along the airfield perimeter for a short distance. What an absolute thrill to see Spitfires! Here was every young man's dream!

For reasons already explained, in 1939, Hurricanes were more numerous than Spitfires, but as the nation braced itself Spitfire production increased. The original Mk I Spitfires were powered by the Merlin II engine and fitted with a two bladed, fixed pitch, propeller made of mahogany. The improved Merlin III was quickly developed, and fitted with a metal twin speed (three-bladed) propeller made by de Havilland. This meant that, as opposed to a fixed pitch propeller, the pilot had two settings: coarse and fine pitch, the pitch being the angle at which the blades bit into the air and the effect of which was akin to changing gear in a car. The Me 109, however, already enjoyed the benefits of a constant speed propeller, meaning that the pilot could rotate the blades throughout 360°, and therefore achieve the perfect pitch in any given situation. This crucial improvement would not be fitted to Spitfires and Hurricanes until June 1940 – only just in time for the Battle of Britain.

At this time, Spitfires were still produced at Supermarine's factory at Woolston in Southampton. In May 1940, a young school leaver by the name of Terry White joined the workforce there as a 'handy lad', recalling many years later that he was 'utterly bewildered by the noise and, as it appeared to me, confusion of what was a very, very busy factory'.

On Dowding's fighter squadrons in Britain, the 'Phoney War' saw life continue much as it had during peacetime. Corporal Fred Roberts:

Flying Officer Arthur Dean Nesbitt, a Canadian flying Hurricanes with 1 (RCAF) Squadron at Northolt. On 15 September 1940, Nesbitt destroyed an Me 109 before being shot down himself and baling out over Tunbridge Wells. Wounded, he was not back in action until 7 October when he was shot up by 109s and forced-landed at Biggin Hill.

Jimmy Belton and I joined 19 Squadron as rookie armourers straight from our six month training course at Manby. Full of enthusiasm we arrived at Duxford expecting to see Spitfires everywhere, only to find everything quiet and more or less closed for the weekend. Of course this was still the 'strawberries and cream and fruitcake for tea' period enjoyed by the pre-war RAF, which was like a posh flying club.

The training of pilots for his 'posh flying club' was something which had caused Dowding great concern. Before the war, pilots went straight from Flying Training School (FTS) to their squadron, where they were trained on the particular fighter aircraft with which their squadron was equipped, and made combat ready. With the advent of war, it was clear that this could not continue, because hard-pressed squadrons would simply not have the time or resources to train replacements. The Air Ministry therefore revealed plans to create special units which would train fledgling fighter pilots to operational standard prior to them reaching their actual units. Of all the RAF's various commands, it was only Fighter Command which objected to this: Dowding felt strongly that the use of operational aircraft for training was a waste. This was an argument Dowding lost, and for once the evidence suggests that the Air Ministry was right. Three training 'pools' were proposed, the first of which was the 11 Group Pool at St Athan, which had eleven Fairey Battles (single-engined light-bombers, soon replaced by the North American Harvard monoplane trainer) and twenty-two Hurricanes on strength. Shortly after the outbreak of war, the course length was halved to four weeks, and syllabus hours were reduced from forty-five to thirty hours per pupil. It was hoped that 300 pilots would be trained to operational standard, per pool, per annum. Still Dowding objected, however, insisting that the 11 Group Pool should only be used to produce replacements for Hurricane squadrons in France, and stating that the proposed 12 Group Pool, destined for Aston Down, was completely unnecessary. The Air Ministry parried by arguing that the lack of group pools would mean a lack of casualty replacements when fighting became intense, and if necessary training aircraft could be taken for operational use. Reluctantly Dowding agreed. In March 1940, the group pools were renamed Operational Training Units (OTU), and a third such unit was added. Nonetheless, during the forthcoming Battle of France, their combined output was barely sufficient to make good the losses of squadrons fighting on the continent, where the standard of training was harshly criticised: new pilots often had only ten hours flying time on Spitfires or Hurricanes, with no high altitude or fighter attack experience. As we shall see, during the Battle of Britain which lay ahead, the situation would deteriorate further still.

Squadron Leader Don Finlay DFC, a former Olympic hurdler and CO of 41 Squadron during the Battle of Britain. Having survived being shot down when previously commanding 54 Squadron, Finlay accounted for several enemy aircraft in the summer of 1940. He survived the war, serving in the post war RAF, but died in tragic circumstances in 1970.

An operational fighter squadron comprised twelve aircraft and pilots, excluding reserves, divided into two 'flights', 'A' and 'B', each commanded by a flight lieutenant. The flights were then sub-divided into two sections of three aircraft, each trio of fighters having its own leader and being identified by a colour. 'A' Flight usually consisted of Red and Yellow Sections, while 'B' comprised Blue and Green. Each section was numbered from one to three, one indicating the leader. 'Blue One' would therefore identify the leader of 'B' Flight's Blue Section. Each squadron was identified by its own two code letters, which were applied to the fighters' fuselages in medium sea grey. Individual aircraft were then further identifiable by a single letter, choosing from A – K for 'A' Flight, and L – Z for 'B'. Each squadron also had its own radio call sign: 'Luton Blue One' therefore identified the leader of 19 Squadron's 'B' Flight. The squadron was under the overall command of a squadron leader, who, in addition to flying duties, was responsible, through his adjutant, for administration, discipline and the general day-to-day smooth running of his unit. In the air, officers and non-commissioned pilots flew together, but on the ground, while off duty, they were segregated in this still very class conscious society. It should not be forgotten that a fighter squadron also included those in behind-the-scenes but nonetheless essential roles: including intelligence officers, airframe riggers, engine fitters, instrument fitters, and armourers.

The operational centre of the squadron was 'dispersal', usually a wooden hut on the airfield in which was situated the orderly clerk and all important telephone. There were also twelve beds on which the pilots rested between sorties. Outside their aircraft were dispersed as a precaution against bombing, facing the centre of the airfield so that pilots could take off with the minimum of delay. During the daytime, pilots learned to leave their parachutes, which they sat on, not in their bucket seats but on top of either the port wing or tailplane with the straps hanging down, meaning that they could seize the two shoulder straps, pull the parachute pack off the wing and move towards the cockpit, all without pausing (on the subject of parachutes, it may interest the reader to know that fighter pilots were only given ground tuition in deploying a parachute, so the first time they actually did so was when abandoning a doomed aircraft!). Pilots wore a flying helmet made of leather, containing radio-telephony earphones, the leads of which were plugged into a socket in the cockpit, in which the helmet and goggles were left, often on the reflector gunsight or control column top. Stout leather flying boots were usually worn, lined with sheepskin, to insulate against the cold in what were unheated cockpits, and a life jacket known as a 'Mae West', after the buxom American actress and for obvious reasons. Oxygen, required at high altitude, was delivered via an oxygen mask, covering the nose, cheeks and mouth, the pilot's eyes being protected by his goggles. With the addition of leather gauntlets, the pilot was thus afforded some protection from fire. What fighter pilots rarely wore, however, in direct contrast to the movies and due to the tight confines of their tiny cockpits, was the bulky, leather and sheepskin flying jacket. Instead they preferred to wear uniform shirts and tunics, although the brightly coloured silk neck scarf was not altogether a pose but necessary to prevent chafing as the pilot constantly screwed his neck around searching for the enemy. Moreover, neck ties shrank in seawater, another valid reason why their use was discarded on operations. On the ground, the fighter pilot famously wore his tunic top button undone.

Sergeant Ken Wilkinson, a Spitfire pilot in 19 Squadron: 'If you were a fighter pilot, top button undone and all that, you were a cocky so and so, but if you were a *Spitfire* pilot you were cockier still!'

Most squadrons worked a four day cycle, on the first day of which pilots would be on 'Stand by' and therefore available to fly within the hour; second day would be 'Available', as in ready to fly in fifteen minutes, and day three would see the stakes upped to 'Readiness' when pilots were ready for immediate take-off. On day four came 'Stand down', when pilots, with their flight commander's permission, could leave the aerodrome. One flight of operational pilots had to remain on the airfield, so this was often used as an opportunity for training. Pilot Officer William Walker was a VR pilot who joined the auxiliary 616 'South Yorkshire' squadron shortly before the Battle of Britain began:

> The early days of war were interesting so far as we were unprepared for what was to come. It is my lasting regret that I did not have more operational training – trying to pick it up with the Squadron straight from flying school was a pretty haphazard affair. For instance, I flew my first Spitfire on June 23rd, 1940, and was declared operational on July 1st.

As we have seen, from the outset the Air Ministry's requirement was that their new monoplane fighters be armed with eight .303 machine-guns, this being rifle-calibre ammunition. The American company Browning won the contract to supply these guns, each weapon carrying a supply of 300 rounds with a rate of fire of 1,200 rounds per minute. Ammunition belts were made up by the 'plumbers' – armourers – with a mix of bullets: ball, armour-piercing and incendiary. The Browning was generally accurate to about 300 yards, after which gravity imposed 'bullet drop'. Many pilots harmonized their guns so that bullets converged at 250 yards, thus producing a lethal cone of fire. Directly in front of the pilot's vision was the reflector lens of his gunsight, onto which were projected illuminated cross-hairs. These lines could be adjusted manually according to which type of enemy aircraft was being engaged: if the bars simultaneously touched both wingtips then true range would be calculated automatically. However, in a twisting, turning, dogfight such methodical operations were impractical. The gunsight was usually therefore pre-set to the wingspan of a particular enemy aircraft type and used as a guide only. Spitfire 'ace' Bob Doe recalls that 'It is incredibly difficult to judge range in the air and I found experience to be the only real help.'

Sergeant Ken Wilkinson. A Volunteer Reservist, after completing operational training he was first posted to 616 Squadron at Kirton, which was rebuilding after being virtually annihilated at Kenley the previous month. Shortly before the Battle of Britain concluded, Wilkinson joined 19 Squadron at Fowlmere and flew operational sorties with the controversial Duxford Wing.

An interesting study of a battle weary Spitfire Mk IA. Pilot Officer David Crook of 609 Squadron poses in his 'office' at Northolt during the Dunkirk fighting. Opposite the Spitfire is a petrol bowser, and further along the perimeter track a Hurricane can be seen.

Connected to each fighter was a mobile starter battery, astride which, sat in readiness, were a couple of 'Erks' – RAF slang for mechanics. The groundcrews, the boss of which was invariably a senior NCO known as 'Chiefy', were accommodated nearby in tents, along with all those personnel connected with squadron maintenance, such as petrol bowser crews, armourers, wireless servicing crews and aircraft fitters. Together, all of these men, not just pilots, constituted the sharp end of Britain's front line.

The 'Phoney War', however, persisted. For the first three months of 1940, little had happened. The Soviets finally overwhelmed the Finns, and U-boats continued to attack Britain's North Atlantic shipping, but, with the exception of the Czechs and Poles, few people had so far suffered unduly from the conflict. In early April, Hitler attacked Denmark and Norway, drawing Anglo-French forces into a hopeless campaign in Norway's inhospitable terrain.

On 13 April 1940, at Bentley Priory, Keith Park received a welcome surprise: he was promoted to air vice-marshal and given command of Fighter Command's prestigious 11 Group. Park was the perfect choice for this vital appointment: he had spent the last two years faithfully helping Dowding create the System of Air Defence, and was therefore fully conversant with its workings. Dowding's strategy was to largely delegate tactical control to his group commanders, and Air Vice-Marshal Park fully understood what was required by his Commander-in-Chief. Still, however, Air Vice-Marshal Leigh-Mallory's 12 Group was considered the most important group, as any aerial attacks from Germany were still expected to approach the east coast and across the North Sea. This had an enormous bearing on the tactics that the RAF decided upon.

It must be remembered that powered flight itself remained a new science, the Wright brothers having made that first historic flight only thirty-six years before the Second World War broke out. Furthermore, monoplanes were newer still: by the declaration of war on 3 September 1939, the Hurricane had only been in squadron service for a year and nine months, and the Spitfire only just over a year – and that was just so far as 111 and 19 Squadron were concerned; other squadrons were still exchanging their obsolete biplanes for the new fighters. Throughout the whole of Fighter Command, therefore, there was very little experience in operating monoplane fighters, and the only fighter pilots who had actually flown them in combat were Germans, in both the Spanish Civil War and Poland. The Air Ministry established the Air Fighting Committee, to research the best methods for attacking enemy aircraft, including the types of formations used so as to maximize concentration of fire. Experiments were conducted by the Air Fighting Development Establishment (AFDE), which concluded that the basic fighter formation should be a tight 'vic' of three aircraft which could bring twenty-four machine-guns to bear simultaneously. This was fine, of course, providing the enemy aircraft encountered was a slow bomber, taking little or no violent evasive action, and which permitted an orderly queue of fighters to line up and destroy it. This was, in fact, what the tacticians foresaw. With Britain being beyond the range of enemy fighters based in Germany, the only aircraft likely to approach these shores was therefore, understandably, considered to be ponderous bombers, these largely intruding over 12 Group. Dramatic and violent events about to unfold on the continent, however, would indicate that the planners could not have been more wrong.

Without warning, on 10 May 1940, Hitler's *Wehrmacht* finally struck against the west, invading Belgium, Holland, Luxembourg and France. Two days later Liege fell, and panzers crossed the Meuse at Dinant and Sedan. The Belgian King immediately regretted his naivety and urgently requested Allied assistance: the BEF now pivoted forward, moving from their prepared defences on the Franco-Belgium border, some sixty miles inside Belgium, over unreconnoitred ground intending to meet the Germans at what was believed to be the *Schwerpunkt*, or point of main effort, i.e. an enemy thrust into Northern France via Holland and Belgium, as in the Great War. German armour was actually, however, undertaking the impossible by pouring through the supposedly impassable Ardennes forest, much further south. Having cleverly disguised the actual *Schwerpunkt*, *Panzergruppe* von Kliest was able to bypass the much vaunted Maginot Line, rendering those defences useless, and punch upwards into

France's comparatively undefended underbelly. The effect was one of paralysis, certainly so far as the French and Belgians were concerned. Once through the Ardennes, the panzers raced for the Channel coast, Erwin Rommel's 7th Panzer advancing with such speed that it was nicknamed the 'Ghost Division'. By 20 May, the Germans, incredibly, had reached Laon, Cambrai, Arras, Amiens and even Abbeville. The absolutely unthinkable had happened. Squadron Leader 'Teddy' Donaldson:

> The French bolted, including their air force. I have never seen so many people running so fast anywhere, so long as it was west. The British Tommies were marvellous, however, and fought their way to the sand dunes of Dunkirk. I was in command of 151 Squadron, and our Hurricanes were sent to reinforce the AASF, flying from Manston to France on a daily basis.
>
> In some respects the Germans were grossly over confident in the air, and so didn't have it all their own way. But every day we had damaged Hurricanes and no ground crews to mend them, dictating that we had to return to Manston every evening. In any event, our airfields in France were being heavily bombed, so had we stayed, although pilots could have got off the airfield to sleep, our aircraft would have taking a beating. 151 Squadron would fly up to seven sorties a day, against overwhelming odds, and on one occasion even stayed on patrol after expending our ammunition so as to prevent the *Luftwaffe* attacking defenceless British troops on the ground.

Amongst Donaldson's pilots was Pilot Officer Jack Hamar, from Knighton in Radnorshire, who, before joining the pre-war RAF, had worked in the family business, a hardware and general store. On 18 May 1940, he found himself not behind the counter but on patrol in a Hurricane, three miles north-west of Vitry:

> I climbed to 7,000 feet and attacked two Me 110s, succeeding in getting onto the tail of one enemy aircraft (E/A). I opened fire at 300 yards with a burst of five seconds. Whilst closing in I noticed tracer passing over my head, from behind, and looking around discovered the other E/A on my tail. I immediately half-rolled away and noticed two Hurricanes chasing another E/A, which was diving to ground level. I followed down after the Hurricanes, and, as they broke away, I continued the chase, hedge-hopping, but did not seem to gain on the E/A. I got within 500 yards and put in a five second burst. I saw my tracer entering both wings, but did not observe any damage. As my windscreen was by this time covered in oil from my own airscrew, making sighting impossible, I broke away and returned to Vitry.

Hamar's combat report is interesting. The Me 110 was a twin-engined 'destroyer', a long range escort fighter, with a top speed of 349mph. The Hurricane – a single-seat and single-engined fighter – had a top speed of only 328mph. A Spitfire, with a top speed of 355mph, would have caught that Me 110. Flight Lieutenant Gerry Edge:

Pilot Officer Jack Hamar DFC, a Hurricane pilot of 151 Squadron, at home with his sweetheart in Knighton, Radnorshire, just before the Battle of Britain began. Tragically, Hamar was killed in a flying accident at North Weald on 24 July 1940 – the very day news was received that he had been awarded the DFC.

During the Fall of France I flew Hurricanes over there with 605 Squadron. After the German offensive began, the roads below were full of columns of civilians and soldiers, all progressing westwards. Once we came upon a Stuka that was strafing a column of refugees. It was plain to anyone, especially from that low altitude, that this was a civilian, as opposed to a military column. I am pleased to say that I shot this Boche down. There were no survivors. Does that concern me? Not at all. Of all the enemy aircraft I shot down, that one gave me great pleasure.

Flight Lieutenant Peter Brothers:

Whilst operating over France as a flight commander in 32 Squadron, I naturally took our latest replacement under my wing to fly as my Number Two. Suddenly I had that feeling we all experience at some time that I was being watched. Glancing in my rear-view mirror I was startled to see, immediately behind me and between my Number Two and me, the biggest and fattest Me 109 – ever! As I instantly took evasive action his front end lit up as he fired. I escaped unscathed, the 109 climbed and vanished as I did a tight turn, looking for my Number Two. There he was, good man, cutting the corner to get back in position, as I thought, until he opened fire on me! Suggesting on the radio that his action

Flight Lieutenant Gerry Edge DFC (right) was a pre-war Auxiliary member of 605 Squadron. Having opened his account during the Battle of France, he was posted to command 253 Squadron at Kenley, scoring further victories until being shot down and wounded. Edge survived the war, but has since died. Pictured at Hawkinge in August 1940, while serving with 605 Squadron, the other pilot is unknown.

Above: Flight Lieutenant Peter Brothers on patrol from Hawkinge during the Battle of Britain. A successful fighter pilot, Brothers survived the war, served in the post-war RAF and is currently Chairman of the Battle of Britain Fighter Association.

Right: Fighter pilot: Flight Lieutenant Peter Brothers DFC, who flew Hurricanes with both 32 and 257 Squadrons during the Battle of Britain. Heavily engaged flying from bases such as Hawkinge, Biggin Hill and North Weald, Brothers destroyed eight enemy aircraft in the summer of 1940, later becoming a wing leader who retired as an air commodore in 1964.

was unpopular, as there were no other aircraft in sight we wended our way home. Not only had he not warned me of the 109's presence or fired at it, he had had such an easy shot but missed. I dealt a blow to his jauntiness by removing him from operations for two days' intensive gunnery training; sadly it did not help him survive.

Fighter versus fighter combat was fast, and all too often confusing. Far too fast, in fact, for the Fighter Command attacks stipulated by the AFDU and geared up to the interception of bombers. In Spain, the Germans had quickly realized that tight formations were useless in combat, so devised the *Schwarm* of four aircraft, flying spread out and in line abreast, like the fingers of an outstretched hand, which, when combat was joined, broke into the *Rotte*, a fighting pair of leader and wingman, which remains the basic fighter formation even today. Pilot Officer Johnnie Johnson: 'We could see the Huns flying this long, stretched out line abreast formation, lean and hungry looking and appearing like a pack of hunting dogs searching for their prey.' In flying such formations, the pilots did not have to concentrate on avoiding collision with each other, and keeping perfect station, but could search for the enemy. Sergeant Reg Johnson:

> Our CO of 222 Squadron, Squadron Leader 'Tubby' Mermagen, was a pre-war aerobatic formation champion, which probably explained his addiction to making us fly our Spitfires in tight squadron formation. We actually flew so tight that our wingtips overlapped. From Kirton he led us off in squadron formation and at times we even landed in squadron formation. We even rolled as a squadron on one occasion! Mermagen was an exceptional pilot, but such training was completely unsuitable for what actually lay ahead.

The losses being suffered by his Hurricane squadrons in France were sufficient to cause Dowding grave concern, since if they were allowed to continue unchecked for sake of what was undoubtedly a lost cause he would not be able to guarantee security of base. In a desperate bid to preserve his strength, on 13 May 1940, Dowding wrote to the Air Ministry, pointing out that although the Air Council considered the minimum number of squadrons required for Home Defence was fifty-two, losses in France had depleted Fighter Command to just thirty-six. As ever, Dowding spoke frankly:

> I must therefore request that as a matter of paramount urgency the Air Ministry will consider and decide what level of strength is to be left to the Fighter Command for the defence of this country, and will assure me that when this level has been reached, not one fighter will be sent across the Channel however urgent and insistent appeals for help may be.
> I believe that, if an adequate fighter force is kept in this country, if the fleets remain in being, and if the Home Forces are suitably organized to resist invasion, we should be able to carry on the war single handed for some time, if not indefinitely. But, if the Home

A *schwarm* of II/JG 27 Me 109s bunch up for the photographer's benefit. In practice they flew more spaced out, thus reducing the risk of collision and ensuring that pilots could concentrate not on their neighbour but on searching for the enemy. In battle, the *schwarm* sub-divided into two fighting pairs, or *rotte*, each comprising leader and wingman and this remains the basis of fighter formations today.

Defence Force is drained away in desperate attempts to remedy the situation in France, defeat in France will involve the final, complete and irremediable defeat of this country.

Fortunately these strong words of wisdom were heeded, but the time rapidly approaching when the Spitfire, preserved for home defence, would at last meet in combat its main adversary: the Me 109.

On 26 May 1940, orders were given for the complete evacuation of Allied troops from Dunkirk. From that day onwards, Fighter Command became devoted almost exclusively to patrols along the line Calais-Dunkirk, some 200 sorties being flown on the first day. As the Royal Navy, supplemented by the heroic 'Little Ships', commenced a shuttle-service across the Channel, Fighter Command's task was to maintain continuous patrols during daylight hours, and this was largely accomplished. Most of these patrols were in squadron strength, although on three occasions single squadrons found themselves heavily outnumbered. The forward bases of 11 Group, such as at Manston and

Hawkinge, suddenly became a hive of activity, as fighters arrived from hither and thither to operate over the French coast. Among them was 12 Group's 19 Squadron, which was roughly handled by Me 109s on 26 May, while attacking a formation of Stuka dive-bombers over Calais. Flight Sergeant George 'Grumpy' Unwin:

We found this gaggle of Stukas and the CO, Squadron Leader Geoffrey Stephenson, a pre-war aerobatic pilot and Cranwell contemporary of Douglas Bader's, led us in a textbook attack: tight vics of three, throttled right back to virtually match the slow target's speed. This was actually suicidal. No-one was looking out for escorting enemy fighters, which suddenly rained down upon us, catching us in a dreadful tactical situation – bunched up and throttled right back. The CO was shot down and captured, and Pilot Officer Watson was killed. It was clear from that point on that the Fighter Command Attacks, which had been practised extensively before the war, were actually completely useless when fighters were about. What the tacticians who wrote the book did not foresee, of course, was

The indomitable Douglas Bader. Having lost his legs in a blameworthy flying accident, Bader overcame this disability to command 242 Squadron during the Battle of Britain. During that time, Bader came up with the 'Big Wing' theory, which although supported by his Station and Group Commander was contrary to the requirements of Fighter Command's Commander-in-Chief. Although believed at the time to have been a great success, recent research indicates that the concept was flawed from the outset and featured massive overclaiming, due to the confusion caused by so many pilots engaging simultaneously.

Hitler's unprecedented advance to the Channel coast, which put even London within the limited range of the Me 109.

That the Me 109 was now able to escort bombers, and undertake *freie hunt* – free-range fighter sweeps – changed everything. Taking aside certain technical advantages that the 109 enjoyed over both the Spitfire and Hurricane, such as fuel injection and 20mm cannon, Fighter Command's almost complete ignorance of fighter versus fighter tactics and formations was the thing most in the enemy's favour. Quite simply, Dowding's pilots would have to learn very quickly – or die.

Nonetheless, many Spitfire pilots opened their accounts over Dunkirk, including that already legendary fighter pilot who had lost both legs in a pre-war flying accident, namely Flight Lieutenant Douglas Bader, a flight commander in 222 Squadron, who destroyed an Me 109 and damaged an Me 110 on 1 June 1940. Squadron Leader 'Tubby' Mermagen:

> When we of 222 Squadron landed, the absolutely irrepressible Douglas Bader stomped over to me and enthused 'I got five for certain, old boy!' Now this was the first time we had met the 109, which were damn good aeroplanes, and everything happened very quickly indeed. To be certain of having destroyed five enemy aircraft (which qualified a pilot to be an ace) in such circumstances was impossible. I said 'You're a bloody liar, Bader!' We credited him with one destroyed and another damaged. Bader was great for morale, though; he used to come stomping into dispersal, for example, saying 'Come on chaps, get out of the way, I want a cup of coffee,' and just barged everyone else out of the way. The chaps loved him for it, he was a kind of buccaneer, really!

The problem of over claiming was a phenomenon of fighter warfare, where everything, as Mermagen says, moved so quickly – in the blink of an eye, the speed of combat could easily confuse and deceive the human brain, and who in their right mind, would hang around to watch whether an enemy aircraft hit the ground from 20,000 feet – to do so would be to court disaster, and invite being shot down oneself.

During the air operations flown as a protective umbrella to the evacuation from Dunkirk, German bombers did, however, get through to the beaches, the beleaguered and desperate troops there bitterly asking 'Where is the RAF?' Indeed, in the eyes of the army, the RAF's esteem sank to an all time low. However, Fighter Command was often operating at high altitude, above cloud and away from the actual beaches, their presence unseen by those on the ground. Had this not been the case, the troops below would undoubtedly had suffered infinitely more at the hands of *Reichsmarschall* Hermann Göring's Luftwaffe. Stretched to the limit of endurance, Fighter Command actually performed essential service: only on one day, 1 June, were really damaging attacks made by the enemy against Allied shipping. Thereafter the evacuation continued at night, which helped the

Flying Officer Arthur 'Art' Yuile, a Canadian serving with 1 (RCAF) Squadron, flying Hurricanes from Northolt. Yuile destroyed one enemy aircraft and damaged another during the Battle of Britain, but was himself shot down and baled out on one occasion and returned to base with a shot up aircraft on another.

hard-pressed fighter pilots given that patrols in strength were only required at dawn and dusk, while ships were leaving or approaching Dunkirk, rather than throughout the long hours of daylight. Air Vice-Marshal Park, in fact, had observed how his fighters fared not just from his Group Operations Room, but from the cockpit of his personal Hurricane, 'OK1'. Park was, of course, having to respond to a scenario for which there were no precedents, but he did so rapidly and effectively – without help from the system, given that radar was of no help in the context of this period of fighting over the French coast. Nonetheless, by 3 June, the evacuation was complete, some 350,000 Allied soldiers having been rescued.

For Hitler, the opportunity to mount a seaborne invasion of Britain was an unexpected bonus of the unprecedented success of his attack on the west. Preparations were hastily made to transport thirty-nine divisions, each 19,000 strong, of the German army across the Channel. Plans were made for the disembarkation in Kent and Sussex of 125,000 men during the operation's first three days. A makeshift invasion fleet was assembled, comprising some 170 large transport vessels, 1,500 barges, and several hundred tugs, trawlers, motor boats and fishing smacks. As the *Kriegsmarine* was hopelessly inferior to the

Royal Navy in warships of every category, the German service chiefs agreed that 'Operation Sealion' would only be feasible if the Luftwaffe could defeat the RAF and therefore command complete aerial superiority over England, before the invasion fleet set sail. The Luftwaffe could then dominate the landing ground's sea approaches and thus repulse any counter attack made by the Royal Navy. Göring stated that 'My Luftwaffe is invincible... And so now we turn to England; how long will this one last? Two, three, weeks?' The *Reichsmarschall* believed that Fighter Command could be annihilated within a month of him launching a major air offensive. Indeed, he estimated that Britain's air defences south of a line from Gloucester to London could be wiped out in just four days, meaning that replacement squadrons from the north of England would have to be sent south, where they too would be destroyed. With Fighter Command thus defeated, Britain would be defenceless against aerial bombardment and, indeed, a seaborne invasion.

To meet this threat, two incomplete armoured divisions (equipped with tanks that were no match for the panzers) and the strongest of some twenty-seven infantry divisions took up position from south and east of a line from Lyme Bay to the Wash. By mid-summer, thousands of civilians and soldiers alike toiled to construct stop-lines of anti-tank obstacles guarding London, the Midlands and the industrial north. The Royal Navy had assembled a striking force of thirty-six destroyers, held ready from the Humber to Portsmouth. However, it could not be guaranteed that an invasion fleet would be sighted before it reached the coast, and, even if it were, a seaborne striking force might not arrive in time to prevent the enemy landing *en masse*. Therefore the success or failure of Britain's air defences, which alone could prevent the enemy from gaining the aerial supremacy required as a pre-requisite to invasion, was the decisive factor. As Hitler therefore prepared to undertake the first occupation of the British Isles in 874 years, on 18 June, Winston Churchill, who had replaced Chamberlain as Prime Minister, stirred the nation:

> The whole fury and might of the enemy must very soon be turned upon us. Hitler knows that he will have to break us in this island or lose the war. If we can stand up to him, all Europe may be free and the life of the world may move forward into broad sunlit uplands. But if we fail, then the whole world, including the United States, including all that we have known and cared for, will sink into the abyss of a new Dark Age made more sinister, and perhaps more protracted, by the lights of perverted science. Let us therefore brace ourselves to our duties, and so bear ourselves that, if the British Empire and Commonwealth last for a thousand years, men will still say '*This* was their Finest Hour'.

During the fall of France, however, Fighter Command had lost 25 per cent of its strength. Flying Officer Frank Brinsden was a New Zealander serving with 19 Squadron:

At squadron level I don't think that we were fully aware of what was going on. We were just keen to have a crack at the Germans, and the prevalent attitude was that we couldn't wait for them to come. Given that the French and Belgians had proved of little use during the defence of their own homelands, we were glad to be on our own. We were absolutely confident that we were better than the enemy, and wanted an opportunity to bloody Hitler's nose.

In June 1940, Pilot Officer David Scott-Malden, a Cambridge graduate with a First Class Honours in Classics, was learning to fly Spitfires at Aston Down, near Stroud in Gloucestershire. During those heady summer days, David and his contemporaries climbed and rolled high in the silent blue, their confidence and exuberance such that he and other pupils flew their Spitfires beneath the Severn railway bridge's arches 'when already safely posted to a squadron and reasonably safe from any complaints to the authorities'. David's diary entries make poignant reading:

Wednesday, June 12th, 1940:
Had a test on a Harvard and passed successfully into Spitfire flight. First solo an indescribable thrill. Felt a pretty king man.
Friday, June 14th, 1940:
Paris falls. Astonishing to think of it in the hands of the Germans. Reynaud declares, 'We will fight on, even if driven out of France.' Marvellous days doing aerobatics in Spitfires.
Monday, June 17th, 1940:
The French give up hostilities. Cannot yet conceive the enormity of it all. I suppose it will not be long before we are defending England in earnest.

How right David was, as Churchill confirmed: 'What General Weygand called the Battle of France is over. I expect the Battle of Britain is about to begin.'

1

OPENING SHOTS:
10 JULY – 12 AUGUST 1940

Quite why 10 July was selected by officialdom is puzzling, given that the air forces of both sides had been skirmishing over the Channel since shortly after the fall of France, and enemy reconnaissance bombers had been active photographing potential targets all over Britain. On 1 July, German troops invaded and occupied British sovereign soil – the Channel Islands – giving a crystal clear indication of what lay in store for the mainland. Being an island, of course, Britain was dependant upon importing supplies from abroad, and such inbound convoys became the focus for German air attacks. These did not, however, start on 10 July; the previous day, for example, very heavy fighting had taken place, with three major attacks developing against convoys in the English Channel. Eight RAF fighters were destroyed that day, three pilots killed and two wounded. One of the latter was 43 Squadron's CO, Squadron Leader George Lott, who lost an eye but, by virtue of the fact that this happened before 10 July, his name cannot be included among the Few. Nonetheless, the remainder of July represented a dangerous time for 11 Group's squadrons in particular, Park's pilots fighting over the sea. Air Sea Rescue (ASR), such as it was, was in its infancy at this time, although German seaplanes ranged far and wide searching for and rescuing downed Luftwaffe airmen. Nevertheless, many pilots and aircrew of both sides would be swallowed up by the Channel's temperate waters, never to be seen again.

Wednesday 10 July Eight convoys were steaming through British coastal waters at dawn. In spite of thick cloud and heavy rain, Fighter Command still mounted standing convoy protection patrols from Exeter, on the south coast, and Wick, near John O'Groats. At 10.00 hours, a substantial convoy, codenamed BREAD, rounded North Foreland, travelling west, and was spotted by a heavily escorted German reconnaissance machine. Spitfires of 74 Squadron were scrambled from Manston, and at 10.50 hours engaged the escorting Me 109s of I/JG 51. Pilot Officer John Freeborn shot up a 109, but both he and Sergeant Tony Mould had to crash land due to battle damage. Soon afterwards a *Staffel* of 109s swept

Flight Lieutenant John Freeborn DFC, a flight commander with 74 Squadron. Pictured here at Hornchurch during the summer of 1940, Freeborn destroyed seven enemy aircraft in the Battle of Britain. Of interest is the starter battery cable plugged into the Spitfire, a Mk IA.

the Dover area, being intercepted by 610 Squadron's Spitfires from Biggin Hill; Squadron Leader A.T. Smith was hit in the port wing and subsequently crash landed at Hawkinge, a small coastal airfield near Folkestone. The 109s withdrew, having suffered no loss.

By early afternoon, radar picked up a large formation assembling over France and heading towards the convoy. At 13.15 hours, one flight of 32 Squadron's Hurricanes were scrambled and soon sighted the incoming raid: twenty-six Do 17s of I/KG 2 escorted by all three *staffeln* of I/ZG 26 (Me 110s), and two *staffeln* of I/JG 3 (Me 109s). This formation therefore comprised around seventy-five enemy aircraft. Reinforcements were rapidly sent to the outnumbered pilots of 32 Squadron: 'B' Flight of 56 Squadron, and elements of both 111 and 74 Squadron, a Fighter Command force of thirty-eight fighters. The ensuing combat was fierce, involving over 100 aircraft. Both 32 and 111 Squadrons' Hurricanes attacked the enemy head-on, although the latter's Flying Officer Higgs collided with a Do 17 and lost his life. While the battle raged, a flight of Kenley's 64 Squadron was vectored to the scene. Given the order 'Buster', the Spitfire pilots

Spitfires of 92 Squadron operating from the grass aerodrome at Pembrey in South Wales. The unit subsequently moved to Biggin Hill and was heavily engaged, emerging as one of Fighter Command's premier fighter squadrons.

rammed their throttles forward and made all haste. Upon arrival, 64 Squadron found the Me 110s, which had been milling around in a defensive circle, beginning to break off and head back to France. The Spitfires harried the enemy 'destroyers' back to the French coast, damaging one 110 over Calais.

The defending RAF fighters, however, did sterling work that day: of some 150 bombs dropped, only one hit its target, sinking a vessel of 700 tons. During the fighting over Convoy BREAD, only one RAF fighter was lost, against two enemy aircraft destroyed. Based at Pembrey in South Wales, however, the keen Spitfire pilots of 92 Squadron were frustrated when scrambled too late to intercept sixty-three Ju 88s which attacked targets at Falmouth in Cornwall and Swansea in South Wales.

Thursday 11 July Clearly the interception of reconnaissance aircraft was paramount, and Fighter Command lost no time in setting about these intruders. Shortly after dawn, 66 Squadron's Squadron Leader Rupert 'Lucky' Leigh and Sergeant Reg Hyde intercepted a Do 17 over Yarmouth, but Leigh's Spitfire was damaged and the Dornier escaped in cloud. Ten minutes later, however, a lone Hurricane, flown by Squadron Leader Douglas Bader, CO of 242 Squadron at Coltishall, caught and destroyed the intruder, which crashed into the sea off Cromer. Another squadron commander, Squadron Leader Peter Townsend of 85 Squadron, was also patrolling alone around this time (the weather being so bad this particular morning that the COs flew themselves, rather than risk their

Squadron Leader Peter Townsend leads the Hurricanes of 85 Squadron on patrol during the Battle of Britain. Such tight formations were found useless in fighter-to-fighter combat, but, given Townsend's experience, it is likely that this formation was adopted on this occasion for the photographer's benefit.

pilots' lives), and attacked a solo Do 17 near Harwich. During the interception, Townsend's Hurricane was damaged, his engine seizing completely and forcing him to bale out. Fortunately this highly experienced pre-war airman and exceptional fighter pilot was rescued after just twenty minutes bobbing around in the cold North Sea. Although the raider escaped, it landed back at base with three wounded crew members. As the battle wore on, some RAF fighters pilots felt it best not to simply destroy enemy aircraft but to send them home badly damaged and with wounded crewmen aboard as a warning to their comrades.

Although Britain was still covered by cloud, the main fighting started early: soon after 07.00 hours, Stukas headed towards a convoy passing through Lyme Bay. The Hurricanes of 501 Squadron's Green Section, Pilot Officer E.J.H. Sylvester (Green One), Pilot Officer R.S. Don and Sergeant F.J.P. Dixon, were *en route* to intercept the ten enemy dive-bombers when bounced by escorting 109s. In the short but sharp engagement that followed, Dixon was shot down; although the 21-year-old pilot baled out, he was never seen again. At Warmwell, near Weymouth in 10 Group, a flight of 609 Squadron's Spitfires were scrambled, arriving over the convoy just as the Stukas attacked. Outnumbered by odds of

Pilot Officer David Crook DFC, an Auxiliary airman with 609 'West Riding' Squadron prepares for take-off at Warmwell in August 1940. Crook was a successful fighter pilot in 1940 but was sadly killed in a flying accident during 1944. Left behind for posterity, however, was his superb first-hand account of 1940, entitled simply *Spitfire Pilot*.

6:1, the Spitfires were routed when the escorting 109s struck, two of the 'West Riding' auxiliary pilots being killed. Although the enemy formation suffered no loss, there were no hits on merchant shipping.

The enemy dive-bombers soon re-grouped for a second raid on the Lyme Bay convoy, but this time their escort was exclusively Me 110s of III/ZG 76. Disastrously, virtually all of the Middle Wallop Sector's fighters were being 'turned around' (re-fuelled and re-armed) when this threat appeared, so the adjacent 11 Group Controller scrambled a flight of 601 Squadron's Hurricanes from Tangmere. Although fifty miles away from the action, the Hurricane pilots pushed their throttles through the 'gate' and made all haste. Upon arrival over Portland, the Me 110s were too high to prevent the Hurricanes' first attack on the Stukas. Flying Officers Cleaver and Riddle soon shot down a dive-bomber each. As the 110s rained down, the 601 Squadron pilots stood firm, destroying one of the escorts. The enemy retired, and 601 Squadron returned to Tangmere without loss. This is a prime example of the fact that the twin-engined Me 110 was just not up to engaging single-engined fighters like Spitfires and Hurricanes; had Me 109s been present, however, as indeed they had that morning to 609 Squadron's Spitfire pilots' discomfort, the Hurricanes would not have had everything their way.

It was to be a busy day for 601 Squadron, which had already destroyed a Do 17 south of the Isle of Wight earlier that day. At 17.15 hours, twelve He 111s and as many Me 110s appeared heading for the Portsmouth naval dockyard. Flying Officer 'Willie' Rhodes-Moorhouse led the charge against the enemy bombers, and a dogfight with the escort developed immediately. Sgt Woolley was unfortunately shot down by 'friendly' anti-aircraft fire, baling out burnt and wounded by shrapnel, but Flight Sergeant Bill Pond attacked an He 111 which took such violent evasive action that it collided with its neighbour and exploded; Flying Officer Cleaver damaged another, and Flying Officer Davis destroyed an Me 110. On what was such a red letter day for 601 Squadron, there must have been quite a party back at Tangmere that particular evening!

Friday 12 July After a night of bombing which left twenty-nine killed and 103 injured, the day fighting revolved around the Convoy BOOTY, steaming south from the Thames Estuary. That day, the Hurricanes of 17 Squadron's 'A' Flight was operating from the Debden Sector's forward base at Martlesham Heath; at 08.00 hours they were up and *en route* to patrol BOOTY, when notified of a substantial incoming raid. The 12 Group Controller scrambled a sizeable force to reinforce 17 Squadron: three Hurricanes of 85, three of 242, six Defiants of 264 and eleven Hurricanes of 151 Squadrons (although 242 and 264 Squadrons made no contact with the raiders). At 08.48 hours, 17 Squadron tally ho'd, having sighted the enemy: two *staffeln* of II/KG 2's Do 17s and likewise of III/KG 53's He 111s – but no fighter escort. Interestingly, 17 Squadron, which had fought during the French campaign, attacked not in the stipulated vic of three, but in pairs. Heinkels, roughly handled by 17 Squadron, were already falling from the sky when Squadron Leader Teddy Donaldson and 151 Squadron arrived; flying with them was Wing Commander Victor Beamish, that legendary Irishman and Station Commander of the North Weald Sector Station. Donaldson charged the Do 17s, but their formation discipline, and thus mutual fire support, proved better than that of III/KG 53's He 111s, so 151 Squadron did not escape unscathed: Flying Officer Allen was hit and never seen again, and several other fighters were damaged. Beamish himself damaged a Dornier, however, which the other Hurricanes set upon and destroyed like a pack of hunting dogs. Just before the party was over, 85 Squadron engaged the He 111s, destroying one but losing Sergeant Jowitt, who was killed.

The raid on BOOTY, dealt with by 12 Group, was the only major threat this day, although small formations of enemy bombers were intercepted hither and thither, the Spitfires of 603 Squadron's Yellow Section shooting down an He 111 which unfortunately crashed on Aberdeen's ice rink, causing civilian casualties.

Bad weather over the Channel had helped conceal Convoy AGENT, traveling south along the Kentish coast. At 14.30 hours the ships were sighted by an He 111 of KG 55's *Geschwaderstab*, but this was promptly destroyed by Squadron Leader Badger and his 43 Squadron, up from Tangmere. Off Portland, reconnaissance bombers also probed British airspace, seeking another convoy,

Hurricane pilots of 151 Squadron at rest between sorties at North Weald. The pilot wearing black pre-war flying overalls is Pilot Officer Jack Hamar DFC, who performed brilliantly during both the Battle of France and Operation DYNAMO. Sadly, he was killed in a senseless flying accident at North Weald early in the Battle of Britain.

Pilot Officer Jack Hamar DFC (standing, extreme left) and pilots of 151 Squadron at North Weald. A regular RAF squadron, the white flying overalls mark out these pilots as pre-war regulars.

238 Squadron operated Hurricanes from bases in 10 Group during the Battle of Britain, seeing much action. This line up was snapped at Chilbolton in 1941 but includes four pilots who saw combat with 238 the previous summer; from left: 2nd – Sgt P. Pearson; 7th – P/O P.J. Morgan, 8th – P/O J.R. Urwin-Mann; 16th – P/O V.C. Simmonds.

but were driven off by 501 Squadron. Sadly, however, Pilot Officer Hewitt was killed when he misjudged a dive and crashed into the sea.

Saturday 13 July Although overcast once more, enemy aircraft sought convoys in the Channel. The first action was fought by 43 Squadron's Blue Section, which chased a Ju 88 from the Isle of Wight almost back to Cherbourg before shooting it down. The convoy that had attracted the Ju 88's attention was in Lyme Bay, and the Germans lost no time in sending fifty bombers to attack it. At 15.00 hours, the Hurricanes of 238 Squadron and Spitfires of 609 Squadron were sent from Warmwell, near Weymouth and in 10 Group's Middle Wallop Sector, to patrol over the convoy. However, expecting to find the ships near Portland, the RAF fighters found only the incoming enemy formation, also seeking the missing ships, the convoy having set a zig-zag course and as a result of which it was some miles away. Two Dorniers were shot down by 238 Squadron, although the victor of one of those combats, the Australian Flight Lieutenant Kennedy, crashed and was killed back at Warmwell. The remaining enemy machines, forty Me 110s of V/LG 1, formed a defensive circle, six miles off Portland, which the RAF fighters were unable to penetrate, although several 110s were damaged.

Another convoy's position, however, was far more dangerous, as it steamed through the Straits of Dover, easily seen from the French coast. Stukas were soon sent to attack the ships, escorted by a whole Gruppe (three *staffeln*) of

JG 51's Me 109s. The presence of so many 109s was bound to bode ill for the RAF intercepting fighters: two Hurricanes of 56 Squadron were subsequently destroyed. Pilot Officer Colin Grey, a New Zealander flying Spitfires with 54 Squadron, chased and destroyed a 109 after a low level chase over the waves, but another Spitfire was damaged by 'friendly' anti aircraft fire.

Sunday 14 July Even though bad weather served to protect the nine convoys steaming through Channel waters, Fighter Command still flew a total of 597 sorties. A convoy off Eastbourne attracted the day's only substantial raid: the whole of IV/LG 1's Stukas, accompanied by thirty Me 109s of JG 3 (and possibly JG 51). Battle was joined when the raiders were intercepted by the Hurricanes of 615 and 151 Squadrons, and the Spitfires of 610 Squadron. Among the 151 Squadron pilots engaged was Pilot Officer Jack Hamar, who later reported vividly on the action:

> At 1500 hours the Squadron was ordered off from Rochford to intercept E/As south of Dover. At approximately 1520 hours, when the Squadron was almost over Dover, a bunch of Me 109s were sighted about 5,000 feet above our formation, in which I was flying Red Two. As it looked as though the E/A were about to attack us, the leader ordered our defensive line astern tactics. As we turned sharply to port, two Me 109s were seen diving to attack the last aircraft in our formation. 'Milna Leader' attacked the leading Me 109 and I the second. I turned inside the E/A, which had pulled up into a steep left hand climbing turn. I closed rapidly and opened fire at about 250 yards with a 45° deflection shot. The E/A seemed to falter and straightened out into a dive. I placed myself dead astern at about 50 yards. I opened fire, closing to almost no distance. I saw a large explosion just in front of the pilot and a large amount of white smoke poured from the E/A, which by this time was climbing steeply. I was then forced to break away quickly due to fire from the rear, lost sight of the E/A and therefore did not see it crash. This action was also witnessed by Flying Officer Forster.

This great combat over the Channel, within sight of the white cliffs of Dover, was actually being witnessed from that vantage point by veteran BBC reporter Charles Gardner, who was sitting in a recording van and whose radio broadcast that evening marked an important milestone in the history of war reporting:

> The Germans are dive-bombing a convoy out at sea: there are one, two, three, four, five, six, seven German dive-bombers, Junkers 87s. There's one going down on its target now – bomb! No! He missed the ships, it hasn't hit a single ship – there are about 10 ships in the convoy but he hasn't hit a single one and – There, you can hear our anti-aircraft going at them now. There are one, two, three, four, five, six – there are about 10 German machines dive-bombing the convoy, which is just out to sea in the Channel.
>
> I can't see anything! No! We thought he had got a German one at the top then, but now the British fighters are coming up. Here they come. The Germans are coming in an

Pilots of 32 Squadron relax at readiness in front of a Hurricane, August 1940. All but one survived the Battle of Britain and the war; Pilot Officer Keith Gillman (second left) was reported missing following combat over the Channel on 25 August 1940.

absolutely steep dive, and you can see their bombs actually leave the machines and come into the water. You can hear our guns going like anything now. I can hear machine-gun fire but I can't see our Spitfires. They must be somewhere there. Oh! Here's one coming down.

There's one going down in flames. Somebody's hit a German and he's coming down with a long streak – coming down completely out of control – a long streak of smoke – and now a man's baled out by parachute. The pilot's baled out by parachute. He's a Junkers 87 and he's going slap into the sea – and there he goes: SMASH! A terrific column of water and there was a Junkers 87. Only one man got out by parachute, so presumably there was only a crew of one in it.

Now then, oh, there's a terrific mix-up over the Channel! It's impossible to tell which are our machines and which are the Germans. There was one definitely down in this battle and there's a fight going on. There's a fight going on and you can hear the little rattles of machine-gun bullets. Crump! That was a bomb, as you may imagine. Here comes one Spitfire. There's a little burst. There's another bomb dropping. Yes, it has dropped. It has missed the convoy. You know, they haven't hit the convoy in all this. The sky is absolutely

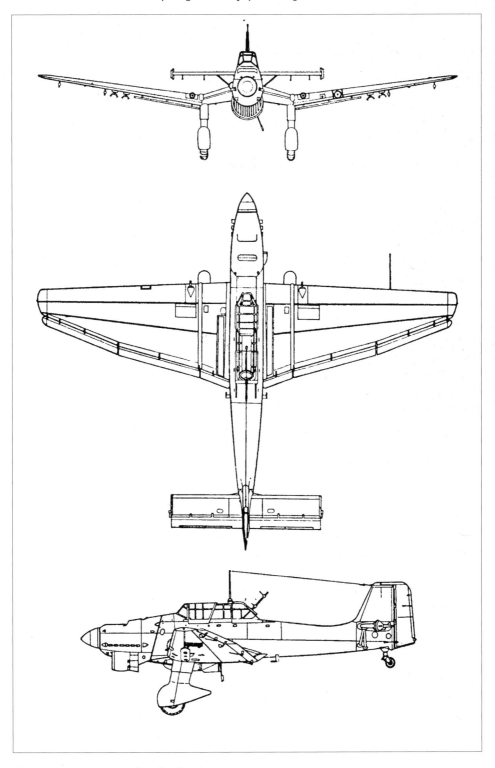

The German Ju 87 or 'Stuka' dive bomber.

patterned with bursts of anti-aircraft fire, and the sea is covered with smoke where bombs have burst, but as far as I can see there is not one single ship hit, and there is definitely one German machine down. And I am looking across the sea now. I can see the little white dot of a parachute as the German pilot is floating down towards the spot where his machine crashed with such a big fountain of water two minutes ago.

Well, now everything is peaceful again, for the moment. The Germans, who came over in about twenty or twenty-five dive-bombers, delivered their attack on the convoy, and I think they made off as quickly as they came. Oh yes, I can see one, two, three, four, five, six, seven, eight, nine, ten Germans hareing back towards France now for all they can go – and here are our Spitfires coming after them. There's going to be a big fight, I think, out there, but it will be too far away for us to see. Of course, there are a lot more German machines up there, 'Can you see, Cyril?' Yes, there are one, two, three, four, five, six, seven on the top layer, one, two, three – there's two layers of German machines. They are all, I think, I could not swear to it, but they were all Junkers 87s.

Well, that was a really hot little engagement while it lasted. No damage done, except to the Germans who lost one machine and the German pilot who is still on the end of his parachute, although appreciably nearer the sea than he was. I can see no boat going out to pick him up, so he'll probably have a long swim ashore. Well, that was a very unsuccessful attack on the convoy, I must say.

Oh, there's another fight going on, away up, now – I think about 20, 25 or even 30,000 feet above our heads, and I can't see a thing of it. The anti-aircraft guns have put up one, two, three, four, five, six bursts, but I can't see the aeroplanes. There we go again – oh, we have just hit a Messerschmitt! Oh, that was beautiful! He's coming right down, I think it was definitely that burst got him. Yes, he's come down. You hear those crowds? He's finished! Oh, he's coming down like a rocket now. An absolute steep dive. Let us move round so we can watch him a bit more. Here he comes, down in a steep dive – the Messerschmitt. No, no, the pilot's not getting out of that one. He's being followed down. What, there are two more Messerschmitts up there? I think they are all right. No – that man's finished. He's going down from about 10,000, oh, 20,000 to about 2,000 feet, and he's going straight down – he's not stopping. I think that's another German machine that's definitely put paid to. I don't think we shall actually see him crash because he's going into a bank of cloud. He's smoking now. I can see smoke, although we cannot count that as a definite victory because I did not see him crash. He's going behind a hill. He looked certainly out of control.

Now, we are looking up to the anti-aircraft guns. There's another! There's another Messerschmitt. I don't know whether he's down or whether he's trying to get out of the anti-aircraft fire, which is giving him a very hot time. There's a Spitfire! Oh! There's about four fighters up there, and I don't know what they are doing. One, two, three, four, five fighters fighting right above our heads. Now there's one coming right down on the tail of what I think is a Messerschmitt, and I think it's a Spitfire behind him. Oh darn! They've turned away and I can't see. Where's one crashing? No, I think he's pulled out. You can't watch these fights very coherently for long. You just see about four twirling machines, you just hear little bursts of machine-gunning, and by the time you've picked up the machines they've gone.

Hello, there are one, two, three, and look, there's a dogfight going on up there! There are four, five, six machines wheeling and turning around. Now – hark at all the machine-guns going! Hark! One, two, three, four, five, six. Now there's something coming right down on the tail of another. Here they come. Yes, they are being chased home! There are three Spitfires chasing three Messerschmitts now. Oh boy! Look at them going! Oh, look how the Messerschmitts – oh boy – look at them going! Oh, look how the Messerschmitts – oh boy – that was really grand! There's a Spitfire behind the first two. He will get them. Oh yes! Oh boy! I've never seen anything so good as this! The RAF fighters have really got these boys taped. Our machine is catching up the Messerschmitt now. He's catching it up! He's got the legs of it, you know. Now, right in the sights, go on, George! You've got him! Bomb – bomb. No, no, the distance is a bit deceptive from here. You can't tell but I think something is definitely going to happen to that first Messerschmitt. Oh yes – just a moment – I think I wouldn't like to be in that first Messerschmitt. I think he's got him. Yes? Machine-guns are going like anything. No, there's another fight going on. No, they've chased him right out to sea. I can't see, but I think the odds would certainly be on that first Messerschmitt catching it. Yes, they've got him down too, yes, he's pulled away from him. Yes, I think that first Messerschmitt has crashed on the coast of France all right!

To many, Gardner's now famous broadcast was inspirational and morale boosting; others wrote to *The Times*, complaining that he had reduced the whole matter of men fighting for their lives to the level of a cup final. They had a point: the first aircraft Gardner saw crash was not a Stuka, in fact, but the 615 Squadron Hurricane of Pilot Officer M.R. Mudie; although rescued from the water, he died in Dover hospital the following day.

Monday 15 July Again the overcast prevented action over the convoys, until a raid came in at 14.15 hours, heading for the Thames Estuary. Three 11 Group Hurricane squadrons were already providing a protective umbrella; although they failed to destroy any enemy bombers, no bombs found their targets.

Tuesday 16 July As already discussed, it is difficult to understand why officialdom decided upon 10 July as the Battle of Britain's start date. From the German perspective the Battle of Britain was fought to achieve aerial supremacy over southern England as a prelude to a seaborne invasion; surely, then, the Battle of Britain cannot be considered to have started until the enemy at least made the decision to invade, and or began the process necessary to achieve that end result? With that in mind, it could strongly be argued that the Battle of Britain actually either started on 16 July, when Hitler issued his Directive No.16, confirming his intention to occupy England, or later, when air operations specifically aimed at wiping out Fighter Command commenced.

On this significant day, fog enveloped Northern France and south-east England, providing an opportunity for the day fighter squadrons to enjoy some

Squadron Leader Crossley DFC (third from right, standing), with some of his pilots at Biggin Hill, July 1940; from left: P/O J.P. Pfeiffer, F/L J.B.W. Humpherson, F/O P.M. Gardner, S/L M.N. Crossley, F/O D.H. Grice, & P/O J.F. Pain; seated, from left: P/O A.K. Eckford, K. Pniak & B.A. Wlasowski.

rare time off duty. Instead of Spitfires, Hurricanes and Defiants droning over convoys, Blenheim night-fighters fulfilled the convoy protection role until midday, when the weather improved sufficiently for 242 Squadron to get up from Coltishall and cover a convoy off Great Yarmouth. Although 238 Squadron sighted some Me 110s off Portland, these were quickly lost in the haze. Fighter Command's only success of the day came at 17.05 hours, when Flying Officer Willie Rhodes-Moorhouse of 601 Squadron shot down a Ju 88 over the Solent.

Wednesday 17 July The abysmal weather continued to prevent the Luftwaffe mounting any major operations, the only substantial threat coming in over the North Sea, from Stavanger in Norway, when a small formation of III/KG 26 He 111s bombed the Imperial Chemical Factory in Ayrshire. One of the raiders failed to return, courtesy of 603 Squadron.

Far to the south, twelve Spitfires of 64 Squadron patrolled over Beachy Head until bounced by Me 109s; Flying Officer D.M. Taylor was shot down and wounded. That evening, 92 Squadron, still based at Pembrey and providing fighter protection to Bristol and South Wales, shot down a Ju 88 over the Bristol Channel, which was no doubt reporting new shipping.

The Battle of Britain was now a week old, and Air Chief Marshal Dowding's system was fighting the defensive battle for survival that he always knew would come, Bill Ellams was an AC1 Airframe Rigger on 611 Squadron's 'B' Flight at Digby:

God I was thrilled when they gave me a Spitfire to look after! We slept in dug-outs on dispersal near the aircraft, and were up every morning at dawn to run up and check everything. Despite it being summer, as the flight mechanic revved up the Merlin, we riggers were straddled over the tailplane, to hold the aircraft down, frozen in the slipstream! Once a Spitfire overrode the chocks and moved forward despite the brakes being applied! I was so cold and numb that I didn't give a damn. Incidentally, the Dunlop air brakes were the weak part of the Spitfire. I must have spent hours of my time upside down in the cockpit adjusting the air valves to synchronise the pressure with the rudder bar.

Whilst on standby we would clean the Spitfires with a wax dissolved in a petrol mixture, let it dry then polish it like hell to get a shine. The crew undertaking this often included the pilot who also mucked in. By doing this we could get an extra 5mph in flight. At Digby we very much regarded ourselves as a team, including the pilot who was more or less considered a friend. We would discuss with him things like the 'hands off' technique. I would place a bit of string doped on the control surfaces or trimming tabs to get perfection – amazing what a little knowledge of aerodynamics could do!

Getting the Spitfire back in the air as quickly as possible was very important to the rigger, mechanic and armourer. Our team would rehearse the routine over and over again. We could all check control surfaces, refuel and rearm in just four minutes. We made short-handled screwdrivers to undo and fasten the *Dzus* buttons which secured the panels. Believe me, these were exciting times! During a panic turnaround, I was passing along the leading edge of the mainplane, the armourer was rearming and reloading the Browning guns when as he was pulling back the striking pin with his toggle he slipped – there was a round up the spout, the bullet passed by my face but I didn't even pause; afterwards, when the kite had taken off, I said a prayer and broke out into a sweat!

Another nasty piece of work was on take-off. The rigger stood by the starter trolley whilst the pilot primed the engine. When the engine fired I had to pass along the leading edge of the mainplane and take out the plug just behind the airscrew, fasten up the little panel with the *Dzus* fastener, run back and pull the chocks away. That airscrew so near one's arm and shoulder was not at all nice, especially as the pilot was anxious to get moving forward to take-off in formation! Many a time I had to duck to let the mainplane pass above my head.

I remember our Sergeant Levenson taking off early one morning in his pyjamas, with flying helmet, jacket, one boot and no trousers – panic stations! He was a shade of blue upon return, but it was no funk. A particular officer pilot even used to spray the inside of his cockpit with lavender water but he was no pansy. Other pilots had lucky charms but I never once saw a frightened face. The comradeship between pilots and groundcrews was wonderful.

Whilst on duty we were never allowed away from the Spitfires, meals were brought out to dispersal. Whilst stood down we had hobbies: I made model aircraft, Gilly Potter grew vegetables, Len Carver made paper knives out of old salvaged flying wire and put Perspex handles on them. Some made a poker and pontoon gang and played with matches, others tried to filter the green dye out of the 100 octane petrol, to sell to the pilots who often had cars but no fuel. I bought an old bicycle and did it up like new, and whilst off duty used to cycle to Lincoln and enjoy egg and chips at the Salvation Army Canteen, price one shilling!

Thursday 18 July With the weather still favouring the defenders, the Luftwaffe's operations remained limited. However, the enemy was by now aware that radar was providing Fighter Command with early warning of their formations approaching, although RDF could not identify individual aircraft types, thus enabling the Germans to set a clever trap: radar noted a large formation building up over the Pas-de-Calais, 11 Group consequently scrambling twelve Spitfires of 610 Squadron to patrol over Dover. Assuming that the raid was largely bombers heading for a convoy in the Dover Straits, the Spitfire pilots were dismayed to be bounced by Me 109s, losing Pilot Officer Litchfield who went down into the sea. The enemy formation was not, in fact, bombers, but exclusively Me 109s, the intention being to provide Fighter Command with a short, sharp, shock.

The motto of Fighter Command was 'Defence: Offence', and this was put to the test when Hurricanes of 111 and 615 Squadrons escorted eighteen Blenheim bombers on a raid to attack enemy invasion preparations at Boulogne. Bombs found their mark, and an Hs 126 communications aircraft, which was foolish enough to blunder into the RAF fighters, was rapidly shot up.

Although no major raids were launched this day, Tangmere's 145 Squadron shot down an He 111 twenty miles off Bognor Regis, in which the *Geschwaderkommodore* of KG 27 was killed. In the North, 603 Squadron was kept busy chasing lone raiders, one of which was damaged by Sergeant J.R. Caister.

Friday 19 July As no less than nine convoys chugged around the British coastline, more squadrons than normal were sensibly sent to operate from forward coastal airfields. The first action was fought off Brighton at 07.40 hours, when 145 Squadron destroyed a lone Ju 88. Sadly, however, this would be a black day indeed for Fighter Command, as Air Chief Marshal Dowding's grave concerns regarding the Defiant were tragically proved correct.

After the Defiants of 264 Squadrons achieved success over Dunkirk, the other Defiant unit, 141 Squadron, harboured similar ambitions. At 08.45 hours, 141 Squadron moved forward from West Malling to Hawkinge, from where, at 12.23 hours, the Squadron was scrambled to patrol twenty miles south of Folkestone. Due to technical problems only nine Defiants took off and headed for their allocated patrol area. *En route*, a *staffel* of ten Me 109s from II/JG 2 pounced on the Defiants, having identified them correctly and attacked head-on,

Pilot Officer Peter de Peyster Brown joined 1 (RCAF) Squadron at Northolt during the Battle of Britain, subsequently destroying a Do 215 and sharing a Ju 88. He is pictured here in the traditional fighter pilots' roll neck jumper.

before another *staffel* of 109s also attacked. Without forward firing armament the Defiants were massacred: five Defiants were shot down in flames, the only aircrew survivor being a pilot picked up, wounded, from the Channel. Another Defiant was pursued and shot down, crashing in Dover. Only four 141 Squadron pilots managed to escape and return to Hawkinge, and two of them were in serious difficulties: Flight Lieutenant Loudon crashed in Hawkinge village, and Pilot Officer MacDougall's aircraft was considered so badly damaged that it was immediately written off.

In that one, dreadful, action, 141 Squadron ceased to exist, having lost seven aircraft and twelve aircrew, leading to the immediate withdrawal of the Defiant as a day-fighter. It is tragic that the Air Staff's incompetence in respect of this matter should have been proven at the cost of so many young lives. In fact, had Squadron Leader John Thompson and the Hurricanes of 111 Squadron not arrived on the scene literally in the nick of time, there would have been no survivors. One of Thompson's pilots, Pilot Officer Simpson, destroyed a 109, but, as the shock waves resounded throughout Fighter Command, it must have felt a hollow victory.

Dover harbour was then attacked, by Stukas, which fled when the Hurricanes of Squadron Leader John Worrall's 32 Squadron, also operating from Hawkinge, appeared. Before 32 Squadron could attack, they were set upon by twelve Me 109s: Flight Sergeant Guy Turner was shot down in flames but rescued from the sea, albeit badly wounded.

Tangmere's 43 Squadron was also engaged by a large force of Me 109s off Selsey Bill. Flight Lieutenant John Simpson baled out with a broken collar bone and a bullet in his leg, and Sergeant John Buck baled out but drowned. The Sector's other squadron, 145, fared better, Red Section shooting down an He 111 of III/KG 55 off Shoreham at 17.55 hours.

There was also action over 10 Group. Stukas attempted to attack the naval installations at Portland but were seen off by 87 Squadron, which damaged a dive-bomber. Finally, back in 11 Group, a cheeky He 115 floatplane, sowing mines in the Thames Estuary during broad daylight, was destroyed by 64 Squadron.

In Berlin, the Reichstag resounded to Hitler's speech appealing for Britain to surrender, so as 'to avert the sacrifices which must claim millions'. Save for continued sorties by Fighter Command, there was no other response forthcoming.

Saturday 20 July The first incoming threat was early: 54 Squadron was scrambled at 05.21 hours but missed the enemy, although shortly afterwards Blue Section of 56 Squadron brought down a Ju 88, one of a small formation caught off Burham. Throughout the morning, lone reconnaissance aircraft were active, 603 Squadron destroying a Do 17 off the Scottish coast. Flying over Convoy BOSOM in Lyme Bay, 238 Squadron saw off three Me 109s before destroying an He 59 that was shadowing the eastbound convoy. As BOSOM passed into 11

One of the classic photographs of 1940: Hurricane pilots of 32 Squadron at Hawkinge in July 1940; from left: P/Os R.F. Smythe, K.R. Gillman & E. Proctor, F/L P.M. Brothers DFC, P/Os D.H. Grice, P.M. Gardner DFC & A.F. Eckford. Situated on the coast near Folkestone, Hawkinge was the closest RAF station to the enemy – just twenty-two miles away across the Channel.

Group's area, another He 59 appeared and shot down a 43 Squadron Hurricane before making off; this success was short lived: 601 Squadron soon found and destroyed the German seaplane.

In anticipation of trouble, Air Vice-Marshal Park ordered up no less than two Hurricane and two Spitfire squadrons from the Kenley and Biggin Hill Sectors to patrol over Convoy BOSOM. This was an unusual deployment, given the numbers of fighters committed, and would confound the enemy, who were taken completely by surprise. At 18.00 hours, Stukas bore down on BOSOM, escorted by around fifty Me 109s and 110s. A huge mêlée began, Park's pilots enjoying the element of surprise, coming out of the sun, into the glare of which the Germans were flying. 32 Squadron charged right through the confused escorts, shooting down two dive-bombers. The escorting Me 110s immediately and wisely went into their usual defensive circle, leaving the Me 109s to tackle the RAF fighters. Three 109s were destroyed by 615 Squadron, against one Hurricane and a single Spitfire. Clearly large formations were useful, providing they could achieve surprise, as in this case, which was Fighter Command's first substantial victory of the Battle of Britain so far. It is also interesting to note how well the Hurricane performed during this engagement, proving that when fighting within certain height bands, where its performance was at its best, Hawker's fighter could, in fact, hold its own.

Sunday 21 July Given the previous day's success, both 10 and 11 Groups mounted convoy protection patrols in squadron strength. This, of course, meant that Fighter Command was flying an increasing number of sorties, which, if continued over time, would be fatiguing on both personnel and machines.

The first enemy fell over Goodwood, a reconnaissance bomber being shot down by 238 Squadron's Red Section at 10.30 hours. A few hours later, at 14.30 hours, the squadron would destroy a similar aircraft over Blandford. At that time, a westbound convoy, codenamed PEEWIT, was attacked off the Needles by a whole *gruppe* of Do 17s, escorted by the usual mixed bag of fifty Me 109s and 110s. 43 Squadron was on hand, however, and went for the bombers before being engaged by the German fighters; Pilot Officer de Mancha collided with a 7/JG 27 Me 109, flown by *Leutnant* Kroker; both pilots were killed. The Do 17s dropped their bombs without result and turned back for France, at which point 238 Squadron arrived to reinforce Badger's 43 Squadron and found Me 110s of V/LG 1 dive-bombing the convoy. The Middle Wallop Sector Hurricanes tally ho'd, and Pilot Officer Brian Considine chased one 110 almost back to France: shot up, it crashed back at base, killing one of the crew.

Monday 22 July Again, the first enemy downed was a reconnaissance machine, at 13.00 hours, this time by 145 Squadron over Selsey Bill. Given the almost complete lack of convoys traversing the Channel, there was otherwise very little activity throughout this day.

Tuesday 23 July Once more enemy air activity continued on a much reduced scale. A Ju 88 shadowing Convoy PILOT off Great Yarmouth was destroyed by 242 Squadron, and a section of 603 Squadron shot down a lone Do 17 some seventy-five miles east of Aberdeen.

Wednesday 24 July An early bird reconnaissance He 111 of KG 26 was damaged by 603 Squadron between Aberdeen and Peterhead, but a Ju 88 operating over the West Country was not so lucky: Red Section of 92 Squadron, up from Pembrey, intercepted L1+DL of 3/LG 1, which was attacking shipping in the Bristol Channel, and shot it down in flames. The raider, which was also attacked by an 87 Squadron Hurricane, crashed in flames on Martinhoe Common at 07.40 hours; two of the crew were captured, the other two baled out too low and were killed. Forty minutes later, 54 Squadron chased off a formation of Do 17s attempting to bomb a convoy in the Dover Strait, but at 11.00 hours another convoy, steaming out of the Medway, attracted a major raid: more Do 17s appeared, but this time escorted by a large formation of Me 109s. The 109s were, in fact, from III/JG 26, commanded by that famous German *experten* Major Adolf Galland, and were making the first of many sorties during the Battle of Britain. JG 26 had only recently moved from Germany to the Channel coast, operating from cornfields at Audembert, near Calais, and equipped with the latest Me 109, the E-4, which enjoyed the benefits of an armoured windscreen and two nose-mounted machine-guns. On this first intrusion over England, II/JG 26, with only ten aircraft, swept ahead of the main formation, but over Dover the *Gruppenkommandeur*, *Hauptmann* Noack, panicked at the appearance of 'thirty Spitfires' (there were actually only nine, of 610 Squadron), aborted the mission but crashed and was killed on landing back at Marquise. Galland's III/JG 26 comprised forty fighters and were engaged by the Spitfires of 54 and 65 Squadrons. Galland's pilots prevented any damage to the bombers, but lost two pilots, one being killed, the other badly wounded and captured. In response the intercepting Spitfires also suffered two casualties, Pilot Officer Johnnie Allen DFC being killed. Galland, who would become one of Germany's most respected and admired fighter pilots and leaders, later commented that his experiences on this sortie reinforced his view that the RAF was a formidable opponent.

When forced to disengage due to fuel reserves, III/JG 26 dived for the deck and skimmed over Kent at low level, roaring over the white cliffs and heading back to the Pas-de-Calais. This power dive was the 109's standard evasive tactic: due to its Daimler-Benz engine being fuel injected, the flow of fuel to the engine was therefore unaffected by gravity, meaning that it did not cut out in a dive, unlike the Rolls Royce Merlin which did not enjoy the benefits of direct fuel feed. The 109, therefore, was always able to outrun a Spitfire in a dive. As III/JG 26 made its hasty exit, III/JG 52 appeared on a *freie hunt* to cover Galland's withdrawal. 610 Squadron, up from Biggin Hill, pounced on the 109s of 7/JG 52 over Margate, destroying two of them (both pilots being killed) for no loss.

This day represents an important development, in that with the German fighter force on the *Kanal* reinforced by JG 26, it was now possible for the enemy to co-ordinate fighter sweeps in advance of the main raid, thus preoccupying and exhausting the defending fighters and leaving the way clear for bombers to attack convoys. At North Weald Sector Station, a tragedy took place on this day. Squadron Leader 'Teddy' Donaldson:

That morning the weather was appalling. I got an urgent telephone call from the AOC. He said, 'The weather is bloody awful, but I have an unidentified aircraft circling Felixstowe at 10,000 feet and I don't like it. As the weather is so bad I must ask you, not order you, if you can go after him.' I turned to my Red Two, Pilot Officer Jack Hamar, and said, 'What about it?' Jack replied, as I knew he would, 'Let's get the bastard!'

Air Vice-Marshal Park said, 'Thanks a lot,' so off we went. Visibility was down to about a quarter of a mile. The danger at North Weald was the international radio masts, which went up several hundred feet, and whilst the controllers could get pilots back to the field, to avoid the masts you had to see them in time.

No sooner were we airborne with wheels up than Group identified the bogey as friendly. We turned around and, flying slowly at 120 mph and only some 60 feet above the ground,

Adolf Galland, the German 'ace' and *Kommodore* of JG 26, prepares for another sortie over England. After the death of his friend Mölders in a flying accident, Galland became general of day fighters, a position he held until 1945. Highly respected by both friends and enemies, Galland was a true *experte*.

I waited for North Weald to reappear, which it did in a few minutes. I ordered Jack to break. To my horror he broke upwards and commenced an upward roll. In a Hurricane it was impossible to carry out such a manoeuvre at that low speed. As I saw him start his right-handed roll, I screamed 'Don't, don't!' down the R/T, but it was too late. Jack stalled and hit the deck upside down.

I was on the ground and beside him within seconds. Jack had had his hood open to improve visibility in the awful weather conditions, which had caused massive head injuries. I was devastated. I absolutely loved the man. Jack had been my Number Two throughout the Battle of France, and was superb. Whatever happened I always knew that Jack would be there, guarding my tail, and, to be fair, looking after me was a hazardous business. Jack did so loyally and even managed to shoot down 6½ enemy aircraft. The half was for a German bomber that we shared: I had damaged it, but it may have limped home, so Jack went and blew it out of the sky.

Only the day before Pilot Officer Hamar's tragic death, 151 Squadron had been notified that his gallantry in the air had been recognised by the award of a Distinguished Flying Cross. Sadly, the 25-year-old was buried at his home town of Knighton, his grieving mother receiving her son's medal from a grateful King in the air raid shelter of Buckingham Palace on 17 September .

At the Duxford Sector in 12 Group, 19 Squadron packed up its troubles and moved to operate from the nearby satellite landing ground at Fowlmere Farm, codenamed G1. This was a wise precaution, so that in the event of Duxford being bombed, not all the Sector's fighters could be destroyed. John Milne was an 18-year-old Halton-trained Flight Rigger LAC on 19 Squadron:

> When we first moved to Fowlmere there was no permanent accommodation. We slept in bell tents, feet to the central pole. A mobile cookhouse accompanied us – one day it caught fire! We dug latrine trenches and spent most of our time out of doors. Nobody seemed to mind. Fowlmere later had Nissen huts, never popular, as condensation dripped down from the underside of the cold steel roof, onto one's bedding and oneself.
>
> Flying from Fowlmere must have been fun! The airfield was far from level and dipped considerably in the corner closest to Duxford. Part of it was overlaid with a metal mesh decking to improve the surface. There were certain features of Duxford and Fowlmere which must remain forever recalled by everyone who served there: the sound of Merlin engines starting up, Spitfires taxying and flying low over the airfield, the smell of glycol coolant leaking onto hot metal, the smell of 100 octane petrol and attempting to strain the green dye from it.

Thursday 25 July Once more, first blood went to an RAF fighter squadron in the north: at 08.30 hours, an He 111 reconnaissance bomber of *Wetterkundungstaffel* 1 (Meteorological Unit) was shot down into the Pentland Firth by Hurricanes of 3 Squadron, which was based at Wick. Four of the crew were missing, but one was rescued from a dinghy twelve miles off Rora Head.

Over southern England, 65 Squadron was first to engage the enemy, destroying a 109 of 8/JG 52 over the Channel near Dover at 12.20 hours; the interesting thing, however, is that not a shot was fired! The fighters were so low over the sea that in his efforts to evade Sergeant Franklin, the enemy pilot hit and crashed into the water.

At 12.46 hours, a *gruppe* of Me 109s was intercepted near Dover by the Hurricanes of 32 and 615 Squadrons. The resulting combat was short and sharp, the enemy pilots disengaging quickly due to being short on fuel, but not before shooting up 32 Squadron's Pilot Officer Daw, who crash-landed back at Hawkinge with a leg wound.

The next incoming threat was a huge raid, comprising three whole *Stukageschwadern*, which successfully bombed an unprotected convoy. 54 Squadron hastened to the scene, but were bounced by Galland's III/JG 26 *Stabsschwarm*, which shot down two Spitfires: one of the pilots, Flight Lieutenant Basil 'Wonky' Way, was killed. A very confused combat then developed when 64 Squadron ran into the whole of III/KG 4's Ju 88s, escorted by some fifty Me 109s. Squadron Leader John Thompson's 111 Squadron was scrambled from

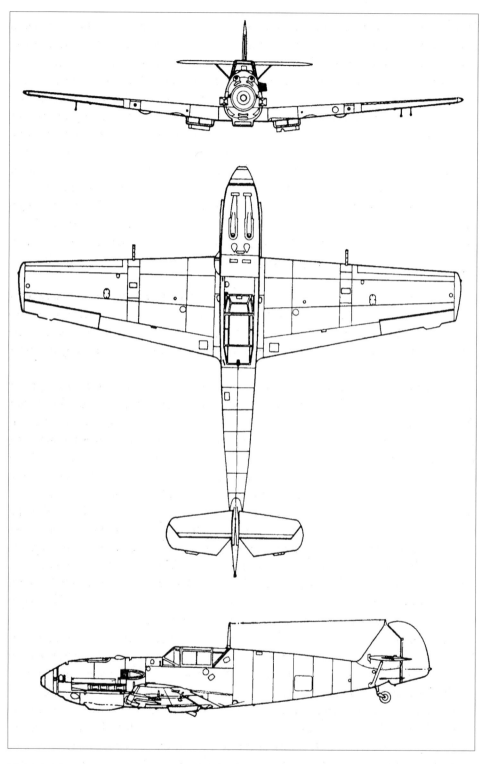

Me 109

Hawkinge, his Hurricane pilots attacking the enemy bombers head on. Attacked from all directions, III/KG 4 abandoned their attack and turned back to France; upon seeing this, the 109s likewise disengaged and withdrew eastwards.

Later that afternoon another dive-bombing attack hit the convoy, which had now passed Dover and was steaming past nearby Folkestone, sinking five ships and damaging for more. Again, there was momentarily no fighter cover when the Stukas appeared, but 56 Squadron attacked the enemy while bombing was in progress. Nine enemy E-boats then appeared, causing the convoy to scatter; one of these German motor torpedo boats rescued a Spitfire pilot, Sub-Lt Francis Dawson-Paul of 64 Squadron, from the sea, although he sadly died in a French hospital several days later. Although both 54 and 64 Squadrons had reinforced 56, the enemy fighters had the advantage of height and sun. Finally, the last attack on this convoy that day came in at 18.30 hours, Biggin Hill's 610 Squadron destroying two Me 109s of 7/JG 52 without loss.

There was fighting too over the West Country. Portland was attacked several times, the three Middle Wallop Sector fighter squadrons flying over 100 sorties in response. The Gloster Aircraft Factory at Hucclecote in Gloucestershire also attracted the attentions of a lone Ju 88, which is worth recounting in some detail.

Although large formations were being used by the enemy in their efforts against convoys, incursions by bombers over England were still seldom undertaken other than for reconnaissance or *Störflug* (harassing attacks) by single aircraft when weather conditions permitted. In these attacks, directed against targets connected with the British aircraft industry, fast and heavily armed Ju 88s would use cloud cover to escape detection before attacking their target and escaping back into the clag. On this particular day, *Unteroffizier* Wilhelm Hügelschäfer, the captain of a Ju 88 of 5/KG 51, based at Paris/Orly, was briefed to make landfall over the Isle of Wight, then proceed inland to Hucclecote. Over England, however, there was very little cloud cover, and as the raider started its turn to pass over the target, it had already been spotted by the defenders. Pilot Officer E.W. 'Bertie' Wootten, a pilot at No. 4 Ferry Pilots' Pool, RAF Kemble: 'We were lying sprawled out on the airfield on what was a lovely day, when we heard the unmistakable *umph umph* of the Ju 88's unsynchronized engines passing overhead.'

Kemble immediately scrambled two Station Defence Flight Hurricanes, flown by Pilot Officers Alec Bird and Richard Manlove, who climbed northwards to 12,000 feet and spotted the raider 500 feet above and likewise northbound. As the Hurricanes closed in, the enemy crew jettisoned their bombs, the pilot, *Unteroffizier* Friedel Dörner, turning SSW, intending to race for the coast. Pilot Officer Bird, whose Hurricane was fitted with the new Rotol constant speed propeller, overhauled Manlove; as anti-aircraft fire burst between the two RAF fighters, the latter watched Bird draw level with the Ju 88 and prepare for a stern attack. Manlove saw Bird 'close right in and deliver his attack from very close

Pilot Officer B.E.G. White and his 504 Squadron Hurricane at Filton in September 1940. Sadly he was reported missing in action while leading 229 Squadron during the Battle for Malta.

quarters before turning away upwards and to port'. At the top of his break-away, Bird's Hurricane suddenly went into a spin. Hügelschäfer remembered feeling 'a severe jolt in the back', and believed that his aircraft had been rammed.

As Bird's Hurricane tumbled from the sky, Pilot Officer Manlove opened fire from long range (500–600 yards), causing the starboard engine to disintegrate and after which parachutes blossomed as the enemy crew abandoned their doomed machine. Manlove also noted that Bird was still in an uncontrollable spin, now down to just 500 feet, when 'a flock of Spitfires arrived'. These fighters were from 5 OTU at nearby Aston Down, and actually comprised an instructor, Flight Lieutenant Prosser Hanks, in a Spitfire, and a pupil flying a Hurricane. Hanks later remembered the incident:

When I first saw the Ju 88 he was well above me and being chased by a Hurricane, presumably Bird's. I went after them, leaving my pupil a long way behind. When the 88 entered cloud, Bird was about 800 yards astern and followed the bomber. I was about 1,000 feet below and continued in the Ju 88's general direction. After a while it broke cloud about 1,000 yards ahead of me, flying quite normally; I saw no damage to it or pieces falling off. I managed to close with it and opened fire. I must admit to having been surprised to receive any return fire and almost immediately the crew baled out.

So, who brought down the Ju 88? Pilot Officers Bird or Manlove or Flight Lieutenant Hanks? If Bird, did he shoot it down, deliberately ram it (why would

Pilot Officer Alec Bird of 4 Ferry Pilots' Pool, based at Kemble in Gloucestershire. On 25 July 1940, Pilot Officers Bird and Manlove scrambled and engaged a Ju 88 bound for the Gloster Aircraft Factory at Hucclecote. In the ensuing combat Bird either collided with or rammed the enemy bomber, bringing it down but losing his own life in the process. Because he was not serving with one of the units officially accredited as having participated in the Battle of Britain, his name will not be found among the Few – even though Pilot Officer Bird made the ultimate sacrifice.

he?), or simply accidentally collide with the raider? Manlove cannot account for Bird suddenly going into a spin, and he did not witness a collision; Hügelschäfer remains convinced that his aircraft was rammed, however. Whatever happened, it is clear that the Ju 88's fate was sealed before the arrival of Flight Lieutenant Hanks, who, once he learned of Bird's fate and the circumstances preceding his involvement, retracted his claim for the enemy bomber's destruction.

Pilot Officer Alec Bird was killed in the resulting crash. His wife, Marjorie, believed that he had a premonition of death: when shopping in Cheltenham only the previous day, her husband spotted a poem in a magazine, saying, 'When I am killed put that on my gravestone and take me back to Yorkshire.' The following day he drove off to the nearby airfield but returned, saying to Marjorie, 'I don't want to leave you today, somehow'. As the 23-year-old requested, the widowed Mrs Bird took Alec's body back to Yorkshire, burying him in Adel churchyard.

The controversial thing is that although pilots like those involved in this particular action saw combat during the Battle of Britain, some, like Pilot Officer Bird, losing their lives in the defence of their homeland, their names will not be found among the Few. Why? Because they did not fly with one of the accredited fighter units decided upon by officialdom when the criteria involved was decided

The Ju 88 engaged by Pilot Officers Bird and Manlove belonged to 5/KG 51, based at Paris/Orly. Here are pictured three crew members of the raider in question, namely, from left, *Unteroffizier* Wilhelm Hügelschafer, *Gefrieter* Gottfried Treue and *Unteroffizier* Friedel Dörner. All three were captured, but a third crewman, *Unteroffizier* Walter Theiner was killed. The 26-year-old enemy airman was buried with full military honours by the RAF at Brimscombe Church, Gloucestershire.

upon. Nonetheless, their contribution and sacrifice remains equally crucial, and must never be forgotten.

Friday 26 July Low cloud and torrential rain, in complete contrast to the previous day, dictated a lull in air operations. III/JG 27's Me 109s flew a *freie hunt*, and at 10.00 hours *Oberleutnant* Dobislav shot down and killed 601 Squadron's Pilot Officer Chaloner Lindsey, whose Hurricane crashed into the Channel two miles off St Catherine's Point. The 20-year-old's body was later washed ashore and buried in France. Later that morning, 2/JG 27 was engaged off Portsmouth, 238 Squadron's Flight Lieutenant Stuart Walch shooting down *Feldwebel* Günther Böer, who was reported missing. During the afternoon, two reconnaissance bombers were damaged by 65 Squadron off Folkestone, but the day otherwise passed without incident. Pilot Officer Richard Jones:

I was a VR pilot, and late in July 1940, after operational training, joined No 64 Squadron, a professional RAF squadron, at Kenley. Upon arrival I remember being met by the CO, an absolutely charming man and a real gentleman in every sense of the word, Squadron Leader A.R.D. 'Don' MacDonell, who was also the Laird of Glengarry. He immediately made us new pilots feel at home, calling us his 'chicks'. We found him to be a quiet but determined leader and an excellent fighter pilot. He looked after the best interests of all who served under him and had the respect of all.

To give us battle experience as quickly as possible, whenever the time allowed, we were paired off with a senior battle-experienced pilot to practise dog-fighting and yet more dog-fighting, to give us both experience and confidence in the Spitfire and combat conditions. We were lucky to have that extra curricular training, which would have been impossible had we been posted to No 64 Squadron later on that summer, and for obvious reasons.

One incident I particularly remember was when we of No 64 Squadron were visited by the Air Minister, Sir Archibald Sinclair. We were all lined up to meet him, standing in front of our Spitfires. He congratulated us on the work that we were doing and in his opening words thanked us as *Hurricane* pilots of *No 12 Group*! Clearly the Air Minister knew not the difference between a Spitfire or a Hurricane, much less the disposition of Fighter Command's fighter groups. We were not impressed.'

Saturday 27 July As a large convoy, codenamed BACON, chugged past Portland, shortly before 08.00 hours thirty Stukas of I/StG 77 took off from Caen, bent upon destruction and escorted by Me 109s of JG 27. Just three 238 Squadron Hurricanes were scrambled from Middle Wallop, but, not surprisingly, they were unable to penetrate the protective screen of 109s. As this raid retired, another was inbound, hitting BACON off Swanage at 09.45 hours. Although six Spitfires and three Hurricanes were already patrolling overhead, the 109 pilots executed their task perfectly, not only keeping the RAF fighters away from the dive-bombers but shooting down Pilot Officer J.R. Buchanan of 609 Squadron in the process: the Spitfire pilot was killed. 609 Squadron was an Auxiliary Air

Force unit, raised locally in Yorkshire's West Riding; personnel were therefore well acquainted, sometimes even related, so casualties were very depressing to morale. Indeed, the Squadron would suffer more casualties over the next month, before its luck changed. Thunderstorms then brought further attacks on Convoy BACON to a halt, although 615 Squadron destroyed an He 59 seaplane off Deal.

By this time, 19 Squadron was experimenting with the Spitfire Mk IB, which lacked machine-guns but was armed with two 20mm Hispano-Suiza cannons. This was, of course, a late response to the fact that the Me 109E had long been armed with two 20mm Oerlikon cannons, the devastating power of which had been made evident to Fighter Command on countless occasions since Dunkirk. Being based in 12 Group, however, 19 Squadron was not given enough opportunities to try out the new weapon, and so as of this day flights began operating from Coltishall, near the Norfolk coast, in the hope of finding action over a convoy. Soon after arrival, 'B' Flight was scrambled and took off in three sections of two aircraft (in itself interesting given that the basic fighter formation was the 'vic' of three). Unfortunately, 19 Squadron's pilots searched in vain for the enemy, although Spitfires of 66 Squadron, also based at Coltishall, destroyed two He 111s of I/KG 53.

Squadron Leader Douglas Bader's 242 Squadron had also been scrambled from Coltishall, meaning that the Controller had left that Sector Station undefended. What was the point of sending off some thirty fighters on such a sortie, which was hardly a crisis? Sergeant David Cox:

> I remember that in June 1940, we of No 19 Squadron were visited at Duxford by the Group AOC, Air Vice-Marshal Leigh-Mallory, who, stabbing his finger at a map on the wall, exclaimed 'My fighters will be here, here and here!' From this I now conclude that he always had in mind to intercept the enemy in numbers, as opposed to what went on down south.

The uneconomic use of so many fighters, however, was contrary not only to the system but equally to the wishes of the Commander-in-Chief, Air Chief Marshal Dowding. This represents, in fact, an early indication of what would become a developing problem with 12 Group, and which, as we will see, eventually became a crisis.

'Down south', an He 111 attacked shipping in Dover harbour, sinking the destroyer HMS *Codrington*. The latter's loss, coupled with reports that the Germans were siting huge railway guns near Calais (able to lob shells into the Dover/Folkestone area, which would become known as 'Hellfire Corner'), the Admiralty withdrew its destroyers from Dover to Harwich and Sheerness on the east coast. As the Luftwaffe's intention was to prevent the Royal Navy operating freely in the Channel, this was a step in the right direction so far as the enemy was concerned.

Flying Officer Joe Pegge DFC, a Spitfire pilot with 610 Squadron at Biggin Hill, destroyed five enemy aircraft and a probable during the Battle of Britain; he survived the war but died while still serving in 1950.

Sunday 28 July At 13.50 hours, a threat developed towards Dover, but, in anticipation of more protracted combat along the Kentish coast, 11 Group had deployed eight squadrons forward to operate from Hawkinge, right on the cliffs above Folkestone. 74 Squadron, however, led by the South African Flight Lieutenant Adolphus 'Sailor' Malan was scrambled from Manston, while simultaneously Hurricanes were sent off from Hawkinge. Although the bombers, inexplicably but possibly due to the appearance of so many British fighters, turned away and flew off towards the south east without attacking any targets, a dogfight ensued between the escorting Me 109s, of I & II/JG 51, and 74 Squadron. Malan himself attacked the leading pair of 109s, shooting one down and badly damaging the second: the evidence suggests that Malan's second target was actually Major Werner 'Vati' Mölders, the leading *experten* and *Kommodore* of JG 51, who was wounded and forced-landed back at Wissant. Pilot Officer P.C.F. Stevenson, in fact, pursued Mölders back across the Channel, but was attacked by I/JG 51's *Oberleutnant* Leppla; although his Spitfire was damaged, Stevenson was unhurt and managed to crash-land back at base. Pilot Officer Johnnie Freeborn's Spitfire was also hit, possibly by *Oberfeldwebel* Schmid, also of I/JG 51. Sergeant Tony Mould was shot down and baled out wounded, but Pilot Officer J.H.R. Young was killed when shot down over the Channel, his Spitfire crashing into the sea near the Goodwin Sands. Both of these 74 Squadron casualties were claimed by III/JG 26, which had also entered the fray, one by the *Kommandeur, Hauptmann* Adolf Galland, whose

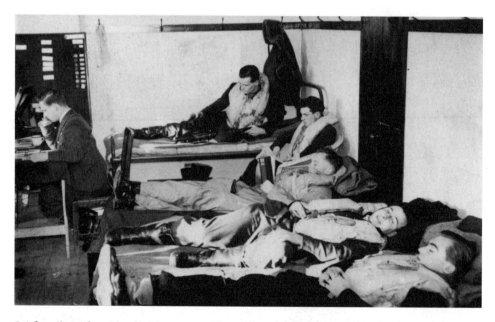

Spitfire pilots of 74 Squadron between sorties at Hornchurch during the Battle of Britain. Kitted out to scramble and take-off at a moment's notice, these pilots are officially at a state of 'readiness'.

Right: 41 Squadron
emerged among Fighter
Command's top scoring
units during the Battle
of Britain, and was
heavily engaged flying
from Hornchurch; from
left: Sergeant John
McAdam, Flying Officer
Tony Lovell DFC and
Pilot Officer Roy Ford.
McAdam was killed the
following year; although
Lovell survived the war
he was killed in a flying
accident in August 1945.
Ford later served as a
test pilot and survived
the war unscathed.

Below: A Spitfire of 234
Squadron on finals at
Warmwell in 10 Group
during the summer of
1940.

Katchmarek (wingman), *Oberleutnant* Müncheberg, destroyed a 257 Squadron Hurricane.

41 Squadron's Spitfires were also in action over the Channel, Pilot Officer George 'Ben' Bennions hurrying to the assistance of Flying Officer Tony Lovell, who was shot down and wounded in the leg; Bennions shot down Lovell's assailant, *Leutnant* Below, who was picked up by the *Seenotdienst* (Luftwaffe air sea rescue service). Following these combats, He 59s were active over the Channel, searching for ditched pilots, two of which were destroyed by 111 Squadron. Spitfires of 234 Squadron were also scrambled from 10 Group's coastal airfield at St Eval, in Cornwall, and destroyed a lone Ju 88 thirty miles out to sea off Plymouth.

The significant thing about the fighting on this day is the clash between Malan and Mölders, both great fighter pilots and legends in their own lifetimes. It is rare indeed to be actually able to provide evidence proving that two such 'aces' met personally in combat, but that was definitely the case here.

Monday 29 July At 07.50 hours, forty-eight Stukas, escorted by some eighty Me 109s, headed for Dover harbour, ignoring two substantial convoys steaming through 11 Group's coastal area. The 109s were high and up sun, thus concealing them from the Spitfires of 41 Squadron which attacked the dive-bombers. The 109s pounced, leaving one Spitfire pilot dead and damaging four other aircraft. The Hurricanes of 501 Squadron, up from nearby Hawkinge, also attacked the Stukas, four of which were destroyed, although the RAF pilots were frustrated by the Dover anti-aircraft barrage insisting on firing into the actual dogfight.

Cleverly, a small force of Ju 88s from II/KG 76 then approached one of the convoys at very low level, thus escaping radar detection, although no damage was caused; one bomber was destroyed when it flew into a balloon cable, another by anti-aircraft fire. A Do 17 then appeared but was seen off by 610 Squadron's Spitfires which were detailed to patrol the convoy from then on. The other convoy was sighted by a Do 17 of *Stab*/KG 2, which was chased all the way back to Belgium by 85 Squadron's Flying Officer Patrick Woods-Scawen, and crash-landed at St Ingelvert. Nonetheless, the convoy was soon attacked by eleven Me 110 fighter-bombers from *Erprobungsgruppe* 210, based at St Omer, escorted by thirty Me 110 *zerstörer* (destroyers) of ZG 26. Two ships were hit and two Hurricanes of 151 Squadron shot down, although neither pilot was hurt; the raiders suffered no loss.

Interestingly, on this day the Deputy Chief of the Air Staff (DCAS), Air Vice-Marshal Sholto Douglas, ordered Fighter, Bomber and Coastal Commands to carry out sharp attacks against enemy E-boat bases, coastal airfields and gun batteries. These attacks, Douglas stated, should be timed to hit enemy airfields immediately after German aircraft had landed following raids on England. Although E-boats could be attacked when their presence was known, airfields were notoriously difficult targets, due to being heavily defended and therefore these attacks were unlikely to be successful. Moreover, the constant enemy air activity over the Pas-de-Calais made it impossible to identify when a raid was in progress until it started moving out across the Channel; due to the speeds of the aircraft involved, the enemy were only five minutes flying time from Dover when thus identified (an observation putting the problem of early interception by 11 Group into sharp focus). In fact, the time from a raid being identified to it re-crossing the French coast was usually no more than thirty minutes. To strike when the German bombers had just landed, therefore, RAF bombers would have to be brought to readiness whenever such a Luftwaffe raid appeared possible. Furthermore, in the wake of having engaged an incoming threat, 11 Group would clearly have difficulty in supplying enough fighters to escort such a counter-attack. Fortunately Air Chief Marshal Dowding's SASO, Air Vice-Marshal Douglas Evill (previously Bomber Command's SASO) recognized these difficulties and felt that such an operation would be most unwise. Having liaised with his opposite number at Bomber Command, and, of course 11 Group's Air Vice-Marshal Park, Evill argued that it would be far better to make such an attack in strength, following extensive reconnaissance and target study. Fortunately Douglas heeded this advice, and the DCAS's potentially suicidal scheme came to nought. This is, however, yet another example of the Air Staff's incompetence, an exasperation that Air Chief Marshal Dowding and Air Vice-Marshal Park would continually fight against and which, unfortunately, would get much worse as the Battle of Britain wore on.

Pilot Officer Wallace 'Jock' Cunningham DFC of 19 Squadron writing home in the pilots' hut at Fowlmere. During the Battle of Britain Cunningham destroyed four enemy machines and shared another. The following year he was hit by flak over the Dutch coast and captured.

Tuesday 30 July Low cloud and drizzle restricted operations, although a section of three 603 Squadron Spitfires bagged a KG 26 He 111 off the Scottish coast (during which combat two of the Spitfires were damaged), and 85 Squadron destroyed an *Erprobungsgruppe* 210 Me 110 off Harwich.

Wednesday 31 July A thick haze made operations difficult for both sides. At 07.00 hours a section of 111 Squadron Hurricanes intercepted and damaged a lone III/KG 76 Ju 88 over the Channel. A solo Do 17, however, was chased by Hurricanes for sixty miles but escaped unscathed.

At 16.00 hours Me 109s from JG 2 began shooting up the Dover balloon barrage and were promptly engaged by 74 Squadron. The interception was unsuccessful for 'B' Flight, which was bounced on the climb by 4/JG 51, two Spitfires of Blue Section being shot down and both pilots killed. Flight Lieutenant D.P.D.G. Kelly, however, managed to hit a 109 before being shot up by *Leutnant* Eric Hohagen. The pilot of the 109 hit by Kelly was wounded and crashed back at Fécamp.

At Coltishall in 12 Group, 19 Squadron was celebrating the award of a DFC to Flight Lieutenant Brian Lane, the commander of 'A' Flight. Pilot Officer Wallace 'Jock' Cunningham:

> We of 19 Squadron were lying in the sun at Coltishall along with Douglas Bader and other 242 Squadron pilots. There was some banter going on and Douglas asked Brian 'What's that?' in his usual cocky fashion, thrusting his pipe at Brian's new DFC ribbon. 'I must get one of those,' said Bader, and, as we all know, he did just that!

Thursday 1 August Low cloud and mist again enveloped England. Although Dowding's squadrons flew numerous convoy protection patrols, there was no action until the afternoon. A section of 145 Squadron chased off a Ju 88 in the Beachy Head area, while another section engaged, unusually, an Hs 126 ten miles south of Hastings; although the enemy reconnaissance machine was destroyed, the rear gunner killed Sub-Lt Ian Kestin, a FAA pilot, whose Hurricane crashed into the sea: the pilot was never found.

The Coltishall Sector 'put up a black' this particular afternoon: the Controller was so preoccupied with shepherding two convoys that he failed to react to a raid by thirty KG 4 He 111s which attacked the Boulton Paul factory at Norwich. Both the factory and nearby Thorpe railway yard was slightly damaged, and forty-three civilians lost their lives. Pilot Officer Wallace 'Jock' Cunningham:

> Flying from Coltishall we routinely flew up and down the North Sea. The graveyard of the Dogger Bank showed up the dangerous task of these underpaid, little appreciated merchant seamen. Hopefully our presence frightened off the odd raid. We sat at low level east of the convoys, looking into the setting sun. Any sign of an attacker and we made a great show, chasing off the poacher. Sometimes when it was judged too dark for the bombers we would be instructed to 'pancake'; once a mile or two west of the convoy we would see AA flashes

– the bomber had watched us against the setting sun and noted our departure.

I recall one thick, misty day over the North Sea trying to find a convoy. I would be vectored onto the convoy's position but at a height of several thousand feet, which was necessary for contact with base. When I descended through the murk to try and find the convoy, trying to guess where fog stopped and sea started, no contact was made. This occupied me for a time but I guess that the Controller decided that if I had so much difficulty, having the benefit of his assistance, then the convoy was safe from attack!

Friday 2 August Off the Scottish coast a small convoy was attacked by ten He 111s of KG 26, two of which were shot down by anti-aircraft fire. Off Harwich, the *Cape Finisterre* was sunk by the crack *Erprobungsgruppe* 210, the Me 110s escaping without loss.

Saturday 3 August Fighter Command suffered no losses, and there was no bombing at all by day.

Sunday 4 August Again bad weather prevented the Luftwaffe from any further assaults. The RAF, however, sent Blenheims of 236 Squadron on a reconnaissance of Le Havre, and one of their number destroyed an 8/JG 51 Me 109 and damaged another.

Monday 5 August Improved weather suggested that there would be action this day. At 08.30 hours, six Spitfires of 64 Squadron relieved 615 Squadron's Hurricanes on patrol between Dover and Beachy Head, and at which point they were attacked by Me 109s of JG 54, the enemy, as ever, possessing the height advantage. A 109 was damaged in the ensuing dogfight, but one Spitfire pilot, Sergeant L.R. Isaac, was reported missing and Pilot Officer 'Art' Donahue, an American volunteer, crash-landed at Hawkinge.

Early afternoon saw more action when an eastbound convoy, steaming through the dangerous Dover Strait, was attacked by Ju 88s. 151 Squadron responded, destroying an escorting Me 109 of I/JG 54 and damaging a Ju 88 for no loss.

Tuesday 6 August Given the recent lack of activity by the German bomber force, eight convoys in total left British shores during this 24 hour period, while two were incoming, all heavily protected by fighters. At 06.15 hours, a section of 85 Squadron Hurricanes destroyed a lone III/KG 3 Do 17 off Harwich.

Wednesday 7 August There was no bombing by day, but the enemy fighter force was attacked by Bomber Command at Haamstede, where 4/JG 54 was bombed while it was taking off to intercept the RAF intruders. Two aircraft were destroyed, five more were damaged and two pilots killed, effectively removing this unit from the battle for over two weeks.

Pilot Officer Harry Welford:

I was an Auxiliary Air Force Hurricane pilot with No 607 'County of Durham' Squadron, based at Acklington, in the north of England. Although we continually practised formation flying, aerial combat and No 1 and 3 attacks, we also flew patrol duties along the NE coast, providing aerial cover to the merchant and fishing convoys. On August 7th, we spotted a Ju 88 weather plane in the distance and flew 100 miles out to sea after it, but we didn't intercept because he made it into cloud just as we came within firing distance. In fact it was stupid of us to go so far out, but in the excitement of the moment one gets carried away even though strict instructions had been dished out to you not to stray too far from the coast. These convoy patrols covered from Acklington to Scarborough but only 5–10 miles out to sea. About this time I had my first flight in a Spitfire, which was a lovely aircraft to fly, not that different to the Hurricane except that in taxying the nose seemed to rear right up in your line of vision, and you had to swing from left to right, this being rather heavy on the brakes and in danger of burning out the brake shoes.

Thursday 8 August If the previous few days had seen a lull in enemy air operations, that now changed with a vengeance. Convoy PEEWIT had tried to negotiate the Dover Strait under cover of darkness, but was tracked by the new German radar near Calais. E-boats attacked at dawn, sinking three merchant ships and damaging several more. Encouraged by the continually improving weather, *Generalfeldmarschall* Hugo Sperrle, commander of *Luftlotte* 3, staged a massive attack on PEEWIT by the Stukas of *Fliegerkorps* VIII. This attack was to be made at mid-day, as the convoy made its way south of the Isle of Wight. Dive-bombers of StG 2, 3 & 77 were escorted by Me 109s of V/LG 1 and both II and III/JG 27. Me 109s of III/JG 26, and II & III/JG 51 swept the Dover area in advance of the main enemy formation.

The advance force of Me 109s provoked a response from the Spitfires of 41, 64 and 65 Squadrons. At 11.45 hours, the CO of 64 Squadron, Squadron Leader Don MacDonnell, the Laird of Glengarry, together with Sergeant Jackie Mann (later famous as a terrorist hostage with Terry Waite), shot down and killed *Oberleutnant* Willi Oehm, an instructor on his first combat mission. Unfortunately the Spitfires came off second best: 64 Squadron's Sergeant Squire was wounded, and Pilot Officer Kennard-Davis died two days later from wounds received; 65 Squadron lost Sergeants Kirton and Phillips killed, and another Spitfire was damaged.

Over the convoy, it was 145 Squadron that scored first blood, penetrating the escort and immediately destroying two Stukas. JG 27 soon rallied, however, and engaged the intercepting fighters, now numbering about thirty, permitting the dive-bombers to attack the convoy, which scattered. Within minutes four ships were sunk and seven damaged. Seven German aircraft were destroyed against five Hurricanes, although sadly all of the RAF pilots were killed.

Sergeant Reg Nutter:

On this and the previous day, three pilots of our Squadron, No 257, Pilot Officer the Hon. David Coke, Pilot Officer Carl Capon and myself provided an escort to a De Havilland Flamingo, pilot by Flight Lieutenant Blenner-Hassett, from Hendon to Northcoates, Manby, Coltishall to Hendon. This trip remains vivid in my memory as the Prime Minister

On 8 August 1940, Pilot Officer Denis Robinson of 152 Squadron was shot-up off Swanage by Me 109s of II/JG 53. Deciding against baling out, the pilot safely force-landed Spitfire K9894 near Wareham – albeit losing a wing in the process!

Sergeant Reg Nutter, a Volunteer Reservist, flew Hurricanes with 257 Squadron at North Weald throughout the Battle of Britain. Following subsequent service as an instructor in Canada, where this unusual picture was taken, he later served as RAF liaison officer with the 7th Armoured Division during the advance into Germany. From a tank equipped with nine radios, Nutter directed aircraft onto their ground targets.

was aboard and persuaded Blenner-Hassett to do some very low flying, purely for his benefit, over the Wash!

On this day we also tried to intercept some bombers attacking a convoy, but were jumped by some enemy fighters. In this, our first major action, we lost three pilots. This, loss, coupled with the recent change in command, caused our morale to drop very sharply.

It then fell to 10 Group to provide a constant fighter screen as the convoy re-grouped off St Catherine's Point. By 16.00 hours, however, some eighty-two Stukas, escorted by sixty-eight Me 109s and Me 110s, were bound for Convoy PEEWIT. South of the unenviable ships, 43 and 145 Squadron attacked, 145 doing so out of the sun and achieving complete surprise. In this initial engagement, II/JG 27 lost its *Gruppenkommandeur, Hauptmann* Werner Andreas, shot down by Flight Lieutenant Thomas Morgan of 43 Squadron. The Me 110s took no part in the air battle but busied themselves with destroying the balloon barrage. As the enemy retired, the scene was positively Wagnerian: burning balloons and

Sergeant Tony Whitehouse, Pilot Officer Bob Dafforn and Sergeant Vic Ekins pose with a 501 Squadron Hurricane in 1940.

ships provided a dramatic backdrop for the thirty or so airmen bobbing around in the sea, hoping for rescue. The convoy itself was decimated, only four ships out of the original twenty steaming safely into Swanage. Suffice to say that the story of Convoy PEEWIT is one worthy of detailed reconstruction, as this was undoubtedly the bitterest fighting seen so far.

Friday 9 August For reasons that would soon become clear to Dowding and his staff, although a resumption of the previous day's heavy attacks were expected, this failed to materialize. A KG 26 He 111 was shot down off the north-east coast by 79 Squadron, a Ju 88 was similarly dispatched by 234 and 601 Squadrons over Falmouth, and another reconnaissance Ju 88 was damaged by 213 Squadron over the West Country. The only action over south-east England occurred at Dover, when JG 51 tried to shoot up the Dover barrage again but were seen off by 64 Squadron.

Saturday 10 August Rain and thunder enveloped England and Northern France, leading to 501 Squadron losing a Do 17 which had bombed West Malling, and 242 Squadron failing to intercept *Erprobungsgruppe* 210's (albeit in any case unsuccessful) raid on the Boulton Paul factory at Norwich.

Sunday 11 August In complete contrast to the previous day, the weather was glorious, heralding the prospect of death and destruction on an increasing scale. The first sign of trouble was another sortie by *Erprobungsgruppe* 210, some aircraft of which attacked the Dover barrage while others dropped sixty bombs on the harbour. An incoming sweep of Me 109s was met head-on over Dover by 74 Squadron, Pilot Officer P.C.F. Stevenson being shot down but rescued after drifting eleven miles out to sea. 32 Squadron's Hurricanes had a similar, fleeting, contact, but 64 Squadron's Spitfires engaged a third *freie hunt* over Bognor Regis and destroyed two Me 109s for no loss.

At 09.45 hours, however, it was clear that a major raid, and probably the day's main effort, was building up over Cherbourg, the Royal Navy's installations at Portland being the likely target. 11 Group scrambled the Hurricanes of 1 Squadron, and 10 Group sent up the Spitfires of 609 Squadron, while six more squadrons were placed at readiness. Soon the largest raid so far dispatched against England – 165 bombers and escorts – approached Portland. By the time the 'bandits' reached mid-Channel, 87, 152, 145, 213, 238, 601 and 609 Squadrons were all *en route* to intercept. At 23,000 feet some five miles south of Portland, the escorting Me 110s started milling about in their usual defensive circles. Squadron Leader Darley and 609 Squadron was first on the scene, and attacked the topmost circle; turning tightly and using deflection the Spitfire pilots cleverly evaded the 110s guns but shot down five of the enemy in an excellent demonstration of air fighting. Most of the other RAF squadrons also engaged these escorts, losses being high on both sides, meaning that the enemy bomber force was able to continue towards Portland unmolested. Only four Spitfires, of 152 Squadron, spotted the He 111s starting their bombing run at 15,000 feet, and the Ju 88s dive-bombing an oil storage depot from 10,000 feet. By then an enormous dogfight was patterning the sky above Weymouth Bay, the enemy reinforced now by JG 27's Me 109s. After the battle the cost was high for both sides: the Luftwaffe lost eighteen aircraft, Fighter Command sixteen Hurricanes and a Spitfire, with fourteen pilots killed.

For the Allied fighter pilots in the water, they knew that their chances of rescue were slim, simply because at this early stage of the war the RAF did not enjoy a formal air sea rescue service, just eighteen high speed launches to search the entire south coast for downed airmen. Frequently pilots, if saved at all, were rescued by chance encounters with a passing trawler, or perhaps, if their plight was being watched by those ashore, by a civilian lifeboat. RAF pilots did not even have inflatable dinghies at this time. Conversely, the German aircrews wore bright yellow skull caps, carried flare pistols, a sea-dye, and one-man dinghies. At strategic points in the Channel, the Luftwaffe had even positioned rescue buoys, called 'Lobster Pots', which contained four bunks with bedding and other essentials that a downed airman might require. Better still were He 59 'ambulance' seaplanes, which were a regular feature over Channel waters during

152 Squadron was based in the West Country, at Warmwell, near Swanage. The Squadron was regularly in action over the Portland area, and later fought over London when 11 Group requested reinforcements from neighbouring groups. On the left is Pilot Officer Dudley Williams, who destroyed four enemy aircraft during the Battle of Britain; the individual at centre is unknown; at right is Pilot Officer Eric 'Boy' Marrs DFC. A professional airman, Marrs destroyed five aircraft during the Battle of Britain, but was killed in action the following year.

the Battle of Britain: controversial targets for RAF fighter pilots who attacked and destroyed them without remorse. An anonymous *Oberleutnant* from ZG 26:

> The coast was some way off and the water was cold. The current was carrying us away from land. My wireless operator had a good idea – he fired a flare. That saved us. German fighters saw us in the water and four Messerschmitts circled overhead. Despite the cold we two smiled at each other, even if we were exhausted and injured. The fighters fortunately signaled a He 59 *Seenotmaschine*, which came and took us aboard a short time later.

After this particularly great air battle, the He 59s were naturally most active: Blenheims from Middle Wallop Sector Station, which had lost six aircraft during the 'Battle of Weymouth Bay', shot one down mid-Channel, and another was

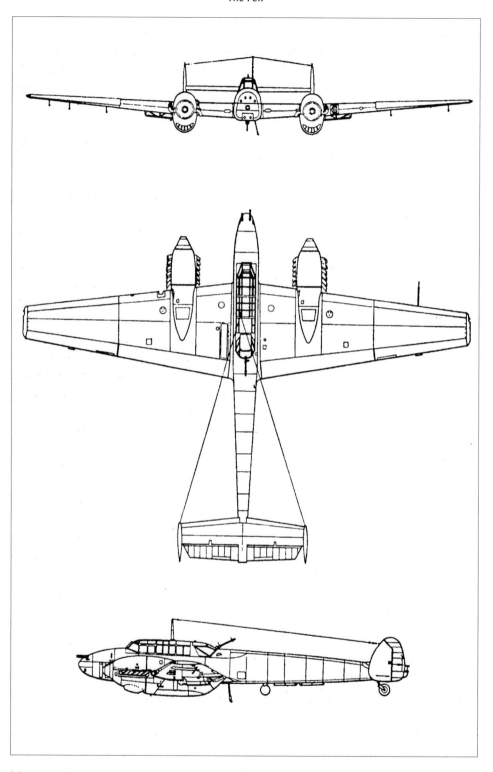

Me 110

destroyed by 610 Squadron, which also clashed with escorting Me 109s and lost two pilots killed. Whether these He 59s were a legitimate target remains a moot point, but what is not in dispute is the fact that the Air Ministry was negligent indeed by not providing our pilots with an appropriate chance of rescue from the Channel's intemperate waters: just how many of the Few were alive after baling out, but simply died of exposure or drowned, will never be known.

The day's fighting was not yet over, however: at 11.50 hours off Harwich, *Erprobungsgruppe* 210, with Do 17s of 9/K.G 2 and Me 110s of ZG 26, attacked Convoy BOOTY, one Me 110 subsequently being destroyed by 17 Squadron, and three more by 74 Squadron. As the enemy withdrew, more raids were immediately incoming, a large formation of Stukas and Do 17s, escorted by Me 109s, hitting another convoy, this time in the Thames Estuary. Again it was the increasingly experienced and successful 74 'Tiger' Squadron that intercepted the raid, damaging several enemy machines, the pilots of which had flown four sorties already that day, and had met the enemy thrice. Cloud was building up, however, preventing 54 and 111 Squadrons from effectively joining battle, and so the worsening weather brought this day's fighting to a close.

On this hard fought day, Fighter Command lost twenty-five pilots killed, the highest number of daily fatalities throughout the sixteen week Battle of Britain.

Monday 12 August So far the enemy had not attacked British radar installations, but, again as will become clear, the main effort on this day was to knock out all stations between the Thames Estuary and Portland.

First, various formations of Me 109s swept over southern England, but the 11 Group Controller wisely did not respond to all, for two good reasons: firstly such incursions could suddenly withdraw before contact, and secondly unless intercepting fighters arc scrambled, such pure fighter sweeps could cause little harm. The early morning *freie hunt* flown by III/JG 26 was among those ignored, but 610 Squadron's Spitfires, scrambled at 07.31 hours, clashed with II/JG 52 high over New Romney. Flight Lieutenant Brian Smith's Spitfire was hit in the cockpit by two 20mm cannon shells; although burned about the hands and face, Smith baled out and was fortunately picked up by the Royal Navy. Three other Spitfires sustained damage in this action, and two Me 109s of Il/JG 52 were destroyed, both pilots being killed.

As indicated by several previous entries, *Erprobungsgruppe* 210, commanded by the vastly experienced and dashing *Hauptmann* Walter Rubensdörffer, was skilled in precision bombing from low level, and not surprisingly *Generalfeldmarschall* Kesselring selected this unit to take out the radar installations. Operating out of Calais-Marck, Rubensdörffer himself led four sections, each of four Me 110s, on what developed into a superbly executed attacks on the Chain Home stations in Kent and Sussex: Dover, Pevensey and Rye were all put out of action, if only for six hours, and that at Dunkirk was damaged. While the radar stations were recovering from these attacks, and therefore not transmitting, a large attack was made on the airfield at Lympne.

An informal snapshot of 152 Squadron, shortly after arrival at Warmwell from Acklington. From left: P/O Warner, Sgt Wolton, P/O Marrs, Sgt Sheppard, P/O Inness, F/L Withall, P/O Wildblood, F/O Deansley, F/L Thomas, F/O Jones, P/O Williams, P/O Bayles & Sgt Ackroyd. The dog, 'Pilot Officer Pooch', was the unit's popular mascot. Sgt Ackroyd is wearing white flying overalls issued to pre-war airmen – he was shot down in flames over Warmwell on 7 October 1940, and died of wounds the next day. His wife, a WAAF on the station, watched her husband's Spitfire plunge earthwards.

Although much damage was caused to this small airfield on the Kentish coast, this was a prime example of how poor Luftwaffe intelligence could be: Lympne was merely used as an emergency field by 11 Group and was, not, therefore, an important link in the system. During this period of radar blindness, two hangars and other buildings were destroyed at Hawkinge – which was an important link in the chain, although it was not a Sector Station and was back on 'top line' within 24 hours.

The next skirmish was won hands down by III/JG 26. Two convoys, ARENA and AGENT, attracted the unwelcome attention of Stukas, which were fortunately driven off by the Hurricanes of 151 and 501 Squadrons. Unfortunately, Adolf Galland's Me 109s pounced on the RAF fighters, shooting down three Hurricanes of 151, and one of 501: two pilots ended up in the sea, but although both were rescued one subsequently died of his wounds.

Next, the whole of KG 51, numbering some 100 Ju 88s, escorted by 120 Me 110s of ZGs 2 and 76, and twenty-five Me 109s of JG 53, came in over the Isle of Wight. As the enemy fighters orbited high above, the bombers divided into two formations. The largest of these skillfully negotiated Portsmouth's balloon barrage and bombed the docks and town, causing great damage and destroying the railway station, oil tanks and shipping; the loss of human life was also high: ninety-six navy personnel and civilians died during this raid. The second, smaller, enemy formation dive-bombed the Chain Home station at Ventnor, on the Isle of Wight. The target was devastated, the bombers not being intercepted, by 152 and 609 Squadrons, until they were withdrawing. As the Spitfires appeared, JG 53 came to the Ju 88s' assistance, destroying two 152 Squadron Spitfires, both pilots being reported missing. In total, KG 51 lost ten bombers during these albeit well executed raids, to either anti-aircraft fire or RAF fighters, and, through intelligent tactics by Air Vice-Marshal Park, the Me 109s were largely kept at bay. Indeed, when the final *freie hunt* came in over Beachy Head, 615 Squadron was waiting for them, shooting down two 109s of JG 54. *Oberleutnant* von Hofe of JG 3 was among the Me 109 pilots escorting KG 51 on that raid:

Six Spitfires dived down from the left, turning towards us. We zoomed up very tightly and they flashed by behind us. We went into a diving turn to the right and the leading 109s of our *Staffel* got behind the Spitfires. All our guns were firing. Two Spitfires went down trailing smoke, one of them exploded after a 1,000 metre dive, the other one flew away trailing white smoke. The other Spitfires turned sharply to meet us and fired away at our *Staffel's* rearmost machines. We then got behind the enemy fighters. The *Kommandeur* set one of them on fire and the English pilot baled out immediately. His parachute blossomed beneath us. The rest of the Tommies dived away, showing us their blue bellies and 'peacock's eyes'. Two of our aircraft reported that they were leaving the formation as both had been badly hit The *Kommandeur* ordered two others to cover and escort them home.

Once again we were flying near the bombers, from which we had been separated in combat. One of them fell back some 200 metres behind the formation. A long white smoke cloud trailed from the right engine. A hit! Some of our fighters covered the machine which lagged further and further behind. The bomber's right propeller was stationary but apparently the machine could maintain its altitude and was still protected by fighters. I certainly hope that it reached the French coast.

British Intelligence reported on the methods and effectiveness of the enemy fighter escorts:

Escorting fighters are dispersed in various positions relative to the bomber formations they are protecting. During the early phase of attacks on this country it was usual for

Canadians: Pilot Officer 'Art' Yuile and 'Dal' Russell at readiness at Northolt in summer 1940. Russell went on to become a particularly successful fighter pilot and leader, awarded the DFC and Bar together with a DSO. He survived the war.

the fighter escort to fly behind and several thousand feet above the bomber formation. If our fighters attacked the bombers, the escort would descend and attack them providing that they (the German fighters) were not outnumbered. If our fighters attacked the enemy fighter escort, the latter would usually form a self-defensive circle, thus ceasing to afford protection to the bombers which they were supposed to be escorting.

Heavy casualties suffered by the bombers led to a change of tactics involving an increase in escorting fighters with new dispositions relative to the bomber formations. Fighters were encountered ahead and on both flanks as well as above and behind the bombers and usually flying in close proximity to the latter. On occasions the individual bomber units were found to be more spaced out with fighters weaving amongst them. Accompanying formations of fighters have also been observed acting as a remote escort of 'freelance' patrols, flying at a great height above and in the vicinity of the bomber formations, but they have rarely taken offensive action.

At 12.50 hours, *Erprobungsgruppe* 210 made a low level attack on Manston aerodrome, immediately followed by a medium level attack by eighteen Do 17s of KG 2. Again much damage was caused to airfield buildings and facilities, but only one Blenheim was destroyed and no Spitfires had been damaged. So, although the enemy pilots believed that Manston had been completely destroyed, within 24 hours this station was also back on 'top line'.

During the evening, coastal towns in Kent were attacked by three formations of twenty Do 17s, and so the day came to a close. Although unbeknown at the time, it was an important one, marking as it did the end of the 'opening shots' and the Battle of Britain's first phase. From the following day onwards, as we will see, the most terrible onslaughts would be unleashed against Britain, as the fighting massively increased in violence and tempo.

As we have seen, on 29 July, the DCAS instructed that enemy airfields should be attacked by Bomber Command immediately after the raiders had landed, the incompetence of such a suggestion being recognised by the SASO who moved to prevent the operation going ahead. The scheme was, however, supported by the AOC of 12 Group, Air Vice-Marshal Trafford Leigh-Mallory, who, on this day and in an expression of support for Douglas's plan, sent the Spitfires of 19 and 266 Squadron to operate from the coastal airfield at Eastchurch. Squadron Leader Phillip Pinkham, CO of 19 Squadron, wrote in his log book that his orders were to 'escort the Battle boys on a beat up of the other side'. This evidence makes even more unbelievable the level of incompetence involved, considering the massive beating Fairey Battle crews had taken during the Fall of France – indeed, such losses alone should have been sufficient to convince anyone that such a proposal was complete folly. It is perhaps unsurprising, however, that Leigh-Mallory, who personally had no experience of fighter warfare whatsoever, unlike every other group commander in Fighter Command, supported such a foolhardy scheme. Apart from demonstrating further incompetence by the Air Staff, this incident also provides an early indication that Leigh-Mallory was not working in concert with his Commander-in-Chief, as he should have been, but inclined towards co-operating with those in even higher office. Air Chief Marshal Dowding's reaction to this business is unknown, and perhaps Evill's timely and positive intervention meant that 'Stuffy', immersed in defending Britain, did not have to waste time and energy dealing with this – indeed, we can only hope that this was the case.

At the end of this first phase, what were the Few's impressions? Pilot Officer H.M. 'Steve' Stephen was a Spitfire pilot with 74 Squadron: 'Looking back, it was July, not August or September that was the most intensive period of fighting. The Germans were bombing convoys and coastal targets, and waves of 109s kept coming over, day in, day out. We were on duty for long periods every day, it was exhausting.'

Because the enemy held the initiative, in that the Luftwaffe chose the time and place to attack and was therefore able to assemble formations over the French coast and gain height before encountering the RAF, Fighter Command was more often than not at a height disadvantage. Radar was essential, but it was not perfect, and the mathematics of time over distance, given the performance of the fighter aircraft in question offset against warning times, meant that scrambling RAF fighters were frequently caught on the climb – the worst possible tactical situation to be in – by Me 109s already up high and positioned up sun. Squadron

Two successful Spitfire pilots of 74 Squadron: Pilot Officer H.M. Stephen DFC (left), who destroyed twelve enemy aircraft during the Battle of Britain, plus two probables and another shared, and Flying Officer John Mungo-Park DFC, whose score during the same period was nine destroyed, one probable and one shared. Stephen survived the war, but Mungo-Park was shot down and killed over France in 1941.

Leader Peter Devitt commanded 152 'Hyderabad' Squadron in the Middle Wallop Sector of 10 Group:

> We were sent forward to fly from Warmwell, very close to the coast, which didn't give us much time to get up there. Middle Wallop was a bit further inland, so really it made more sense to leave us there so that we had more time to climb to an appropriate combat altitude. The lack of air sea rescue provision also concerned me very greatly, and I told Group, in simply understood terms, that this needed rectifying quickly.

Devitt was twenty-seven during the Battle of Britain, and married with two children; a stock broker who had made his money with Lloyd's before the war. One of his pilots, Pilot Officer Roger Hall, described him as 'a debonair sort of chap, an excellent pilot and a very capable leader'. LAC Ray Johnson was an armourer on 152 Squadron:

> Warmwell was a grass airfield inland of Weymouth and not far from the army camp at Bovington. In fact it was adjacent to the spot where Lawrence of Arabia was killed on his motorcycle. About a week or so after our arrival the Station Commander, a Group Captain, had the whole station parade; until then we had all operated from the concrete apron in front of the hangars, but the Groupie's address was to change all that. It went something like this: 'One of these days in the not too distant future, the Hun is going to appear over those Purbeck Hills and knock three kinds of shit out of us. Therefore No 152 Squadron will disperse to the far side of the airfield in an effort to ensure that minimum damage will be occasioned. The hangar will only be used for major inspections and repairs.' He was right, we were hit, several times.

Pilot Officer Michael Appleby:

> My Squadron, No 609 'West Riding', was an auxiliary unit, although I was a Volunteer Reserve pilot. Towards the end of July, Dowding ruled that all pilots should have at least eight hours stand down time in any 24, and at least 24 hours continuous time off once a week. To enable us to do this we had a further intake of newly qualified pilots, including a second from the VR stable, namely John Bisdee. Being Orderly Officer one evening I took a phone call from a newly posted pilot, who wanted to know if it would be possible for him to postpone his arrival until the next day, as he wanted to see his parents in London on the way down from training school. To this I agreed. Next day arrived the 'Green Eyed Monster' – Noel Agazarian, of French and Armenian ancestry, who had been sent down from Oxford, having intended to read for the Bar. He was by nature a cosmopolitan and brilliant linguist, but English education discovered the athlete in him and his flying was typical of his slapdash but brilliant improvisation. He did survive the Battle of Britain but was later killed in the Middle East.
>
> On July 18th I did five sorties, on one of which, a patrol of Lyme Regis, Swanage and Weymouth, I acted as Section Leader, that is the leading aircraft of a section of three, but

Members of 152 Squadron's groundcrew at Warmwell during the Battle of Britain. Although a less glamorous role, the essential contribution of 'Erks' such as these cannot be overlooked. It was these men who kept the 'kites' on 'top line', and upon whom the pilots relied.

nothing of any event occurred so as the weather closed in we returned and patrolled base for half an hour before landing. On August 8th, I flew four times, on one of those sorties as number two to Squadron Leader Darley when he put me in such a position over some Me 110s attacking a convoy that I had nothing to do but press the firing button, and both the engine cowlings and cockpit canopy came off as the aircraft was seen to dive into the sea, much to the delight, we subsequently heard, of the Royal Navy.

The strain of waiting at dispersal, I will never forget, was greatly emphasised by the field telephone; every time it rang everyone would just stop until the operator answering would call out, perhaps, 'Sergeant so and so required in Sick Quarters', at which point we all promptly relaxed. On the other hand, when it was a scramble, we all rushed to our aircraft, preceded by the fitter and rigger, popped into the cockpit, set our parachute and safety harnesses, quite tight too, and having got the throttle mixture control and airscrew pitch controls set, the fitter operated the starter battery and the engine started. Then off we would go, taking off in formation, and after that, who knew what would happen?

2

ADLERANGRIFF:
13 AUGUST – 18 AUGUST 1940

During the previous few days, it was clear that the enemy was no longer focusing on convoys but had changed tack, attacking instead coastal radar installations and forward aerodromes. Although hundreds of reconnaissance sorties were flown over England, German intelligence had frequently misinterpreted the information collated. The Luftwaffe planners did not understand how Air Chief Marshal Dowding's System of Air Defence worked; although the fact that radar was important had been grasped, how it fitted into the chain and how radar generated information was fed into the system was not. Moreover, the crucial significance of Sector Stations had not been fully appreciated, and the importance of various airfields, such as those at Eastchurch, Lympne and Gosport, some of which were Coastal and not Fighter Command bases, was wrongly recorded. During this phase, however, the really heavy fighting began, although due to this poor intelligence picture the Germans would waste much time and resources attacking targets that were not of any particular significance to their mission: the destruction of RAF Fighter Command.

Tuesday 13 August This day was chosen for Göring's much vaunted *Adlertag* – 'Eagle Day' – the raids launched on 13 August heralding the great *Adlerangriff*, or 'Attack of the Eagles'. For all of this Wagnerian rhetoric, the weather was nonplussed, bad weather seeing the huge dawn attack postponed. One *kampfgeschwader*, KG 2, commanded by *Oberst* Johannes Fink, could not be recalled, however, due to a mix up in radio crystals, so although their escorting Me 110s returned to France, Fink's seventy-four Do 17s continued droning over the Channel towards England. KG 2's target, in a scenario so typical of this phase, was the Isle of Sheppey, and specifically the naval base there together with Eastchurch airfield – neither of which were significant to the system. Nonetheless, due to Air Vice-Marshal Leigh-Mallory supporting the DCAS's plan to attack enemy E-boat bases, elements of two Spitfire squadrons, 19 and 266, were temporarily detached to Eastchurch. Sergeant David Cox:

Armourers, also known as 'plumbers', re-arming Pilot Officer David Crook's Spitfire between combats at Warmwell on *Adlertag*, 13 August 1940. The starter battery is plugged in, and the pilot's parachute awaits on the tailplane.

I was awakened by the bombing at about 0730 hours. I rushed out of my room, which was in a wooden hut, into a corridor where I met Flight Sergeant Tofts, who was in charge of servicing 'B' Flight's aircraft. He grabbed me by the arm and we ran into the only brick shelter available, a urinal, and Tofts pushed me onto the floor saying 'This is no time to be squeamish, lad!' Thirty odd people were killed in that raid, although fortunately none from our No 19 Squadron.

The 19 Squadron Operations Record Book (ORB), however, did record that Eastchurch had been 'Most thoroughly bombed'. According to the 266 Squadron ORB, over 100 high explosive and incendiary bombs were dropped by thirty Do 17s, which hit all hangars, destroying all ammunition and 'much equipment', and damaging the water supply; sixteen airmen were killed and one Spitfire destroyed.

The bad weather had, in fact, assisted KG 2's unescorted approach to Sheppey, only one RAF fighter squadron, 74 Squadron, managing to find and intercept Fink's raiders before reaching their targets. It was the Hurricanes of 111 and 151 Squadrons, however, which executed the greater damage, shooting down five Dorniers. Some Me 109s managed to get up early that morning, in spite of the *Adlertag* postponement: III/JG 26 flew an uneventful *freie hunt* in advance of

KG 2's raid, but 1/JG 2 clashed with 43 Squadron's Hurricanes over Shoreham, losing the *Gruppe* Adjutant, *Oberleutnant* Paul Temme, who was shot down and captured.

In what seems to have been a confused situation given the postponement, the unescorted Ju 88s of KG 54 then left the French coast, heading for the army airfield at Odiham and Royal Aircraft Establishment (RAE) at Farnborough, both being situated in Hampshire. Although KG 54 was recalled just after crossing the British coast, the Hurricanes of 43 and 601 Squadrons, up from Tangmere, pounced on the bombers, shooting down two: one of these exploded so violently upon impact that no trace of it was ever found. A third raider was so damaged over England that the pilot gave the order to abandon the stricken machine; only one crew man did so before the Ju 88 was brought back under control and managed to limp back to base. The hapless airman who took to his parachute, *Gefreiter* Gerhard Neissel was captured. The confusion of enemy signals then turned to chaos: the Me 110s of ZG 2 were not told that their mission to escort other elements of KG 54 to Portland had been cancelled. Over the British coast, ZG 2 found no friendly bombers but some very hostile RAF fighters which shot down and destroyed one 110.

By mid-afternoon the weather had improved sufficiently for the main attack to be unleashed. A huge German formation was reported incoming at 15.30 hours along a forty mile wide front. Some thirty Me 110s escorted 120 Ju 88s of KG 54 and LG 1. JG 27's Me 109s provided the escort to nearly 100 Stukas, while the 109s of II/JG 53 swept ahead on this massive *Valhalla*. This was an enormous formation, comprising over 300 'bandits' and aimed entirely at targets in 10 Group. The state of anxiousness in the Middle Wallop Sector Station Operations Room can only be imagined, as the Duty Controller, Wing Commander David Roberts, quickly assessed and deployed the forces available to him as this massive phalanx of enemy aircraft bore down upon him. The Spitfires of 152 Squadron sighted the II/JG 53 *freie hunt*, but the 109s had insufficient fuel for combat and so streaked back to France. In view of the huge weight of numbers involved with this incoming threat, Roberts scrambled every available Spitfire and Hurricane from the Sector Stations of Middle Wallop and Tangmere, and the forward airfields at Warmwell and Exeter: throttles pushed right forward, the RAF fighter pilots climbed desperately to combat altitude.

Although intercepted by two squadrons of Hurricanes, LG 1 fought its way up the Solent to Southampton, where damage was caused to the port and adjacent residences. Fortunately the Spitfire factory at Woolston escaped any significant damage, probably because at this time German intelligence believed that the factory was producing bombers. Over Portland, KG 54's bombing was disrupted by Spitfires and Hurricanes, which also saw off the escort. If spectators were not already being greeted to the biggest air battle so far, being fought out from Portland to the Isle of Wight, things were just about to become even more dramatic.

Sergeant Laurence 'Rubber' Thorogood, a Volunteer Reservist flying Hurricanes with 87 Squadron, poses with Flight Lieutenant 'Widge' Gleed's AL-K. Thorogood was a successful fighter pilot who later flew in the Far East and survived the war. He died in 2001.

Short of fuel, the Me 109s detailed to escort the Stukas bound for Middle Wallop, had to turn back before the dive-bombers reached Lyme Bay. Squadron Leader George Darley's 609 Squadron, which up to that point had suffered several heart-felt casualties, now had revenge, the Spitfires turning the interception into a veritable 'turkey shoot': 5/StG 2 lost six (of nine) Stukas destroyed, and a further aircraft damaged. Pilot Officer Michael Appleby:

> This was a very big raid, intercepted by various squadrons, 609 Squadron claiming many enemy aircraft destroyed without loss to ourselves. I did not personally claim any aircraft destroyed but I was credited with a Ju 87 and an Me 110 damaged. This was both a turning point for our Squadron, and a great success for our CO, George Darley, because of the tactics he had adopted in getting us in the right position at the right time, providing the information received from our radar people was reliable.

Interestingly, in his book, *Spitfire Pilot*, 609 Squadron's Pilot Officer David Crook described his part in the action, which involved a fleeting engagement with the withdrawing escort:

...at this moment I saw about five Me 109s pass just underneath us. I immediately broke away from the formation, dived on the last Me 109 and gave him a terrific burst of fire at very close range. He burst into flames and spun down for many thousands of feet into the clouds below, leaving behind a long trail of smoke.

I followed him down for some way and could not pull out of my dive in time to avoid going below the clouds myself. I found that I was about five miles north of Weymouth, and then I saw a great column of smoke rising from the ground a short distance away. I knew perfectly well what it was and went over to have a look. My Me 109 lay in a field, a tangled heap of wreckage burning fiercely, but with the black crosses on the wings still visible. I found out later that the pilot was still in the machine. He had made no attempt to get out whilst the aircraft was diving and had obviously been killed by my burst of fire. He crashed just outside a small village, and I could see everybody streaming out of their houses and rushing to the spot.

The record, however, proves that all three Me 109s of 5/JG 53 lost in this clash with 609 Squadron crashed in the sea. The wrecked enemy aircraft seen by Pilot Officer Crook could not, therefore, have been the Me 109 that he had shot down, but more likely one of the three Stukas which crashed in Dorset that afternoon. It is, of course, easy to understand how such simple mistakes are made, but this observation also highlights the historian's difficulty in piecing together an accurate chronicle.

Returning to the action, while 5/StG 2 was being massacred by Darley's Spitfires, the remaining Stukas, unable to find their target, beat it for home. LG 1 was no more successful, mistakenly bombing Andover instead of the all important Middle Wallop Sector Station – the Operations Room of which was controlling the RAF fighters during this battle. While the raid on Southampton had been successful, the threat to Middle Wallop had been summarily dealt with.

At 17.00 hours a threat later developed over Kent, directed at Rochester airfield, which was, again, not a Sector Station but just a forward airfield. Also unable to find their target, the raiders consequently dropped their bombs randomly. Quarter of an hour later all three *gruppen* of JG 26 flew a *freie hunt* over the Kentish coast in advance of forty Stukas bent on attacking the Coastal Command airfield at Detling. II/JG 26 was engaged by 56 Squadron, which lost four Hurricanes in the ensuing dogfight: three pilots baled out, one badly burned, while the fourth crash-landed at Hawkinge. 65 Squadron, however, shot down *Unteroffizier* Hans Wemhoner, who was captured, but this enemy fighter diversion was completely successful: not only had four Hurricanes been shot down for the loss of a single 109, but the path was clear for the dive-bombers to pulverize Detling. Again, however, this was not a Fighter Command airfield, and of no consequence, therefore, to the system. Nonetheless, sixty-seven personnel were killed, including the Station Commander, and twenty-two aircraft were written off.

During a combat over the Channel, Pilot Officer Rupert Smythe of 32 Squadron had a lucky escape when a German bullet ripped through his flying helmet. The Hurricane pilot escaped unscathed, and shows off his trophy to Flight Lieutenant Peter Brothers DFC back at Hawkinge.

As the day drew to a close, the Germans had lost forty-four aircraft destroyed and thirteen damaged; Fighter Command had lost thirteen fighters with three pilots being killed. Only 266 Squadron's single Spitfire had been destroyed, and the other forty-six aircraft written off by bombing that day were not fighters. Of course these facts and figures only became known long after the event, so at the time the impression of both sides was that their efforts that day were commendable. The Germans, however, had expended much of the days effort in attacking targets unconnected with the system, but Fighter Command's intercepts were poor: all too many squadrons had failed to find their targets due to cloud: had the enemy effort been directed against really vital targets, then the close of play would have been firmly in the away team's favour.

Wednesday 14 August Having flown so many sorties the previous day, it is not surprising that enemy air activity was somewhat reduced this day, but that is not to say that the resulting action was not violent, fast and furious. Some eighty Stukas, this time of II/StG 1 and 1V/LG 1, set course for Dover, possibly intending to bomb Hawkinge, with both I and III/JG 26 as close escort. II/JG 26 flew an appended *freie hunt*, there being around 100 Me 109s airborne. 11 Group responded at 11.50 hours by scrambling two Hurricane squadrons, 32 and 615, and two of Spitfires, 65 and 610. A huge dogfight subsequently developed over Dover, involving somewhere approaching 150 fighters. Once more the excellence of the *Jagdwaffe* was demonstrated: nine Spitfires and Hurricanes were shot down, two pilots being killed, while the only enemy loss was 1/JG 26's *Feldwebel* Gerhard Kemen, who was shot down by 32 Squadron's Pilot Officer R.F. Smythe and captured (many years later, the complete tail section and other substantial parts from Kemen's fighter were discovered at a scrapyard and are now on display at the Kent Battle of Britain Museum, Hawkinge). The Stukas, however, did not attack Hawkinge, apparently confused by the maelstrom of fighters dueling around them. Instead, the Goodwin lightship was sunk, and a *staffel* of Me 109s destroyed eight balloons of Dover's barrage.

While this great dogfight was underway, Rubensdörfer's *Erprobungsgruppe* 210 cleverly used the confusion as a diversion while it suddenly attacked Manston, a Sector Station, at very low level. Personnel of 600 Squadron, manning a makeshift 20mm anti-aircraft gun, hit *Unteroffizier* Steding's Me 110, which collided with the aircraft of *Leutnant* Brinkmann; of the two two-man aircrews involved, only *Gefreiter* Schank, Steding's gunner and radio operator, survived. This was another brilliant attack by this crack unit, which left another fifty craters in Manston's runway.

Interestingly, *Luftflotte* 3's raids on this day were a complete contrast to the huge *Valhalla* dispatched against 10 Group on *Adlertag*: instead of mass formations, nine *ketten* (vics of three bombers) were sent to attack individual targets in the West Country. Spread out over 100 miles, Brand's fighters played cat and mouse with Sperrle's raiders, some of which reached their targets. In total seven of these raiders were destroyed throughout the day, the most significant by

This He 111 of 9/KG 27, briefed to attack Cardiff Docks, was shot down by Flight Lieutenant Bob Stanford Tuck DFC of 92 Squadron. The bomber forced-landed on the Mendips, the five man crew being captured unhurt.

Flying Officer John Dundas and Pilot Officer David Crook of No 609 Squadron. This aircraft was one of the KG 55 *Stabskette* (Staff Flight), which had successfully bombed Middle Wallop, causing damage to 609 Squadron's offices and hangar, killing two airmen. The He 111 crashed and exploded in the Royal Navy Armaments Depot at Dean Hill, near East Dean. Within the wreckage were found the remains of none other than the *Geschwaderkommodore*, *Oberst* Alois Stockl, *Oberleutnant* B. Brassier, the KG 55 navigation officer, and *Oberst* W. Frank, *Luftgau* VIII's Chief of Staff. The damage caused to Middle Wallop was hardly worth the loss of such skilled and experienced officers.

Thursday 15 August It was clear to all that the tempo of battle was now significantly increasing, and that the main fury of the enemy was directed at 11 Group, and, to a lesser extent, 10 Group. Pilots in 12 Group, among them the indomitable and ever restless Squadron Leader Douglas Bader, were confused and frustrated as to why their comrades further south were engaging overwhelming odds on a daily basis, while their own days were still spent flying mundane convoy protection patrols and playing patience. Pilot Officer Denis Crowley-Milling: 'Naturally Douglas wanted to get us of 242 Squadron into the

Sergeant James Cowley of 87 Squadron pictured at Exeter during the Battle of Britain. A regular airman, Cowley's Hurricane was damaged by Me 109s over Portland on 14 August 1940; he forced-landed near Bridport, slightly wounded.

Flying Officer Henry MacDonald Goodwin, an Auxiliary killed in action over the Solent while flying Spitfires with 609 Squadron on 14 August 1940. The 25-year-old was taken home to Chaddesley Corbett in Worcestershire and buried next to his brother, Pilot Officer Barrie Goodwin, who was killed flying Hurricanes with 605 Squadron earlier that fateful summer.

action. He used to say, "Why don't they get us airborne when the Germans are building up over the Pas-de-Calais?" He felt that we could then proceed south and meet the enemy formation at combat altitude head on.'

Frustrating though it was for 12 Group, under the provisions of the system theirs was nonetheless a crucial role, as Air Chief Marshal Dowding himself had explained to Air Vice-Marshal Leigh-Mallory in a letter dated 1 October 1939:

> Now I have delegated tactical control almost completely to groups and sectors, but I have not delegated strategic control, and the threat to the line must be considered as a whole and not parochially. The units at Debden and Duxford may be urgently required at short notice for the defence of London and, although they have been put under you to balance the number of stations in groups, this function of theirs must not be overlooked.

Another fundamental role of the 12 Group squadrons was to provide cover for 11 Group's airfields in the event of Air Vice-Marshal Park's fighters being engaged further forward. Nonetheless, Douglas Bader in particular sulked and stormed, unable to accept that his was a lesser role in what was clearly a critical and epic aerial conflict In challenging his Commander-in-Chief's System of Air Defence, however, the young Acting Squadron Leader Douglas Bader was insubordinate, and clearly misunderstood the factors involved. For example, the limitations of early radar meant that it was virtually impossible, due to the general high volume of air activity over the French coast, to identify when a raid was actually building up. The first indication of an incoming raid was inevitably, therefore, when the plots began moving towards England cohesively. The time and speeds involved therefore made it impossible for 12 Group to be scrambled, travel to and meet the enemy as Bader suggested. Moreover, the CO of 242 Squadron was also unable to grasp why 11 Group was not responding to the larger German formations in strength, instead of using 'penny packet' formations. Again, however, these tactics, intended to preserve Fighter Command's limited resources and prevent them being wiped out *en masse*, as was Göring's intention, had been decided upon after extremely careful consideration by two of the most experienced fighter tacticians in the world at that time: Air Chief Marshal Dowding and Air Vice-Marshal Park; who, then, was *Acting Squadron Leader* Bader to challenge the judgement of such men?

The Luftwaffe was not only based in Northern France, but also in Scandanavia. Air Chief Marshal Dowding was ever conscious of the fact that a major attack could be delivered across the North Sea, to the industrial Midlands or north of England, so he had no choice but to constantly base fighter squadrons in those areas, ready to respond to such a threat. Had he concentrated his force in the south, and used mass fighter formations against raids coming in from France, the remainder of the British Isles would have been unprotected. The most efficient squadrons, however, were clearly required in the south and south-east, and so Air Chief Marshal Dowding rotated his squadrons, after a spell in the main combat zone, squadrons were sent north to re-fit, being relieved by units having completed that process at such northerly bases as Catterick and Leconfield. In this way, should the Luftwaffe attack in strength from their bases in Norway, they would still be met by Spitfires and Hurricanes, and yet, at the same time, Fighter Command's strongest squadrons were always in 10, 11 and, to some extent, 12 Groups.

If ever evidence was required that Air Chief Marshal Dowding's system worked, it came on 15 August. Also on the same day friction between 11 and 12 Groups erupted, which would have far-reaching and negative consequences for both Air Chief Marshal Dowding and Air Vice-Marshal Park.

Reichsmarschall Göring, however, was not entirely satisfied with the progress of his *Adlerangriff* thus far and so held a conference at Karinhall, his opulent home, with senior Luftwaffe commanders. From now on, Göring decreed, the emphasis of operations was to be the destruction of the RAF. Shipping was only to be attacked when the opportunity arose and circumstances were entirely favourable to the Germans. *Störflug* were to continue against targets connected with the British aircraft industry, but attacks against radar sites were to cease completely on the grounds that in spite of the effort expended, not one station had been put out of action. Still placing great faith in Stukas, the Luftwaffe commander's memorandum also detailed exactly how the dive-bombers were to be escorted, emphasizing that Me 110s were in short supply and so had to be used 'economically'. Crucially, this document makes clear the fact that the enemy underestimated the advantages that radar gave the defenders, and abandoning attacks against such targets represented a grave tactical error.

Dawn reconnaissance flights over England were followed by a period of quiet, as the weather slowly improved. While the commander of 11 *Fliegerkorps*, General Lorzer, was absent at the Karinhall conference, the decision whether to launch a massive attack against England, from Edinburgh to Exeter, rested on the shoulders of *Oberst* Paul Deichmann. With all aircrews standing by and improving weather, Lorzer's Chief-of-Staff courageously gave the order to go.

The first targets attacked were the coastal airfields at Hawkinge and Lympne. Fortunately, Squadron Leader Harry Hogan's 501 Squadron had been scrambled from Hawkinge just minutes before the raid. When the raiders appeared, a large formation of Stukas escorted by Me 109s, Hogan's Hurricanes were patrolling near Dover and pounced on the Hawkinge attack force. Two dive-bombers were shot down before the 109s of II/JG 51 counter-attacked, shooting down two Hurricanes and damaging a third. Fortunately both downed British pilots baled out and survived the traumatic experience unscathed. 54 Squadron's Spitfires were also patrolling near Dover when the raid came in, and Squadron Leader James 'Prof' Leathart led his pilots to attack the bandits heading for Lympne. JG 26 was providing the escort to the Stukas in the process of pulverizing the little airfield at Lympne, and successfully parried 54 Squadron's thrust; the Manston based squadron lost two Spitfires in the process, although both pilots survived. These two targets, however, were successfully dive-bombed: a hangar and other installations were destroyed at Hawkinge, and Lympne was devastated. Again, however, German intelligence was wanting, as although Lympne, conveniently situated on the Kentish coast near Dungeness, was sometimes used as an emergency landing ground by damaged fighters, it played no part in the system.

Although Manston was strafed by low flying Me 110s, the next raid was completely unpredictable, as *Luftflotte* 5 mounted a huge raid against north-east England. Flying from their bases in Norway, seventy-two He 111s of I and II/KG 26, escorted by twenty-one Me 110s of I/ZG 76, took off soon after 10.00 hours, bound for Sunderland, while fifty Ju 88s headed for the airfields at Driffield. Confident that RAF fighter opposition would be negligible, the Germans were about to receive a telling demonstration of the brilliance of Air Chief Marshal Dowding's system.

As this huge raid approached their coastline, the 13 Group Controller, for whom such an occurrence was a completely new experience, scrambled five fighter squadrons based between Catterick in Yorkshire to Drem on the Firth of Forth. Over the Fame Islands, 100 plus bandits were tally ho'd. Squadron Leader Ted Graham: 'I was leading No 72 Squadron, and the German formation was quite a sight, something I will never forget, and I must confess to have reported the enemy in a rather excited manner!'

In 72 Squadron's initial charge, two Me 110s went down into the North Sea, including the *Kommandeur* of I/ZG 76, *Hauptmann* Werner Restemeyer, whose aircraft exploded. Pilot Officer Harry Welford:

At 1230 hours we of 607 Squadron were going off duly for 24 hours leave when the whole Squadron was called to readiness. We heard from the Group Operations Room that there was a big flap on, that is a warning of imminent enemy action along the NE coast. We waited out at dispersal points, al Flights, for half an hour, then scrambled in Squadron formation. I was in a feverish state of excitement and we quickly took off and climbed to our operational height of 20,000 feet, ready to patrol the coast. We kept receiving messages over the R/T of 40 or 50 plus bogeys approaching Newcastle from the north. Although we patrolled for over half an hour, we never saw a thing. Just as I was expecting the order to pancake, I heard the senior flight commander shout 'Tally Ho!', and Tally Ho it bloody well was! There, on our port side at 9,000 feet, must have been 120 bombers, all with swastikas and German crosses as large as life, having the gross impertinence to cruise down Northumberland and Durham's NE coast. These were the people who were going to bomb Newcastle and Sunderland, where our friends and families lived, we being an auxiliary unit raised from that local area.

I'd never seen anything like it. They were in two groups, one of about 70, the other about 40, like two swarms of bees. There was no time to wait and so we immediately took up station and delivered No 3 attacks in sections. As only three Hurricanes at a time, flying along nicely in formation, attacked a line of 20 bombers, I didn't see how their gunners

Flight Lieutenant Ted Graham, pictured with his 72 Squadron Spitfire at Acklington, before the Squadron moved south for the Battle of Britain. Graham saw action on 15 August 1940, when the Luftwaffe sent a large but unescorted raiding force across the North Sea to attack Sunderland and Driffield. Known as the 'Junkers Party', the sortie confirmed the folly of sending bombers to England in daylight without fighter escort.

could miss us. We executed our attack, however, and despite the fact that I thought it was me being hit all over the place, it was their machines which started dropping out of the sky. In my excitement, during the next attack I only narrowly missed one of our own machines whilst doing a split arse breakaway – there couldn't have been more than two feet between us! Eventually, spotting most of the enemy aircraft dropping down with only their undercarriage damaged, I chased an He 111 and filled the poor devil with lead until first one, then the other, engine stopped. I then enjoyed the sadistic satisfaction of watching the bomber crash into the North Sea. With the one I reckoned to have damaged with my first attack, these were my first bloods, and so i was naturally elated.

The other RAF squadrons engaged were similarly successful, in what had become another turkey shoot. Although it reached the north-east coastal area, the raid was turned back before Sunderland was bombed. Now KG 30's Ju 88s appeared on the scene, the Controller anticipating that this new raid was bound for the important fighter airfields at Leconfield and Church Fenton. The Spitfires of 616 Squadron – at thirty minutes notice to fly – and the Hurricanes of 73

Squadron's 'B' Flight were rapidly scrambled from Leconfield. Pilot Officer Hugh 'Cocky' Dundas:

> As we of 616 Squadron were having lunch and at 30 minutes notice, we really thought that the Controller had taken leave of his senses, but he was insistent, all the time the Controller becoming increasingly excited. A phone call to the Officers' Mess, where we were dining, sent us running to our cars, and as we sped around the perimeter track we saw our groundcrews urgently preparing our Spitfires for flight. Disembarking, we ran to our aircraft and took off urgently. The Controller's still excited voice ordered us to head out to sea and intercept a big raid incoming south of Flamborough Head. I have to say that the whole scenario appeared most unlikely, but we welcomed anything that broke the monotony of convoy patrols.
>
> We flew at top speed, not as a squadron or even in flights or sections, but individually we raced across the coast and out to sea. About 15 miles out to sea I saw them, to our left front and slightly below, twin-engine German bombers, flying in a loose and scattered formation towards our coastline. I switched on my reflector sight, setting the range for 250 yards, and turned the gun button to fire. I curved towards the nearest bomber, the rear gunner of which fired at me but this stopped after my first burst. The bomber fell back, gushed black smoke and fell steeply towards the sea. All around Spitfires were jockeying for position to fire at enemy aircraft, jostling each other out of the way to get in a shot. I then chased a damaged bomber, which was heading out to sea, but by the time I shot it down I was a long way out and the sky was empty. As I was running low on ammunition by that time, hot and elated I decided to return to Leconfield.
>
> I landed 25 minutes after take off. The rest of the Squadron straggled in, singly or in pairs, and, looking at the blown canvas patches over their gun ports, everyone seemed to have fired. The Squadron claimed eight Ju 88s destroyed, four probables and two damaged. None of our Spitfires were even damaged.

In spite of the heavy losses inflicted upon KG 30 during the 'Junkers Party', some raiders reached their target – not the fighter stations at Leconfield or Church Fenton – but the bomber base at Driffield, where ten Whitleys were destroyed and others damaged. Seven Ju 88s were destroyed, but in both actions only one RAF fighter, a 605 Squadron Hurricane, was damaged. Had Air Chief Marshal Dowding concentrated his fighter force in the south, these raids would have reached their targets unopposed. As things stood, *Luftflotte 5* had taken a pasting, losing eighty-one aircrew and never again attempted such an enterprise. The inadequacy of the Me 110 as an escorting fighter was finally proven beyond doubt, as was the folly of bombers venturing forth anywhere over England without the protection of Me 109s. Of course in this case the distance from Norway to the north-east coast of England was far too great for the Me 109, indeed even the Me 110s had to use auxiliary fuel tanks. Moreover, having been briefed to expect no serious opposition, the enemy aircrews must

Pilot Officer Hugh 'Cocky' Dundas, an Auxiliary flying Spitfires with 616 Squadron. On 22 August 1940, Dundas became another victim of Major Mölders when shot down in flames over Dover. Baling out wounded, Dundas later flew with distinction throughout the war; one of Douglas Bader's 'inner sanctum' at Tangmere in 1941, by 1945 Dundas was a highly decorated group captain and fighter ace.

have been demoralized to have been so roughly handled by so many Spitfires and Hurricanes. The elation of 13 Group can only be imagined, and whatever celebrations took place that night were wholly justified.

At 14.15 hours, *Luftflotte* 2 staged its second major effort of the day. Two *gruppen* of JG 26 swept over Kent in advance of eighty-eight KG 3 Do 17s, closely escorted by 130 Me 109s from JGs 51, 52 and 54, tasked with attacking the airfields at Eastchurch and Rochester – again targets of no significance to the system. While this raid was materializing, a fast plot was tracked incoming over towards Harwich, as a consequence of which the 11 Group Controller scrambled 17 Squadron from Martlesham Heath, the forward coastal airfield in the Debden Sector. This was a wise move, as twenty-five Me 110s and Me 109s of *Erprobungsgruppe* 210 once more confounded the defenders by sweeping in at low level and plastering Martlesham. With the huge KG 3 raid simultaneously incoming, the 11 Group Controller had no choice but to require assistance from 12 Group. Sergeant David Cox:

> The attack on Martlesham Heath, near Ipswich, was brilliantly executed by Erich Rubensdörfer, *Erprobungsgruppe* 210's approach going completely undetected until just a few minutes from the target. Taking into account the distance from Fowlmere to Martlesham, 60 air miles, our chances of contacting the enemy were nil. Even taking into account an *optimistic* speed for our Spitfires of 300 mph, it would take 12 minutes from take-off to reach Martlesham Heath. In any case, at our altitude, 2,000 feet, I doubt that our cannon-armed Spitfire Mk IBs were capable of that speed, as its maximum speed was not achievable until 19,000 feet. I would therefore suggest that 280 mph was the most likely maximum speed for height, but even at 300 mph 19 Squadron could not achieve the impossible.

The raiders were intercepted by three Hurricanes of 17 Squadron and nine more of 1 Squadron. South of Harwich, the Hurricanes of the latter's Red, Yellow and Green Sections were attacked by Me 109s. Red Section bore the brunt of this attack: Flight Lieutenant Brown baled out and was rescued by a trawler, but Pilot Officer Browne and Sergeant Shanahan were both killed. Pilot Officer Matthews sighted and engaged the enemy raiders bombing Martlesham, damaging one. Pilot Officer Mann was attacked by an Me 110 from behind, shaking off his assailant only to be hit by an Me 109 on which he turned the tables: opening fire from astern, the Hurricane pilot blew the 109's canopy off before setting the enemy fighter alight. Another Me 109 attacked Green Two. Pilot Officer Tim Elkington:

> The enemy aircraft started to climb and turn to the left, but I turned sharp left and came in behind him, giving a short burst with no noticeable effect. I again fired at the enemy aircraft from astern as it straightened out and went into a steep climb. I gave him a two second burst from astern and above. The engine belched fumes and it turned over on its

back, staying there for about three seconds, and then turned over and dropped like a plummet into the sea. I circled round but saw no-one get out.

In the ensuing engagement, however, the Me 109s destroyed three RAF fighters, killing two pilots.

Air Vice-Marshal Park was furious about the bombing of Martlesham, but for the reasons outlined above 19 Squadron could hardly be blamed. Although 12 Group complained that they had been called for too late, due to the absolute bare minimum of warning involved, the 11 Group Controller was neither to blame. Unfortunately, both groups appeared to overlook the fact that Rubensdörfer had, once again, trounced the defences by sneaking in beneath the radar screen at high speed and causing chaos. Nonetheless, the frustration of both 11 and 12 Groups can be fully appreciated: there would be many more arguments between the two over the weeks ahead.

The raid directed at Eastchurch and Rochester had still to be dealt with, however, so there was no respite as yet. 64 Squadron contacted the JG 26 *freie hunt*, losing three Spitfires, one of which crash-landed near Calais. Two Hurricanes of 111 Squadron were damaged as was another belonging to 151 Squadron. JG 26 suffered no losses. In fact, the *Jagdfleigern* closely escorting KG 3 provided an impenetrable shield around the bombers, which devastated Rochester and caused great damage to the adjacent Short Brothers factory which produced Stirling bombers.

Hawkinge and other targets in 'Hellfire Corner', including the Foreness Chain Home Low station, were then attacked by KGs 1 and 2, which were escorted by the Me 109s of I/LG 2. As if the defenders were not now hard pressed enough, more waves of enemy aircraft simultaneously bore down on targets in the 10 Group area. South-east of the Isle of Wight, 43 Squadron tally ho'd sixty Ju 88s of LG 1 and forty Me 110s of ZG 2, bound for the Sector Station at Middle Wallop. Once more the airspace over the Solent and Southampton was the scene of more fighting, as two more Hurricane squadrons and a Spitfire squadron joined the fray. The enemy bombers' navigation was disrupted, however, and instead of concentrating their attack on Middle Wallop as planned, Odiham and Worthy Down were also bombed; the damage at all three airfields was fortunately slight. On this occasion, 601 Squadron – the so-called 'Millionaire's Mob' – up from Tangmere performed superbly, massacring 4/LG 1.

An air battle also raged over Portland, where naval installations were once more dive-bombed by Stukas. Exeter's two resident Hurricane squadrons, 87 and 213, waded into the escorting Me 109s and 110s, a force some eighty strong, being reinforced soon afterwards by the Spitfires of 234. Four of the Spitfires were shot down, Pilot Officer Richard Hardy famously being hit far out to sea and making a wheels down forced landing in France, where both he and his aircraft were captured. Still, however, the day had yet to draw to a close, as more plots appeared on the table at Uxbridge.

Wounded fighter pilots convalesced at the Palace Hotel, Torquay. There the young officers formed a band, the singer is none other than Flight Lieutenant James Brindley Nicolson, the only fighter pilot to win a Victoria Cross in the Second World War. Shot down in flames by an Me 110 over Southampton on 16 August as Nicolson prepared to bale out his assailant appeared in front of his Hurricane; climbing back into the furnace Nicolson destroyed the enemy aircraft before finally taking to his parachute, badly wounded. The incident was witnessed by watchers in both the air and on the ground. Sadly he was killed in the Far East in 1945.

Hauptmann Adolf Galland's III/JG 26 swept ahead of heavily escorted Do 17s intending to bomb the Sector Station at Biggin Hill. Unmolested by RAF fighters, however, the formation bombed West Malling by mistake, which was a new and as yet non-operational aerodrome. Once again, Rubensdörfer was back over England, his elite unit bent upon destruction at the Kenley Sector Station. Although missing the scheduled rendezvous with his proposed Me 109 escorts, Rubensdörfer pressed on, but, shortly before 19.00 hours, mistakenly bombed Kenley's satellite field at Croydon. Nonetheless *Erprobungsgruppe* 210's bombing was accurate, causing much damage: six servicemen were killed along with sixty-two civilians and 192 more were injured due to there having been no air raid warning. Shortly before the bombs fell, however, Squadron Leader Jon Thompson's 111 Squadron had scrambled from Croydon, the Hurricanes falling upon the withdrawing Me 110s. Rubensdörfer himself was shot down and killed by Thompson, the *Kommandeur's* machine crashing in flames at Rotherfield. 32 Squadron was also engaged and the Hurricanes collectively executed great damage, at last, on this thorn in the defenders' side: *Erprobungsgruppe* 210 lost seven aircraft in total, three from the *Stabschwarm*, which was wiped out. At last, the action of 15 August was over.

The Luftwaffe had flown over 2,000 sorties this day, a figure that would not be surpassed. Never again, however, would *Luftflotte* 5 attempt a mass raid against north-east England. The inadequacies of both the Me 110 and Stuka were further emphasised, as was the poor standard of enemy intelligence. Once more, though, the brilliance of the enemy fighter pilots had been demonstrated, as had the tenacity of the defenders, who had destroyed seventy-five enemy aircraft and sent fifteen more back to their bases damaged and with wounded crewmen aboard. Although the Martlesham raid provided the first occasion for open hostility between 11 and 12 Groups, the excellent performance of 13 Group showed clear evidence that Air Chief Marshal Dowding's strategy was working.

Friday 16 August Having been hit the previous day, the new Fighter Command airfield at West Malling was being repaired when KG 2's Do 17s appeared overhead shortly before 11.00 hours. The ensuing further damage ensured that the airfield remained non-operational for several more days. On this occasion the raiders escaped unscathed.

An hour later, three further threats of 100 aircraft each appeared on the plotting table. Over the Thames Estuary the Spitfires of 54 Squadron intercepted the Hornchurch bound raiders of II/KG 2, which for some reason turned about before reaching their target, and engaged the escorting Me 109s of JG 54 in a running battle back to France. That successful fighter pilot from New Zealand, Pilot Officer Colin Gray, claimed two 109s destroyed, German records indicating that I/JG 54's *Unteroffizier* Rimmel was wounded when he crash-landed with combat damage back at St Ingelvert, and 3/JG 54's *Feldwebel* Knedler was reported *vermisst*. Two Dorniers were also lost, and another returned to France badly damaged, while the Spitfires suffered no loss.

Another 150 bandits were then incoming high over the white cliffs of Dover, 11 Group responding by scrambling three squadrons of Spitfires and two of Hurricanes. The latter charged the enemy bombers head-on. Flight Lieutenant Gerry Edge:

> They didn't like that head-on attack, you know, but you had to judge the break-away point exactly right. If you left it to the last 100 yards then you were in trouble, due to the fast closing speeds, but once you got the hang of it a head-on attack was a piece of cake. When you opened fire you would kill or badly wound the pilot and second pilot. Then you'd rake the whole line as you broke away. On one attack, the first Heinkel I hit crashed into the next.

Perhaps Flight Lieutenant Henry Ferriss, up with 111 Squadron from Croydon, misjudged the all-important break-away: he collided with a 7/KG 76 Do 17 and was killed when his Hurricane crashed in flames at Sheephurst Farm, Marden.

Squadron Leader Rodney Wilkinson's 266 Squadron had moved from Wittering in 12 Group to Hornchurch just two days previously, and had yet to see any intensive combat during the Battle of Britain. At Wittering, Wilkinson's Spitfires flew the usual round of monotonous convoy protection patrols around the east coast, chasing off lone enemy raiders. Since Dunkirk, however, the Squadron had not clashed with the Me 109; time and time again throughout the summer of 1940, inexperienced squadrons would move into the combat zone only to be decimated on their first substantial intercept. They were unprepared for the massively increased and vicious tempo of battle caused by the presence of Me 109s – the experience was simply traumatic, as 266 Squadron was about to discover.

As *Hauptmann* Karl Ebbighausen led his II/JG 26 *Stabsschwarm* back out over Deal, heading back to Marquise, Squadron Leader Wilkinson led seven 266 Squadron Spitfires down to attack the enemy escort fighters. In the subsequent combat, Ebbighausen disappeared, the third II/JG 26 *Kommandeur* to be lost in just three months. The 266 Squadron formation, however, was virtually annihilated: Squadron Leader Wilkinson crashed in flames and was killed at Eastry Court, near Deal, and Pilot Officer N.G. Bowen's Spitfire also became a 'flamer', the 20-year-old pilot being killed, his fighter crashing at Adisham. Spitfire N3095 was also set alight, but fortunately Flight Lieutenant S.H. Bazley baled out with burns and minor injuries. Sub-Lieutenant Henry La Fone Greenshields, a Fleet Air Arm pilot serving with Fighter Command during this desperate hour of need, was reported missing: pursued over the Channel and shot down by *Leutnant* Gerhard Müller-Dühe of III/JG 26, his Spitfire crashed and burnt out in Calais, the 22-year-old pilot being buried in France. Pilot Officer S.F. Soden's Spitfire was badly damaged and forced-landed near Faversham, the pilot slightly wounded; Sergeant Eade came off best: although his aircraft was badly damaged over Canterbury, the pilot was unhurt. Of the seven Spitfires that Wilkinson had led into battle just a few minutes earlier, by the combat's conclusion five had been shot down, with three pilots killed, including Wilkinson himself, two more wounded and a further aircraft damaged. This outcome was absolutely disastrous, 266 Squadron being withdrawn from the front line a few days later.

The third enemy formation, also comprising over 100 aircraft, progressed towards targets further west: Tangmere Sector Station, the Ventnor CH radar station, and the navy base at Lee-on-Solent. StG 2's Ju 87s dived out of the sun, executing a highly successful attack which damaged all hangars together with other essential facilities and services. A number of Spitfires and Hurricanes were also destroyed on the ground, together with all aircraft on charge with the Fighter Interception Unit, which included the first operational Bristol Beaufighter night-fighter. Casualties were high: fourteen RAF personnel and six 'civvies' were killed while forty-one more were injured.

The Stukas failed to escape unscathed, however, 1 and 43 Squadrons shooting down seven of their number and damaging three more. Over Portsmouth, the former's Pilot Officer Elkington sighted and chased an Me 109, but was in turn attacked from behind by another enemy fighter. As Elkington's Hurricane burst into flame, the pilot's rapid exit from his cockpit was impeded by a trapped radio lead; after climbing back in and disconnecting the wire, he at last managed to fall free of his doomed fighter and safely deploy his parachute. Among those watching the drama from their homes on Hayling Island was none other than Pilot Officer Elkington's mother, blissfully unaware that the pilot who had narrowly escaped death and was now drifting earthwards beneath a silk canopy was her son! Elkington had actually become the eighteenth victim of one of the enemy's most dangerous *experten*: Major Helmut Wick, *Kommodore* of JG 2 'Richthofen'. In his log book, Elkington wrote the following of this traumatic experience:

> CO leading. In Berry's Section. On to Portsmouth and ran into 100+ Huns there. Got split up doing X over. Ran into eight 109s. Went after one and three others were behind. Cannon hit starboard tank and burst into flames; ended up by the Nab Light. Baled out and landed at West Wittering, landing on my —! Berry blew me onto land with his slipstream. Taken to West Sussex Hospital by ambulance. Chute pinched! Baled out from 10,000 feet at 1340 hours.

Over Bognor Regis, the Hurricanes of 601 Squadron attacked the Tangmere raiders, but Pilot Officer Billy Fiske's aircraft was badly damaged. Returning to Tangmere, Fiske forced-landed, but his stricken aircraft was strafed as it careered across the cratered runway. The Hurricane burst into flame; although the pilot was rescued, he died the next day. Billy Fiske is a unique casualty of the Battle of Britain given that he was the first American volunteer to make the ultimate sacrifice, having volunteered for aircrew duties with the RAF just two weeks after war broke out and, of course, when the United States was still neutral. Fiske was from a privileged background, his father being an international banker based in Paris. During the 1930s Fiske had lived in England and graduated from Cambridge, but it was at winter sports that he truly excelled: at St Moritz he set a record for the Cresta Run, and in 1932 was captain of the American Olympic team that won a gold medal in the bobsled event. Fast cars were another passion, and when only nineteen years old Fiske drove the first Stutz car at Le Mans. Today, his grave can be seen at Boxgrove Abbey, Sussex, and a memorial plaque in St Paul's proclaims 'An American citizen who died that England might live'. The other two formations from the incoming threat that claimed the life of Billy Fiske successfully attacked naval stations at Lee-on-Solent and Gosport; although damage was caused, this is further evidence of how lacking Luftwaffe intelligence was: neither airfield was connected with Fighter Command and were therefore inconsequential to the defence of Britain. Nonetheless, the Gosport raid became the subject of high drama.

Pilot Officer Peter Hairs of 501 Squadron, pictured at Tangmere. Hairs opened his account during the Battle of France, also destroying an Me 109 during the Battle of Britain, after which he largely served as a flying instructor, being made an MBE in 1946.

On 14 August, 249 'Gold Coast' Squadron had flown south for a tour of duty in the combat zone, joining 10 Group at Boscombe Down in Dorset. Inland of Portland and not far from Southampton, the Boscombe squadrons found themselves heavily engaged. On 16 August, Flight Lieutenant Eric James Brindley Nicolson led 249's Hurricanes up from Boscombe at 13.05 hours on a patrol of the Poole – Romsey line at 15,000 feet. Enemy activity was seen over Gosport , and Nicolson, Red One, led Red Section (Pilot Officer Martyn King, Red Two, and Squadron Leader Eric King, Red Three) towards the trouble. A squadron of Spitfires, however, beat the Hurricanes to it, and so 'Nick' turned Red Section about and set off back to join 249 Squadron. Climbing, the sun behind them, Red Section was in a dangerous tactical position indeed: Me 110s swooped out of the dazzling sunlight, hitting all three Hurricanes.

Squadron Leader King, who was flying with 249 Squadron as a supernumerary squadron leader to gain combat experience prior to taking command of Teddy Donaldson's 151 Squadron, managed to escape with only slight damage and returned safely to Boscombe. Pilot Officer King, however, baled out but his canopy, damaged by a cannon shell, collapsed at 1,500 feet and the pilot fell into the garden of 30 Clifton Road, Shirley, Southampton; there the 19-year-old died in the arms of a local resident, Fred Poole. Fate, however, had great things in store for Red One.

Flight Lieutenant Nicolson's Hurricane was hit by four cannon shells, one of which set the gravity fuel tank ablaze. His cockpit became an inferno, but as he prepared to bail out an Me 110 – possibly his assailant – suddenly presented itself as a sitting duck right in front of the blazing Hurricane. 'Nick' therefore climbed back into the flames and gave chase. His left foot already wounded by shrapnel, 'Nick' watched horrified as the skin on his throttle hand incinerated and his instrument panel was reduced to molten metal. Satisfied that his attack on the Me 110 had been successfully pressed home, Nick, by now badly burned about the hands, face, neck and legs, baled out. As he descended through the air battle, the wounded British pilot played dead, hanging limply in his parachute harness, not wanting to attract bullets from a murderous enemy pilot. Narrowly missing high-tension cables in the built up area of Southampton, shortly before Flight Lieutenant Nicolson landed in Mr Strange's field at Burrowdale Road, Millbrook, he was fired upon by a Home Guard sergeant armed with an antiquated 12-bore, the pellets peppering his right side. A butcher's boy pedaled his bicycle furiously in the direction he had seen the airman descending, and, having established the badly injured pilot's identity, set about the Home Guard NCO with his fists! Suffering third degree burns from the waist downwards and bleeding from his shotgun wound, before being administered morphine he managed to dictate a telegram for his pregnant wife, Muriel, in Yorkshire.

Flight Lieutenant Nicolson's road to recovery began at the Royal Southampton Hospital, and after a spell at the Halton RAF hospital he was sent, with other fighter pilots wounded during the Battle of Britain, to convalesce at the Palace Hotel, Torquay. Pilot Officer William Walker (see 26 August):

> A telegram arrived for Nick, whose response was simply 'Well, what d'ya make of that?' He was genuinely puzzled, and not a little embarrassed, that of the hundreds of brave deeds performed by RAF fighter pilots that summer, his had been singled out for this very great honour. At first Nick got into trouble for being improperly dressed, because he refused to stitch the maroon ribbon on to his tunic. In the end I think he adopted the attitude that he was accepting the medal on behalf of us all. He was a very good sport, in fact. We enjoyed playing together in a four-piece band that we two formed with other wounded pilots at Torquay.

The citation, published in the London Gazette that day, commented that: 'Flight Lieutenant Nicolson has always displayed great enthusiasm for air fighting and this incident shows that he possesses courage and determination of a high order by continuing to engage the enemy after he had been wounded and his aircraft set of fire. He displayed exceptional gallantry and disregard for the safety of his own life.'

On 25 November, Nick, accompanied by his wife, mother and both sisters, attended an investiture at Buckingham Palace where the still confused fighter pilot received his Victoria Cross from the King. This was, of course, not only the only Victoria Cross awarded to a fighter pilot during the Battle of Britain, but, indeed, throughout the Second World War. Twenty-one other Victoria Crosses were awarded to RAF personnel, but due to the speed and individual nature of fighter combat, finding witnesses to 'signal acts of valour' was more often than not impossible. Having occurred over a densely populated area, this was not the case with Nicolson's combat. Sadly, however, Nick, who was later awarded a DFC, would not survive the war: on 2 May 1945, he was killed when flying as a passenger in a B-24 Liberator bomber which crashed into the Bay of Bengal due to an engine fire and after a raid on Japanese installations at Rangoon. The 29-year-old Wing Commander J.B. Nicolson VC DFC has no known grave and is remembered on the Singapore Memorial.

As Nicolson was being admitted to Royal Southampton Hospital, however, on 16 August 1940, the fighting still raged over England. Following diversionary feints, two *schwarm* of Me 109s strafed Manston late in the afternoon, destroying a Spitfire. Shortly afterwards, at 17.05 hours, KG 27's He 111s and their Me 110 escorts were incoming over Brighton while another plot appeared Biggin Hill bound. Seven RAF fighter squadrons intercepted these two formations, which consequently wheeled around and returned to France.

There was also action this day in the 12 Group area, much to the delight of 19 Squadron's 'A' Flight. Both flights of that squadron had spent a boring day at Coltishall, flipping a coin to determine whether 'A' or 'B' went for tea first. The coin favoured Flight Lieutenant Wilf Clouston's 'B' Flight, so Flight Lieutenant

Brian Lane's 'A' Flight remained at readiness. A few minutes later, at 17.30 hours, Lane and his pilots were recalled to Duxford, but shortly after take off were advised that there may be some 'trade' further south, an 'X', or unidentified incoming plot, having appeared on the radar screen. Anticipating, as more often than not was the case with such things, the X Raid to be nothing more than an unidentified friendly aircraft, 'A' Flight was stunned when, about thirty miles south of Harwich, they ran into, in Lane's own words, 'about 150 Huns!' Enemy bombers, protected by forty–fifty Me 110s which were stepped up behind their charges, together with Me 109s 1,000 feet above and to starboard of this main formation, were flying southwards. Then the seven cannon-armed Spitfire Mk IBs of 19 Squadron's 'A' Flight pounced, in two sections of three and four aircraft. These Spitfires, however, were the experimental aircraft trialing 20mm cannon, one in each wing, but no machine-guns. The Hispano-Suiza cannons were intended to be mounted upright, but due to the Spitfire's thin wing section they had been side-mounted, with custom-made chutes fitted to eject spent shell casings. On the ground this worked perfectly, but in combat, with the added stresses and strains imposed by speed, torque and gravity, the ejection chutes frequently jammed. When the cannons worked, though, the results were devastating.

Sergeant Jack Potter 'pursued an Me 110 and fired at very short range from above and saw almost the whole of his starboard engine disappear. He flicked over to port and as he did so a large piece of front section broke away.' When later asked by the Squadron Intelligence Officer whether he thought the claim a certainty, Potter replied, 'Well, I knocked the port engine out of the wings, and the nose as far as the windscreen fell out as well, but he might have got home with hell of a draught in his face!'

Flight Sergeant George 'Grumpy' Unwin:

I attacked one of the Me 110s and gave him a short burst. He half rolled and went down almost vertically. I could not see what happened to him because I was attacked by another. I out-turned him and found myself with a perfect target at close range. My starboard cannon had a stoppage but I fired the remainder of my port cannon's ammunition into the 110. Bits fell off it and he went into a steep dive, during which the tail came off. I followed him down and when I emerged from cloud saw a splash in the sea, which I assumed was him.

Pilot Officer Wallace 'Jock' Cunningham also destroyed an Me 110 before his cannons jammed, but those of Flight Lieutenant Lane and Sergeant Bernard 'Jimmy' Jennings refused to fire at all. Years later, Jock commented that 'I remember mainly Jennings on the R/T bemoaning his jammed 20mm cannon, full of indignation at the unfairness of life in general.'

Unusually, the Me 110s had no rear gunners, and the Me 109s took no part in the engagement. In his log book, Sergeant Jennings recorded that he suspected the enemy formation to have been practising. The pilots' frustration with their cannons, however, was evident from the daily entry in the 19 Squadron ORB: 'Results would have been at least doubled had we been equipped with either cannon and machine-guns or just eight machine-guns.' For 19 Squadron there would be further frustrating combats ahead before the problem was resolved.

Saturday 17 August There was no action during the day, Göring having summoned many of his fighter and bomber commanders to a conference at Karinhall, his opulent country estate near Berlin.

In an effort to make good the heavy losses suffered over the past week or so, certain Polish and Czech fighter squadrons were made fully operational, among them 310 (Czech) Squadron at Duxford. The Czechs rapidly became popular and earned respect. Wing Commander R.B. 'Woody' Woodhall:

> Most of the Czechs had reported in French uniform, having fought with the French until France fell. Upon arrival they spoke little English and had to be converted onto Hurricanes. They were therefore provided an English squadron commander, Squadron Leader Douglas Blackwood, and English flight commanders, namely Flight Lieutenants Sinclair and Jeffries, in addition to an English flying instructor and interpreter. The Czech CO was Squadron Leader Sacha Hess, who was quite famous in Czech air force circles. Much older than the rest, at 45, he was a first class pilot and a dedicated fighter.
>
> Our first problem was to overcome the language difficulty, so I rang the BBC with the result that the interpreter and I spent a day at Broadcasting House where we recorded a series of orders, first in English followed by Czech, covering everything from 'Scramble' to 'Pancake'. The BBC quickly sent us several copies of these records, and in a very short time the Czechs were conversant with orders in English alone.
>
> 310 Squadron had a spare Hurricane (needless to say the oldest and slowest) which was always at my disposal, and as a result, albeit on the few occasions when I could spare the time from my other duties as Station Commander and Sector Controller, I flew on operations with the Squadron as rear-end Charlie.

Squadron Leader Douglas Blackwood: 'I cannot speak highly enough of the Czechs' fighting qualities, although they did not always know what was expected of them; they were very keen on attacking enemy aircraft whenever they saw them, no matter what the circumstances.'

Flight Lieutenant Gordon Sinclair: 'I have nothing but praise for my fellow (Czech) pilots who were a wonderful bunch of people, totally determined to kill Germans. They went about this task with great enthusiasm and courage, and I found it tremendously comforting in battle to be surrounded by such pilots!' Corporal Bill Kirk was a clerk attached to 310 Squadron:

> The Czechs were first class and anxious to have a go. It became a tradition for British personnel serving with 310 Squadron to replace our top tunic buttons with a Czech Air Force example. I was amongst the personnel sent to form 310, and in our office we processed all the admin from leave passes to Air Ministry orders. Working hours were

Squadron Leader Douglas Blackwood (wearing peaked cap), CO of 310 (Czech) Squadron, and one of his flight commanders, Flight Lieutenant Gordon Sinclair (in forage cap), pictured at Duxford in September 1940 with Czech pilots. The Squadron flew as part of the controversial Duxford Wing.

unspecified, you just went to work until the job was done. I lived in the barrack block at Duxford and we all got on famously with the Czechs. They were always keeping fit, playing volley ball, and were very keen generally.

For us on the ground it was tremendously exciting knowing that our aircraft were going into action, and upon return we all looked anxiously for those Hurricanes with blown gun port patches, indicating that the guns had been fired. It could also be distressing, talking to a chap in the Mess only for him to be a 'goner' the next day. Our office was almost on the airfield, so we were very close to the pilots and aircraft. They were exciting times.

Pilot Officer 'Teddy' Morton:

I received my commission in late June 1940, and was posted to RAF Duxford for supernumerary duties in Operations. The VR letters on my tunic still shone brightly, they were so new. Several of us arrived together, including an elderly pilot officer who was a retired solicitor. We were all introduced to the Station Commander, Wing Commander Woodhall, who noticed that the old lawyer was wearing a Boer War medal ribbon but none from the Great War. When asked where his 1914–18 ribbons were, the old boy replied that he had been too old for active service in that conflict! In view of his obviously extensive life experience, the Wing Commander made him Assistant Adjutant to 19 Squadron, to help the Adjutant write casualty letters.

At that time, the Duxford Sector Controllers were Wing Commander Woodhall, Squadron Leader K.C. Horn (who had commanded a Strutter squadron in the Great War and whose brother was a successful Sopwith Camel squadron commander), Squadron Leader Marsden, Squadron Leader Stanley Cooper, and Squadron Leader Livivosk. As dawn broke each day, if on duty at Ops 'B', the Controller would be resting (i.e. asleep and only to be disturbed if necessary). Straight after dawn I would telephone Wing Commander Woodhall on his direct line and inform him of the situation over southern England. There was dire trouble if ever 'Woody' wasn't given this brief first!

As an embryonic controller, a 'Wingless Wonder' or 'Penguin', I always made it my business to get to know as many pilots as possible, so as to gain their trust and understand the problems they faced in the air. All of us on the ground, of course, wanted to help them as much as possible.

The WAAF plotters in Duxford's Operations Room were known as 'Woody's Beauty Chorus'. Jill 'Half Pint' Pepper:

In 12 Group there were long periods with little action, so we got plenty of time to chat to the Observer Corps on our headphones. Voices, however, can be very misleading and we often got a shock when meeting the bloke in person!

After Dunkirk things got livelier and we were kept busy on our watches, concentration and calmness being essential to get the plotting right. The planes went up and it was always exciting when we heard 'Tally Ho!' over the intercom. We felt then that we were doing our bit to help stop the bloody Huns. It was sad, though, when some of our aircraft failed to return, even if we did not know the pilots personally.

There were often dances in the big hangar and whenever I hear 'In the Mood' I'm back there again and can see the Station Controller, Wing Commander Woodhall, complete with monocle, playing his saxophone with great enthusiasm!

Sunday 18 August Following the previous day's conference at Karinhall, the Luftwaffe continued its assault on Fighter Command's airfields. At 10.54 hours Spitfires made the day's first kill over Manston when 54 Squadron's Pilot Officer Colin Gray destroyed an enemy reconnaissance machine. Such intruders were, needless, to say, active all over southern England, gathering information on the disposition of Dowding's fighters. By 12.30 hours, the radar showed so much enemy air activity over the French coastal areas that every single available fighter pilot and aircraft were brought to readiness throughout 11 Group. Eight minutes later 54 Squadron was scrambled from Hornchurch to meet an incoming raid comprising over 300 bandits, followed by nine more RAF fighter squadrons.

This time, the targets selected by the Luftwaffe were both crucial Sector Stations: Biggin Hill and Kenley. KG 1 was briefed to send sixty He 111s to

Hauptmann Horst Tietzen of JG 51, the tail of his Me 109 showing eighteen victories. On the afternoon of 18 August 1940, Tietzen was killed in action with Hurricanes of 501 Squadron. Of interest is the pilot's *schwimmveste*, inflated by a compressed air bottle (and with oral inflation as back up), which was superior to the RAF's 'Mae West'.

attack the former, KG 76 the latter with forty-eight Do 17s and Ju 88s. The tactics for Kenley included an audacious low-level strike by 9/KG 76, and with the Me 109s of JGs 3, 26, 51, 52 and 54, together with the Me 110s of ZG 26, providing both escort and diversionary fighter sweeps, the scene was set for another fierce combat.

Oberleutnant Gerhard Schöpfel, the *Staffelkapitän* of 9/JG 26 led III/JG 26, in Major Galland's absence, on a *freie hunt* with a *gruppe* of Me 109s from JG 3. These forty fighters crossed the British coast high over Dover, twenty-five miles ahead of the main raiding force, representing a massive phalanx of black-crossed aircraft bent upon destruction. To the south-west, the Do 17s of 9/KG 76 flew at low-level towards Beachy Head, sneaking in beneath the British radar screen.

As the Germans struck inland, air raid sirens wailed and lives were once more disrupted and service personnel and civilians alike sought refuge in shelters. By 13.00 hours, 17, 54, 56, 65 and 601 Squadrons were patrolling the Canterbury–Margate line, intending to parry any thrust at the fighter stations north of the Thames. Four more squadrons climbed to defend Biggin Hill and Kenley, but 11 Group still had reserves, Air Vice-Marshal Park keeping nine further squadrons at readiness.

Me 109Es of 9/JG 26 at Caffiers, August 1940. Operating from temporary airfields, the German fighter force congregated in the Pas-de-Calais for the main assault on England. The aircraft in the foreground is that of *Oberleutnant* Gerhard Schöpfel, who destroyed four Hurricanes of 501 Squadron over Canterbury in as many minutes on 18 August 1940.

Certain of the RAF fighters, however, were, yet again, in a dangerous tactical position as they clawed for height while reaching their patrol objectives. At 13.30 hours over Canterbury, Schöpfel, high up and concealed by the sun, watched the Hurricanes of 501 Squadron climbing in vics of three. Covered by his *kameraden*, the 27-year-old *experte* dropped towards the enemy, achieving total surprise: attacking unseen and out of the dazzling sun, within seconds both 'weavers' were dispatched, their fate unseen by the remaining Hurricanes. Unable to believe his luck, Schöpfel then downed the rearmost aircraft which was soon plunging earthwards in flames. Still, however, 501 Squadron continued climbing in tight formation, completely unaware of their comrade's fate or that death still stalked them. Pilot Officer Kenneth Lee: 'I was the fourth Hurricane Schöpfel dispatched. I got a lump of shrapnel in my right calf and the engine caught fire. I baled out sharpish.'

This was a classic fighter attack, achieving complete surprise and out of the sun, so perfectly executed as to have been unprecedented. It was also a graphic condemnation of RAF fighter tactics: of the four 501 Squadron pilots shot down,

Oberleutnant Julius Neumann of II/JG 27, preparing to take off in his Me 109. On 18 August 1940, Neumann was shot down, crash-landing on the Isle of Wight where he was captured.

The Hurricane-equipped 501 Squadron was in the line throughout the entire Battle of Britain, and unsurprisingly suffered the most casualties. These pilots of 501 are pictured at Kenley in September 1940; from left: Sgt T.G. Pickering, F/O D.A.E. Jones, F/O V.R. Snell, Sgt S.A.H. Whitehouse, unknown, Sgt R.J.K. Gent, F/S P.F. Morfill, next two unknown, P/O R.C. Dafforn and P/O S. Witorzenc (Polish). Both Gent and Dafforn lost their lives on active service during WW2.

three were wounded, one was killed, and all four Hurricanes were destroyed. As Schöpfel withdrew, other 109s fell on the hapless Hurricane formation, but no more were lost.

The main enemy formation inexorably droned on towards Biggin Hill and Kenley, the low-level raiders of 9/KG 76 whipped over the rooftops and approached their unsuspecting target. As the first Dornier appeared over Kenley's southern most hangars, the airfield became wreathed in a veritable maelstrom of shot and shell. Six of the raiders were either destroyed or damaged by ground defences and defending fighters, but the damaged caused was significant. Indeed, so much dense smoke was billowing over Kenley that the high level Ju 88 raiders were unable to execute their proposed precision dive-bombing attack and so headed for their alternative target of West Malling.

By 13.24 hours, a running battle had developed all the way from Kenley to the coast, tying down many defending fighter squadrons and which gave KG 1 a clear run in to attack Biggin Hill. Most bombs fell on the runway and in a wood to the east of it. Over Cranbrook, five 65 Squadron Spitfires found and shot up a straggling KG 1 He 111. The Spitfires were led by Flying Officer Jeffrey Quill, the Supermarine test pilot who, to his great credit, had volunteered to fly with Fighter Command and gain first-hand combat experience. Flying Officer Jeffrey Quill:

> In 65 Squadron we did not fly the useless formation comprising vics of three, but instead our four sections flew in line astern. This could be rapidly opened out sideways and, like the German line abreast *schwarm*, required much less concentration. August 18th, however, was a hectic day and we suffered a fatal casualty, Flying Officer Franek Gruszka. The trouble was that our two Poles, Szulkowski and Gruszka, were inclined to go off chasing the enemy on their own, so determined were they. None of us saw what happened to Gruszka, and back at Hornchurch Szulkowski was very upset that his friend was missing.

Michael Wigmore, an 11-year-old schoolboy, excitedly watched the air battle overhead: 'A Spitfire's engine was screaming as the plane came down, very close to me. It crashed with a loud thud at a 45° angle and immediately burst into flame. It was completely out of control and the pilot made no attempt to pull out of the dive.'

The RAF fighter had crashed into the remote Grove Marshes at Wickhambreux, near Canterbury, where it lay undisturbed until 1971 when amateur aviation archaeologists excavated the site, discovering human remains. In an unacceptable and controversial catalogue of error, for which the authorities have to accept responsibility, however, the pilot's remains were not formally recovered by the RAF until 15 April 1974: as of that day, Flying Officer Gruszka, a victim of the intense air fighting of 18 August 1940, was no longer missing. The gallant Polish

Flying Officer Franek Gruszka, a Pole serving with 65 Squadron at Hornchurch. On 18 August 1940, Gruszka was reported missing; in 1971, his aircraft and human remains were controversially recovered by aviation archaeologists near Canterbury. The pilot was subsequently buried with full military honours at Northwood.

airman was subsequently buried with full military honours at Northwood. Pilot Officer David Glaser:

> In 65 Squadron we were very fond of our two Poles. I was really only a youth and both Gruszka and Szulkowski were experienced and respected pilots in their own air force before the war, I looked up to them. They were having a hard time coming to terms with the language and so on, and I used to try and teach them English during the time we spent at readiness. It is incredible to think of Gruszka lying out in those marshes all those years, and 'Ghandi' Drobinski, another Polish pilot in 65 Squadron, and I were very angry when we heard about what went on at his crash site during the 1970s. At least our missing man was respectfully treated and buried in the end.

As the enemy withdrew, Air Vice-Marshal Park's fighters harried the raiders all the way back to the Channel. Kenley had been severely damaged, with many casualties, but Biggin Hill had suffered comparatively little. Some damage was caused to hangars and three Lysanders were destroyed at West Malling, but there were no casualties. Losses of aircrew and aircraft were high for both sides,

Pilot Officer Boleslaw Drobinski (Polish), more commonly known as 'Ghandi' because he was so thin! Posted to 65 Squadron at Turnhouse while the unit was recuperating from its tour in 11 Group, Drobinski's account as a fighter pilot was not opened until 1941, after which he became an ace.

but even before these raids had completely crossed back over the British coast, *Luftflotte* 3 was already assembling over the French coast for another major assault.

This attack involved the greatest number of Stukas so far unleashed during the Battle of Britain, but again their designated targets represented further errors by Luftwaffe intelligence: the naval airfields at Gosport, Ford and Thorney Island, and the *funkstation* (radar station) at Poling, near Littlehampton. In total, 109 Stukas were flung at these targets, escorted by a staggering 157 Me 109s. To meet this threat, 11 Group called upon 10 Group for assistance, and soon sixty-eight RAF fighters were scrambled. Soon dive-bombers were raining down on their targets, and the sky along a twenty-five mile front, from Bognor to Gosport, became a mass of twisting and turning aircraft, aero-engines, gun fire and exploding bombs providing the backing soundtrack to this absolute turmoil. Although damage was caused at all three airfields, this was irrelevant to Britain air defences, and other radar stations were able to overlap and cover the hole created by Poling being temporarily put out of action. StG 77, which had attacked Thorney Island, had been particularly hard hit, by 43, 152 and

601 Squadrons together with Blenheims of 225 Squadron, losing ten Stukas destroyed. Thereafter, all went quiet, for a couple of hours at least.

Having attacked Biggin Hill and Kenley, *Luftflotte* 2 now sallied forth to hit the sector stations of Hornchurch and North Weald: fifty-eight Do 17s of KG 2 were dispatched to the former target, fifty-one He 111s of KG 53 to the latter. The two formations of bombers were escorted by 140 Me 109s and Me 110s, drawn from JGs 3, 26, 51 and 54, and ZG 26. Of this impressive fighter force, only twenty-five Me 109s of JG 51 were allocated a close escort to the Hornchurch raiders, while twenty ZG 26 Me 110s would shepherd KG 53 to North Weald. The remaining Me 109s were tasked with a *freie hunt* to soften and divert RAF defences ahead of the bombers.

The 11 Group Controller brought thirteen squadrons either to a state of immediate readiness or scrambled them to patrol specific lines. Having called upon 12 Group for assistance, similar orders were passed to four of Air Vice-Marshal Leigh-Mallory's squadrons. Soon the first of these squadrons, 56 Squadron, was in action of the Essex coast, intercepting those raiders bound for the Squadron's home station at North Weald, the Hurricanes being rapidly reinforced by 54 Squadron's Spitfires. As these fighters were forced to withdraw, having expended their ammunition, five more RAF fighter squadrons barred the enemy's path to North Weald.

The Hornchurch raid was intercepted by the Hurricanes of 32 and 501 Squadrons, but were unable to penetrate the enemy escorts. II/JG 51 pounced on 501 Squadron, *Hauptmann* 'Joschko' Fözö shooting down Flight Lieutenant George Stoney, who was killed; years later, Harry Hogan, 501 Squadron's CO, remembered that 'Stoney's was a great loss. He was an exceptional officer and definitely destined for air rank.' The Squadron's two Polish pilots, Flying Officer Stefan Witorzenc and Pilot Officer Pavel Zenker, avenged Stoney's death by shooting down two Me 109s, both pilots being killed. Squadron Leader Mike Crossley's 32 Squadron was attacked by III/JG 26. *Leutnant* Gerhard Muller-Duhe was shot down in flames and *Oberleutnant* Walter Blume was badly wounded and captured, but three Hurricanes were destroyed, including that of the CO, who took to his parachute.

So far only one German bomber had been lost, but as the enemy continued towards their targets the unpredictable British weather intervened, completely covering both airfields with cloud. Unable to see their target, the Germans had no option but to wheel about and return to France, harried all the way back over England. Ultimately the raiders lost four bombers destroyed and ten fighters destroyed, offset against Fighter Command's loss of ten fighters (three pilots killed). The defenders were jubilant, it being believed at the time that the enemy's target was actually Chatham dockyard, and that RAF fighter opposition was responsible for turning the raids about.

In total, on this day the Luftwaffe had flown 970 sorties, and lost sixty-nine aircraft destroyed or damaged beyond economic or practical repair; ninety-four

Squadron Leader Mike Crossley was an exceptional Battle of Britain airman in every sense. His efforts during the Battle of France were recognized with a DFC in June 1940, and his leadership of 32 Squadron during the summer of 1940 was acknowledged with the DSO in August. Crossley survived the war but died in South Africa during 1987.

German aircrew were killed, forty were captured and twenty-five were wounded. From this point onwards the hard-hit Stukas played no further part in the aerial assault against England. The forces committed by Fighter Command were much stronger than the enemy expected, again illustrating how lacking was Luftwaffe intelligence: Air Chief Marshal Dowding's pilots flew 927 sorties, losing thirty-one fighters, ten pilots killed, twenty wounded.

So ended the main events of what British historian Dr Alfred Price dubbed years later 'The Hardest Day' (see bibliography).

3

TARGET 11 GROUP:
19 AUGUST – 6 SEPTEMBER 1940

During the previous phase, in Churchill's words 'the whole fury and might of the enemy' had been flung at Fighter Command, and yet the outcome remained indecisive. Göring once more called his principal officers to Karinhall and again harangued them, singling out the fighter leaders for particular attention. The fighting since *Adlertag* indicated that no serious impression had been made upon Fighter Command's strength – in spite of the huge number of sorties flown and heavy losses sustained by the Luftwaffe. In Göring's opinion this was mainly due to a lack of aggression by his fighter pilots, which was simply untrue. The real problem was that the Me 109, like the Spitfire and Hurricane, was designed and intended as a short-range defensive fighter, not a long-range bomber escort machine. Operating without auxiliary fuel tanks at the extreme of its limited range, the Me 109 pilots had precious little time for combat over England – if they were to maintain sufficient fuel reserves to return home safely. The RAF fighters, however, were operating over their homeland and therefore at short-range, so in that respect enjoyed an advantage. Moreover, the twin-engined Me 110, envisaged as a long-range escorting fighter, was simply inferior to the single-engined Spitfires and Hurricanes, but this Göring refused to accept, and inexcusably blamed not the machine but his aircrews. During the subsequent conference, Göring decreed, among other things, the following:

1. That *Luftflotten* 2 and 3's principal task from this point on was to 'inflict the utmost damage possible on the enemy fighter forces'.

2. Armed service promotion often comes with an accrued seniority, and not necessarily due to experience and or ability. In the RAF, for example, there were many fighter squadron commanders, and even a group commander, who had little or no fighter or up-to-date combat experience; among their subordinates were often younger men with greater current combat experience and therefore potentially better and more appropriate leaders. The same was true of the Luftwaffe, and this Göring not only recognised but rectified. In a bid to achieve a more aggressive outlook, many young *gruppenkommandeure* were

promoted and replaced older, more staid, *geschwaderkommodore*. For example, Adolf Galland handed over III/JG 26 to Gerhard Schöpfel and became *Kommodore*.

3. Regarding German fighter tactics, it has often been claimed by historians that Göring insisted upon his Me 109s providing inflexible and close escorts to the bombers – much to the chagrin of his fighter leaders who preferred the freedom and initiative provided by the *freie hunt*. Göring's memorandum of 19 August, however, does not support this claim: 'In the actual conduct of operations, commanders of fighter units must be given as free a hand as possible. Only part of the fighters are to be employed as direct escorts to our bombers. The aim must be to employ the strongest possible fighter forces on free-lance operations, in which they can indirectly protect the bombers, and at the same time come to grips with under favourable conditions with enemy fighters. No rigid plan can be laid down for such operations, as their conduct must depend on the changing nature of enemy tactics, and on weather conditions.'

4. Attacks on targets connected with the British aircraft industry to continue when weather conditions were favourable, as they were forecast to be over the next few days, and by both day and night. The intention was to destroy the 'relatively small number of aircraft engine and aluminium plants.'

5. Bomber and fighter commanders were to achieve maximum co-operation by means of conferences before each attack.

In summary, Göring concluded that:

> We have reached the decisive period of the air war against England. The vital task is to turn all means at our disposal to the defeat of the enemy air force. Our first aim is the destruction of the enemy fighters. If they no longer take the air, we shall attack them on the ground, or force them into battle by directing bomber attacks against targets within the range of our fighters… Once the enemy air force has been annihilated, our attacks will be directed as ordered against other vital targets.

In the main, much of what Göring said made sense, although this new directive saw the German assault deflecting away from attacking radar stations, an important feature of the previous phase. This suggests that Luftwaffe intelligence still failed to appreciate the full value of Dowding's chain of such stations; putting these sites out of commission should have been an absolute priority. Moreover, this represented the third change of direction since the battle began. Pilot Officer Johnnie Johnson:

> The great thing in war is to devise a plan and stick to it, no matter what. A perfect example of this in action was the American daylight bombing offensive from 1942 onwards: at first their losses were horrendous, due to a lack of long-range fighter support, but they kept at it and eventually, really once the Mustang, Thunderbolt and Lightning fighters appeared, all of which were designed as long-range escorts, produced some terrific results: accurate precision bombing from high altitude. During the Battle of Britain, Göring kept changing

his mind, first switching this way but then soon afterwards changing tack. This is exactly what you must not do. After the war I got to know the German ace 'Dolfo' Galland pretty well and he agreed that Göring was wrong to do this.

On the same day that Göring held his latest conference at Karinhall, Air Vice-Marshal Park took stock of the battle to date and issued a memorandum to his controllers in 11 Group:

1. Despatch fighters to engage large enemy formations over land or within gliding distance of the coast. During the next two or three weeks, we cannot afford to lose pilots through forced landings in the sea;

2. Avoid sending fighters out over the sea to intercept reconnaissance aircraft or small formations of enemy fighters;

3. Despatch a pair of fighters to intercept single reconnaissance aircraft that come inland. If clouds are favourable, put a patrol one or two fighters over an aerodrome which the enemy are approaching in clouds;

4. Against mass attacks coming inland, dispatch a minimum number of squadrons to engage enemy fighters. Our main objective is to engage enemy bombers, particularly those approaching under the lowest cloud layer;

5. If all our squadrons around London are off the ground engaging mass attacks, ask No 12 Group or Command Controller to provide squadrons to patrol aerodromes Debden, North Weald, Hornchurch;

6. If heavy attacks have crossed the coast and are proceeding towards aerodromes, put a squadron or even the Sector Training Flight, to patrol under clouds over every sector aerodrome;

7. No 303 (Polish) Squadron can provide two sections for patrol of inland aerodromes, especially while the older squadrons are on the ground refueling when enemy formations are flying overland;

8. No 1 (Canadian) Squadron can be used in the same manner by day as other fighter squadrons.

As ever the astute Air Vice-Marshal Park was carefully preserving his resources, these instructions being sensibly directed at preventing wastage through pilots being lost in the sea or the use of large formations which might be wiped out *en masse*. Also, and as per his Commander-in-Chief's specified System of Air Defence, 12 Group was to be called upon to patrol his airfields north of the Thames when their fighter squadrons were engaged further forward. With both sides reappraised and briefed, the new phase began.

Monday 19 August After the massive effort of the previous day, and given the changing tactical direction being decided by on high, the Luftwaffe's activity over England was much reduced. KG 51 sent thirty Ju 88s to attack Southampton, two others attacking the Llanheath oil tanks at Pembroke Dock, the resulting fire taking twelve hours to bring under control. Another KG 51 raider, bound for

Sergeant Laurence 'Rubber' Thorogood of 87 Squadron, pictured at Bibury during the Battle of Britain with Hurricane AL-G, usually flown by Flying Officer Watson.

RAF Little Rissington, was intercepted by Spitfires and shot down into the sea off Bognor Regis, and a similar fate met another KG 51 crew briefed to attack the small airfield at Bibury, also in Gloucestershire.

The Auxiliary pilots of 616 Squadron, based at Leconfield in 12 Group, were posted to Kenley on this day. Pilot Officer Lionel 'Buck' Casson remembers:

We were a confident lot. Up north we had chased about after reconnaissance jobs and enjoyed great success during the 'Junkers Party' off Flamborough Head a few days before. We thought air fighting was pretty straight forward, I suppose. When we were posted to Kenley the Squadron went off, and I just said 'Cheerio, see you later', as I was to follow on August 24th with a replacement Spitfire we were awaiting.

Pilot Officer William Walker:

I was amongst the 15 pilots of 616 Squadron who flew south to Kenley, which we found to be in quite a state. The Mess there was quite a sombre building, far removed from the modern, light and cheerful Mess at Leconfield. Kenley had been bombed on several occasions prior to our arrival and many scars bore witness to the damage and loss of life.

Pilot Officer Lionel 'Buck' Casson, an Auxiliary member of 616 Squadron, fought throughout the Battle of Britain and destroyed a Do 17. On 9 August 1941, he was responsible for accidentally shooting down Wing Commander Douglas Bader over France in an incident of 'friendly fire'. Casson himself was shot down *en route* home, and, like Bader, ended up in the 'bag' for the duration. A dedicated airman, Casson continued to serve with the post war Auxiliary Air Force and was awarded the AFC.

An atmosphere of purpose prevailed and the Squadron had to respond to a life of far greater activity than at Leconfield, where only a few raids had disrupted our lives.

Having relieved Squadron Leader Don MacDonell's 64 Squadron, which flew north to Leconfield, 616 Squadron would find the tempo of battle over the 11 Group area incomparable; for those who survived, the next few days would be unforgettable.

During the afternoon, there was also a little action in 12 Group. Sergeant David Cox:

Green Section of No 19 Squadron, comprising Flying Officer Leonard Haines, Flight Sergeant Harry Steere and myself, were given a vector of 90°, which was the direction of the east coast. We flew at about 2,000 feet, under 10/10ths cloud. As we approached the coast near Aldeburgh, the cloud started to break up and I, who was flying on the left and looking out to sea, saw a twin engined aircraft. As was the rule, being the pilot who had the enemy in sight, I took over the lead. At about 300 yards I opened fire with my cannons in a quick burst of about three seconds. I then broke away allowing Haines and Steere to attack. On making my second attack I saw the port engine catch fire, which rapidly enveloped the whole aircraft. Three of the crew baled out, but Haines insisted that it was an Me 110 bomber, which had a crew of two. As Haines was a senior flying officer I entered the kill in my log book as a 110, but German records made available after the war confirmed that I was right, it was actually a Do 17 of 7/KG 2.

The Squadron's cannons, however, were still troublesome and the CO, Squadron Leader Pinkham, busied himself testing the Spitfire Mk IB and reporting on his experiences to Fighter Command. Given that the Me 109E had long been armed with two wing mounted 20mm Oerlikon cannon, it was certainly a deficiency that the RAF needed to quickly resolve.

Tuesday 20 August Cloudy weather saw various German reconnaissance aircraft operating over England throughout the morning, until *Erprobungsgruppe* 210, led by Erich Rubensdörfer's successor, *Hauptmann* von Boltenstein, raced in at low level to attack the airfield at Martlesham Heath. Fortunately most bombs missed the target on this occasion, and Flight Lieutenant Ken Gillies, a flight commander in 66 Squadron, destroyed one of the raiders over the North Sea; sadly, however, Gillies himself would not survive the Battle of Britain.

By early afternoon the cloud had dissipated sufficiently for KG 3 to send twenty-seven Do 17s, escorted by thirty Me 109s of I/JG 51, to attack Eastchurch. 615 Squadron destroyed a bomber over the target, and 65 Squadron's Spitfires also intercepted while the enemy was withdrawing; that being so it is surprising that there were not more combat claims.

Two days earlier a squadron of Poles, 302 Squadron, had been declared fully operational at Leconfield in Yorkshire. On this day the new Squadron, much to the bloodthirsty Poles' delight, scored its first kill when Green Section destroyed a Ju 88 of 8/KG 30 off Flamborough Head.

Wednesday 21 August Poor weather over England again dictated a reduced level of Luftwaffe sorties. In order to keep the defenders at full stretch, numerous formations of up to three enemy bombers intruded on a wide front over England. The airfield at St Eval was bombed by Ju 88s of 1/KG 54, destroying or damaging a number of 236 Squadron Blenheims. It was, however, a costly day for the enemy: fourteen Do 17s and Ju 88s were lost on operations over England, while another raider returned to base damaged and carrying wounded crewmen.

Thursday 22 August During the morning, a huge enemy gun ensconced in a railway tunnel near Calais began hurling shells at Convoy TOTEM, which was steaming through the Dover Straits. Some 100 costly shells later the gunners gave up, having not scored a single hit!

Poor weather again prevented operations, but shortly after lunch TOTEM was attacked by Von Boltenstein's Me 110s, but 54 and 610 Squadrons prevented the convoy being hit, although one Spitfire and pilot was lost in the process.

During the evening, 616 Squadron, newly arrived in 11 Group, flying in vics of three, patrolled high above Dover. Higher still were Me 109s, which bounced the unsuspecting and inexperienced Spitfire pilots. Pilot Officer Hugh 'Cocky' Dundas:

Suddenly my aircraft was hit so hard that I assumed a heavy anti-aircraft shell was responsible. Thick white smoke filled the cockpit. I could see nothing, and as the Spitfire went into a spin, I was pressed, hard, against the side of my cockpit. I was terrified and just sat there thinking that this was the end, until a voice in my head told me to open the hood and get out, which I did. Centrifugal force still pressed me into the cockpit and I got stuck, half in, half out. With the ground perilously close I managed to fall clear. My parachute opened and I watched as my Spitfire exploded in a field. I landed a couple of hundreds away from my burning aircraft, my left leg was bleeding and my left shoulder was dislocated.

The following day I discovered the humiliating truth: I had not been shot down by our own ack ack, as I thought, but by an Me 109 none of us had even seen.

It was not a good start to 616 Squadron's Battle of Britain proper, but much worse was to follow.

On this day, another new squadron arrived in 11 Group: Squadron Leader Philip Hunter's 264 Squadron, which flew in to Hornchurch. This unit was equipped with the Boulton Paul Defiant, which had been forced upon Dowding by the DCAS, Sholto Douglas (see Prologue). Over Dunkirk the Defiants had at first recorded success, the enemy assuming them to be Spitfires or Hurricanes and attacking from the rear, only to be rudely awakened by the Boulton Paul fighter's rear gun turret. It did not take the Germans long to realize, however, that the Defiant completely lacked forward firing armament.

Friday 23 August Again low cloud restricted air operations over England, but the Luftwaffe again probed the defences using small formations. An He 111 was destroyed by Spitfires off Fair Isle, and a Do 17 of *Stab* KG 2 was hit in the port engine by ground fire during a *störflug* to attack factories in Coventry. At 09.20 hours, the raider forced landed at Wickham Brook. The crew was captured.

Following Göring's Karinhall conference of 19 August, it had been decided to move practically all of *Luftflotte 3*'s Me 109s to the Pas-de-Calais where they operated from makeshift airfields. This gave *Luftflotte 2* an overwhelming provision of escorts, but even so the 109s would still only have sufficient fuel for twenty minutes of combat given a radius of penetration as far as London – the extreme limit of their range, even from the Pas-de-Calais. The few *Emils* (Me 109E) left in Normandy and Brittany, however, were hard pressed to penetrate very far at all over Dorset and Hampshire, given the much longer sea crossing involved. RAF intelligence reported on the enemy fighter tactics:

> Escorting fighters are dispersed in various positions relative to the bomber formations they are protecting. During the early phase of the attacks on this country it was usual for the fighter escort to fly behind and several thousand feet above the bomber formation. If our fighters attacked the bombers, the escort would descend and attack them providing that they (the German fighters) were not outnumbered. If our fighters attacked the enemy fighter escort, the latter would usually form a self-defensive circle, thus ceasing to afford protection to the bombers which they were supposedly escorting.
>
> Heavy casualties suffered by the bombers led to a change of tactics involving an increase in escorting fighters with new dispositions relative to the bomber formations. Fighters were encountered ahead and on both flanks as well as above and behind the bombers and usually flying in closer proximity to the latter. On occasions the individual bomber units were found to be more spaced out with the fighters weaving amongst them. Accompanying formations of fighters have also been observed acting as remote escort or 'freelance' patrols flying at a great height above, and in the vicinity of, the bomber formations, but they have rarely taken offensive action.

Saturday 24 August Clear skies heralded a resumption of heavy fighting. The first big raid, comprising forty bombers escorted by sixty Me 109s. Bombs were dropped on Dover and Ramsgate, but so tight was the enemy fighter screen that the bombers escaped unscathed. 85 Squadron, up from Croydon, managed to penetrate the Me 109s but had to break off its attack when the Dover barrage began; Sergeant Sammy Allard, however, shot down 9/JG 26's Feldwebel Artur Beese, who was picked up from the Channel by the *Seenotdienst*.

264 Squadron's Defiants were operating from Manston on a daily basis, and were re-fuelling when the airfield was once more attacked. Taking off amidst exploding bombs, Squadron Leader Hunter led his Defiants off to engage the enemy. Just minutes later, the *Kommandeur* of I/JG 3, Major Güther Lützow, shot

down two Defiants over the Channel, the crews of which were reported missing. Squadron Leader Hunter and his gunner, Pilot Officer Fred King, were last seen pursuing a Ju 88 over the sea, but also failed to return. This represented another tragic confirmation that Air Chief Marshal Dowding had been absolutely right about the Defiant, and that the DCAS was wrong.

Manston was, in fact, hit repeatedly that day, the damage being so bad that the airfield was nearly abandoned. Hornchurch too was bombed, and sadly more Defiants were lost in its defence. North Weald was also hit and damaged during the afternoon. By 16.00 hours, all of 11 Group's squadrons were committed, and so Air Vice-Marshal Park called upon 12 Group to cover his beleaguered airfields.

At 15.45 hours, 19 Squadron went off from Fowlmere in, according to the Squadron's ORB, 'a panic take-off'. As Flight Lieutenant Brian Lane later wrote, the Squadron perfectly understood their role: '...after lunch we were ordered off to the London area as a covering patrol while other squadrons down there were refueling after battling with the Boche'.

Over the Thames Estuary, Flight Lieutenant Lane's 'A' Flight caught the North Weald raiders; his Red Section tackled the escorting Me 110s while Green Section fended off the Me 109s. Although three Me 110s were subsequently claimed destroyed, Lane's pilots once more experienced exasperating cannon stoppages. Brian Lane corresponding log book entry, however, confirms the destructive power of 20mm cannon fire:

Had a bang at an Me 110 but had to break away as tracer was coming over my head from another behind me. He appeared to be hitting his fellow countryman in front of me but I didn't wait to see if he shot him down. Had a crack at another and shot his engine right out of the wing – lovely! Crashed near North Foreland. Last trip in BLITZEN III!

There was also 'trade' over the 10 Group area, Portsmouth suffering the highest number of casualties so far inflicted in an air raid since the war began: 154 dead, including many naval personnel, and 237 injured.

Sunday 25 August During the day, German fighters prowled up and down the Channel, hoping to provoke a reaction from Fighter Command, but the RAF sensibly ignored these otherwise punitive sorties.

At 16.00 hours, a huge raid of some 300 aircraft approached Weymouth, before separating into three formations to attack Portland, Weymouth and the coastal airfield at Warmwell. Over Portland, Squadron Leader John Dewar's 87 Squadron, up from Exeter, went for the bombers while Squadron Leader 'Uncle' George Darley's Spitfires of 609 Squadron mixed it with the escorting fighters, which included Me 109s of JG 53. 17 Squadron's Hurricanes defended Warmwell, although two hangars and the Station Sick Quarters were hit, and the Station's communication lines were severed. Over Portland, the CO of 17 Squadron, Squadron Leader Cedric Williams, came off second best in a head on attack against an Me 110: his Hurricane's port wing came off, the aircraft spinning into the sea; Williams was never seen again.

Leading Aircraftsman Geoff Gwillam: 'It was a shame when Cedric Williams was killed. He was very popular with all of us, even us 'erks' on 17 Squadron. He definitely wasn't one of those snobby officers.'

Leading Aircraftsman Ray Johnson:

We armourers were working on the airfield when we saw about a dozen twin engined aircraft approaching Warmwell at 8–10,000 feet and drop their loads. It was all over in a matter of minutes. They were pretty accurate: the hangar and a number of aircraft were either destroyed or damaged, and then delayed action bombs kept exploding for the next few days. There was also a number of casualties amongst the ground personnel. As practically all our waking hours were spent at the dispersal point at the wooded end of the airfield, for years after in any panic the standard call was 'Away to the woods!'

After this raid withdrew, *Luftflotte* 2 sent more bombers to attack Hawkinge. Major Adolf Galland led all three gruppen of JG 26 on a *freie hunt* in advance of this raid, Over Dover, Galland's fighters bounced the Spitfires of 610 and 616 Squadron, which lost one Spitfire each: the former's Flying Officer Gardiner baled out safely, but the latter's Sergeant Westmoreland was killed. *Oberleutnant* Kurt Ruppert, *Kapitän* of 3/JG 26, chased another Spitfire across the Channel to Calais, where he shot it down. The pilot, Sergeant Wareing of 616 Squadron, was captured. Pilot Officer William Walker:

We were very unsure of ourselves at this time. Everything happened so quick, and of course our formations of vics and lines astern were all wrong. There was so little information available to us. Very little was passed on by those squadrons that we relieved as they just couldn't wait to get the hell out of it! Fighting in the south, where the 109s always seemed to have the advantage of height and sun, was very different indeed to chasing about after unescorted bombers up north.

Monday 26 August Pilot Officer William Walker:

It was still dark when the orderly awoke me with a cup of tea at 0330 hours that morning, just two days after my 27th birthday, which had passed unnoticed amid the current level of activity and excitement. I drank my tea slowly and gradually awakened to another day. It seemed such a short while since we had been stood down the previous evening, at about 2100 hours, and after which a few beers refreshed our spirits before bed. However, I dressed and went down to breakfast, always a quiescent occasion at the unearthly hour of 0400 hours! The sound of aero engines could be heard in the distance, indicating that the groundcrews were already busy. One was so accustomed to the drone of engines that it passed almost unnoticed amidst the clatter of cups and plates.

Pilot Officer William Walker, a Volunteer Reservist serving with 616 'South Yorkshire' Squadron of the Auxiliary Air Force. Having scrambled from Kenley, on 26 August 1940, Walker was shot down over the Channel by the German *Oberkannone*, Major Werner Mölders. Baling out with a bullet in his ankle, Walker was fortunately rescued by a passing trawler.

Hauptmann Joschko Fözö, *Staffelkapitän* of 4/JG 51, recounts a successful combat over England. An *experte*, Fözö survived the war and died in 1995.

Flight Lieutenant Denys 'Kill 'em' Gillam AFC DFC. A professional airman in 616 Squadron, Gillam was the backbone of his squadron during the period in August when the unit was virtually wiped out at Kenley. He destroyed seven enemy aircraft during the Battle of Britain, and survived being shot down himself on 2 September. He was later posted to 312 (Czech) Squadron as a flight commander. On 8 October 1940, he took off and immediately engaged a Ju 88, scoring what was both the unit's first kill and probably the quickest victory of all time.

Following breakfast I joined other pilots outside the Mess. We all climbed aboard a lorry and were driven to dispersal, to remain at readiness where a hut and and a few tents constituted 616 Squadron's base. A few days earlier the Duke of Kent had visited us at our modest location to wish us well.

That day I was allocated Spitfire R6633, and was to fly in Yellow Section, led by Flying Officer Teddy St Aubyn, a former Guards officer. The plane stood within 50 yards of our hut and so I walked over and placed my parachute in the cockpit with the straps spread apart and ready for wearing immediately I jumped in. Two of the groundcrew stood by the plane with the starter battery plugged in. I walked back to the hut as the sun rose and added a little warmth to a chilly start. Pilots sat about either reading or exchanging the usual banter that had become routine. We had spent many months in this way, which was now a way of life. At 0800 hours our second breakfast arrived at dispersal, and was just as fulfilling as our breakfast of four hours earlier: coffee, eggs, bacon, sausages and toast to replenish our undiminished appetites.

Throughout Fighter Command, this was the typical start to a fighter pilot's day.

It was not until around 11.30 hours that the first big raid was incoming above Dover: forty He 111s and twelve Do 17s, escorted by eighty Me 109s, bound for Biggin Hill and Kenley. Air Vice-Marshal Park responded with seventy RAF fighters, among them seven Spitfires of 616 Squadron's 'A' Flight. Pilot Officer William Walker:

The telephone rang in the dispersal hut and a shout of 'Yellow Section, scramble! Patrol Dungeness/Dover Angels 20!' sent me running to my plane. I leapt onto the wing and was in the cockpit, parachute strapped on, within seconds. I pressed the starter and the engine fired immediately. The groundcrew removed the plug from the cowling and pulled the remote starter battery clear. I waved the chocks away and taxied the aircraft, followed by my Section Leader and Sergeant Ridley, to the end of the runway for take-off. Within minutes Yellow Section was airborne. We head east, climbing quickly and passing through cloud, reaching our patrol course in some 15–20 minutes. We flew in wide formation and had been airborne for about an hour without sighting any enemy aircraft when suddenly several Me 109s appeared.

Over Dungeness the hapless Spitfires were bounced, having been unfortunate enough to have been espied by Major Werner Mölders who was leading all three *gruppen* of JG 51 on a *freie hunt*. Flying Officer Teddy St Aubyn's Spitfire was hit in the coolant system, the pilot crash landing at Eastchurch; Flying Officer George Moberley crashed into the sea and was killed, as was Sergeant Marmaduke Ridley who crashed near Dover. St Aubyn was the fifteenth kill of *Oberleutnant* 'Pips' Priller, *kapitän* of 6/JG 51, while Moberley and Ridley are believed to have been killed by *Hauptmann* 'Joschko' Fözö, *kapitän* of 4/JG 51. Only one of 616 Squadron's pilots brought his guns to bear, Flight Lieutenant Denys 'Kill 'em' Gillam, of Blue Section:

On arriving at 10,000 feet we were ordered to intercept two 40 plus raids. We climbed to 11,000 feet and discovered about 100 Me 109s all around and above us. I ordered line astern and we formed a circle. One Me 109 appeared on Blue Two's tail, so I turned on to it and fired at it down to 4,000 feet. I then followed it through cloud and on coming out saw the aircraft hit the water straight ahead.

Gillam's victim was *Leutnant* Hoffman of 7/JG 51. Major Mölders himself, as usual attacking from behind and slightly below, aimed at Spitfire R6633 and claimed his twenty-seventh kill. Pilot Officer William Walker:

When the 109s hit us I banked steeply to port, towards a 109, but suddenly my machine was raked with bullets. I never even saw the one that attacked me. The flying controls ceased to respond and a sudden pain in my leg indicated that I had been hit. Baling out seemed to be a sensible option. My two comrades of Yellow Section had both vanished.

I pulled back the hood and tried to stand up but realised that I had not disconnected the radio lead, which was still plugged in, and had to remove my helmet before I was free to jump. The aircraft was still banking to port, so jumping out was easy. I was still at 20,000 feet and pulled the ripcord immediately. A sudden jerk indicated that all was well and that I was on my way down. I looked around but could not see a single aircraft. Below there was 10/10ths cloud. I had no idea where I was. It seemed to take ages to reach the clouds and passing through I realised that I was still over the Channel. Thinking that I would soon land in the sea prompted the thought that I had better remove my heavy flying boots. I did this and let them fall. I watched them spiral down for what seemed like ages and then realised that I was much higher than I thought. I inflated my Mae West and eventually landed in the sea. I easily discarded my parachute and could see the wreck of a ship sticking out of the water a few hundred yards away and swam to it. I reached it and climbed on, sitting there for about half an hour until a fishing boat came alongside and I clambered aboard. I was now extremely cold from my immersion and wet clothes.

The fishermen gave me a cup of tea, well laced with whisky, as we headed for land. When about two miles offshore an RAF launch came alongside and I was transferred to it. By this time the tea concoction had worked quite disastrously on my cold stomach. Fortunately there was a loo aboard to which I retired, with some relief. I was still enthroned when we reached Ramsgate harbour. An aircraftman kept knocking on the door and enquiring whether I was okay. It was some time, however, before I was able to emerge! I was carried up the steps to a waiting ambulance, by which time quite a crowd had gathered and gave me a cheer as I was put in the ambulance. A kind old lady handed me a packet of cigarettes, so I decided that being shot down was perhaps not such a bad thing after all!

This had been a catastrophe for 616 Squadron. Since having arrived at Kenley a week previously, seven out of fifteen Spitfires had been lost, four pilots killed and an equal number wounded. The Squadron Clerk, clearly a master of the understatement, recorded the action as 'a most unfortunate engagement'. Pilot Officer Buck Casson:

Having arrived at Kenley with the replacement Spitfire on August 24th, the following day Tom Murray and I were loaned to 615 Squadron, a Hurricane unit with which 616 shared Kenley, because they were short of pilots and we both had experience on Hurricanes. After 616 was badly mauled on August 26th, however, we had to return to 616, which was rapidly running out of pilots too.

Pilot Officer William Walker:

I was driven to Ramsgate Hospital, which had been badly bombed, where doctors tried to remove the bullet in my foot. This proved too great an undertaking, so I was put to bed; I was absolutely freezing cold and it was a further five–six hours until I felt my circulation returning. The following day it was decided that I be moved, still with said bullet lodged in my ankle, to RAF Hospital Halton. *En route* we stopped off at Kenley so that I could collect my belongings, and the driver took me to dispersal so that I could say farewell to any remaining pilots. It proved a sad occasion, however, as the Squadron had suffered severe losses and very few pilots actually remained operational.

By the time we arrived at Halton it was almost 2200 hours, a 14 hour journey. Having not eaten since breakfast I was starving. Although the kitchens were closed at that late hour, a wonderful night nurse produced a wonderful and appropriate meal: scrambled eggs!

After breakfast the following morning, doctors appeared and attended to the officers in my large ward of 20 beds. Nobody came to see me, however, and apart from my wound getting rather painful, I was starting to worry about gangrene. The previous 48 hours had been rather traumatic to say the least, so my concern was not entirely unjustified!

At noon the head doctor, a group captain, did his rounds. As he passed my bed he asked what I was in for. I told him that I had a bullet in my leg. He said 'Oh yes, and who is looking after you?' When I told him that I had yet to see a doctor despite having arrived the previous night, I thought that he was going to have a convulsion! He literally exploded and his wrath remains a vivid memory. Never were so many doctors torn off a bigger strip. It was action stations from then on, and within just 10 minutes I was in the operating theatre.

When I regained consciousness, the surgeon was beside my bedside. He said, 'I think you may like to have this,' and handed me an armour-piercing bullet. He then told me that as he was prising open the bone in my leg to extract the bullet it shot out and hit the ceiling of the Operating Theatre! I still possess the bullet today as a cherished souvenir.

Fortunately my sense of humour never quite left me, and when a doctor later asked how my accident happened I assured him that I was not the victim of an accident, but of a determined attempt on my life by a German fighter pilot!

On 26 August, there would be many 'attempts' on the lives of fighter pilots from both sides.

264 Squadron also intercepted the day's first raid, finding the Do 17s unescorted over Herne Bay. As 264 attacked, Me 109s intervened, shooting down a further three Defiants. This time, however, it was not entirely one-sided, in spite of the Defiant's total unsuitability for day-fighting, claiming the destruction of six bombers. 1 (Canadian) Squadron's Hurricanes, up from Northolt Sector Station, also managed to get through to the bombers, but lost three aircraft with a pilot killed. Low on fuel, the forces of both sides then withdrew.

The next raid confused the defenders as it appeared to be heading towards London, forcing Air Vice-Marshal Park to commit all of his available fighters. The ack ack barrage over Colchester, however, persuaded most of the bombers to turn about, only six Do 17s penetrating to Debden and bombing that airfield. Given the number of RAF fighters on the scene, the futility of pressing on to Hornchurch was obvious, and so the remaining raiders also wheeled around and headed home. It is interesting that on this occasion the bombers were largely unprotected, mainly due to the high number of Me 109s engaged on *freie hunt*, leading to bomber commander's urgently requesting that this tactic cease forthwith.

Once more 11 Group had called upon 12 Group to protect the airfields north of the Thames. Debden, however, was hit. Sergeant David Cox:

> As 19 Squadron was patrolling at 10,000 feet and above 10/10ths cloud, we did not see the raid which actually came in at 1,000 feet. It appears that the Observer Corps had accurately reported the raid at 1,000 feet, but 11 Group assumed this to be a mistake and so sent us off at Angels 10. The subsequent intelligence reported claimed that Debden had been damaged because 'the Spitfires from Fowlmere were too slow in getting off the ground' but that was certainly not the case.

The above account, however, does not necessarily support the fact that 11 Group had called for reinforcements too late – it would appear that 19 Squadron was over Debden in good time, but cloud and misinformation concerning height caused the problem. Pilot Officer Teddy Morton:

> The 11 Group controllers definitely called for 12 Group too late. By the end of August there was a certain amount of hostility between the respective operations rooms. 11 Group accused us of being too late, we said that they called for us too late. Whenever 12 Group squadrons arrived after the action, we would suffer sarcastic remarks from the 11 Group Controller. The situation was not good.

Wing Commander 'Woody' Woodhall:

> In those early days, RDF information was not very accurate, particularly regarding height and numbers of aircraft, and of course there was a time lapse of several minutes before

Wing Commander Victor Beamish AFC (fourth left), Station Commander of North Weald, poses with pilots of 151 Squadron, including the Commanding Officer, Squadron Leader 'Teddy' Donaldson DSO (third left) and his wingman, Pilot Officer Jack Hamar DFC (fourth right). Having already fought in France, 151 was heavily engaged during the early stages of the Battle of Britain.

the information reached the Sector Operations Room. The Sector Controller therefore had to use intelligent guesswork to direct his fighters on an intercepting course, and to position them up-sun, above the enemy. To begin with, the operations table in 12 Group only extended to the north bank of the Thames, and enemy plots were only passed to us when they reached this point. In 11 Group, however, enemy plots were received whilst the enemy was still over France. Command Operations Room had the whole picture, of course, but in my opinion there was insufficient liaison between 11 and 12 Groups.

Luckily, Wing Commander Victor Beamish, the Sector Commander at North Weald, was a good friend of mine, so I extended our operations table to the south and as far into France as St Omer; as soon as North Weald was informed of enemy activity we kept the tie-line telephone open, and the plots were passed from North Weald to Duxford. In that way we obtained earlier warning, but in spite of this, we were frequently scrambled too late because we were not allowed to fly over 11 Group territory unless asked for by them. It was frustrating to see an enemy raid plotted on our board, obviously going for a target in 11 Group, then to wait on the ground, with the pilots in their cockpits for 15–20 minutes, and finally to be scrambled too late to get into the fight.

Flying Officer Frank Brinsden: 'During late August 1940, we of 19 Squadron always felt a bit cheated as we always seemed to be late off the ground and

On 27 August 1940, 32 Squadron was withdrawn from 11 Group to rest and re-fit at Acklington in Northumberland. This is the interior of the Squadron's pilots' hut there; note the wireless, and model aircraft used for recognition training. At left is Flight Lieutenant Peter Gardner DFC, the Squadron's 'Spy' (Intelligence Officer) and Flight Sergeant McCloughlin (groundcrew).

therefore late to intercept; we often arrived over the battle zone only to find all gone home.'

Another of Duxford's squadrons, however, did engage on this day, namely the Czechs of 310 Squadron who intercepted the Debden raiders and destroyed an Me 109, the Squadron's first kill. *Luftflotte* 3 then sent fifty He 111s of KG 55, escorted by Me 110s and a lesser number of Me 109s, but this raid was turned about by RAF fighters from 10 and 11 Groups before the target, the ports of Southampton and Portsmouth, were reached.

Tuesday 27 August After 12 Group's failure, for whatever reason, to protect 11 Group's airfields the previous day, Air Vice-Marshal Park wrote, outlining the problems as he saw them, to Air Vice-Marshal Evill, Air Chief Marshal Dowding's SASO. The chain of command and protocol dictated this to be the correct course of action for Park to pursue his grievance and rectify the situation. It was the SASO's job to deal with such issues, and a meeting before the two fractious group commanders can only be considered appropriate, and may well have prevented the more serious problems that subsequently arose. The SASO, however, did nothing, and therefore, albeit unintentionally, contributed greatly to the even more serious problems between 11 and 12 Groups that lay ahead. Indeed, it can be considered that on this day any previously existing liaison between the two groups broke down: Air Vice-Marshal Park instructed his controllers that in the event of reinforcements being required, requests were not to be routed directly to 12 Group, but instead through HQ Fighter Command. These were critical days, the focus of Luftwaffe daylight operations being targets in 11 Group. The effective cover of his airfields by neighbouring groups, therefore, was of paramount importance to Air Vice-Marshal Park, but to route such requests through Fighter Command would undoubtedly waste precious minutes.

Although the weather was fine, the day saw no major attacks materialize. Two German reconnaissance aircraft were destroyed by RAF fighters; a Spitfire was hit by return fire from a Ju 88 off Portland, the pilot baling out, and Squadron Leader Harry Hogan, CO of 501 Squadron, returned to Gravesend with a glycol tank damaged in combat with a Do 215 over the Channel.

The reprieve provided an opportunity for certain hard-pressed and exhausted squadrons to be removed from the front line and sent north, to rest, re-build and re-train. This was a good system in that battle weary squadrons were stood down, but their places were inevitably taken by inexperienced units, like 616 Squadron, which found themselves completely unprepared for the traumatic change in tempo caused by the presence of Me 109s. Repeatedly such squadrons suffered their greatest losses on their first few sorties.

At Turnhouse in Scotland, 603 'City of Edinburgh' Squadron prepared to fly south and relieve 65 Squadron at Hornchurch. 'B' Flight of 603 Squadron had been detached to operate from the nearby airfield at Montrose, where the pilots had formed a close association with the local children. As 'B' Flight's Spitfires dived one by one and roared over the hamlet where their young friends lived, on the road the children had spelt out two words in white rocks: 'Good luck'. Sergeant Jack Stokoe:

Only a year before the Battle of Britain began, my contemporaries and I were pursuing our civilian careers whilst learning to fly with the VR in our spare time. The majority of us were 18–19 years old. Being aircrew, when called up, in September 1939, we were automatically given the rank of sergeant, which at first caused some dismay amongst the ranks of professional sergeants, many of whom had taken 20 years to reach that exalted rank!

Most of us only had 50–60 hours flying on elementary types like Tiger Moths and Magisters when we were called up. After a brief spell at Initial Training Wing (ITW) to instill some discipline into us, we had about 100 hours on Harvards at Flying Training School (FTS), which included a few trips actually firing guns. We were then posted to an OTU, in my case Aston Down, before being posted to an operational fighter squadron – with just 10–15 hours on Spitfires recorded in our log books.

603 was an auxiliary squadron, and there were only three of us NCO VR pilots. By the time we went to Hornchurch I had 70 hours on Spitfires, so counted myself most fortunate as I could easily have gone straight from OTU to a front line fighter squadron – as so many young pilots did – and in which case I would not have rated my chances of survival very highly. I had even already seen, although not engaged, German reconnaissance bombers over northern Scotland.

Among the squadrons relieved during this lull was 32 Squadron at Biggin Hill. Flight Lieutenant Peter Brothers:

Of our pre-war pilots, in 32, who were experienced chaps, there were some who had been shot down and baled out unhurt, or burnt, or wounded, or both, but none were killed. Our losses were the 'new boys' who never had the time or opportunity not only to learn or be taught the tricks of the trade, but also to know the performance advantages and limitations of their aircraft and how to exploit them. Tragically, they paid the ultimate price for this inexperience.

Wednesday 28 August Across the Channel, the Germans had neither been idle so far as their fighter force was concerned. The temporary airfields around the Pas-de-Calais had been a hive of activity, as the *jagdgeschwadern* prepared for the next onslaught against England.

The day's first raid came in over Deal, where the heavily escorted bombers separated into two formations, heading for the airfields at Rochford and Eastchurch. Three Hurricane squadrons attacked over the Kent coast, diverting the escorting fighters, providing an opportunity for the Defiants of 264 Squadron to attack the Rochford bound He 111s of KG 53. Pilot Officer Carnably destroyed one of the bombers, and Sergeant Lauder damaged another. Then Major Adolf Galland and his JG 26 *Stabschwarm* fell upon the hapless Defiants: Squadron Leader Garvin and Flight Lieutenant Ash were shot down and baled out, although the latter was subsequently dead when found – possibly shot by a German fighter while defenceless beneath his parachute; Pilot Officer Whitley and Turner were killed when their aircraft became a flamer, and Pilot Officers Kenner and Bailey were also killed. Pilot Officer Bailey and Sergeant Hardy were also shot down but unhurt. Of the eight Defiants that escaped back to Hornchurch, only three were serviceable. 264 Squadron had virtually ceased to exist, and this engagement provided further, tragic, confirmation of the Defiants complete unsuitability to daylight fighter combat.

Meanwhile the Hurricanes of 79 Squadron mixed it with I/JG 26: Flight Lieutenant G.D.L. Haysom's aircraft was damaged and he forced landed at Tenterden, and another pilot baled out safely. Two of Galland's *Stabschwarm*, however, were also shot down over Kent, both of whom were captured. The raiders reached Rochford but their bombing was inaccurate, due to the heavy barrage put up by the airfield's ground defences, and little damage was caused.

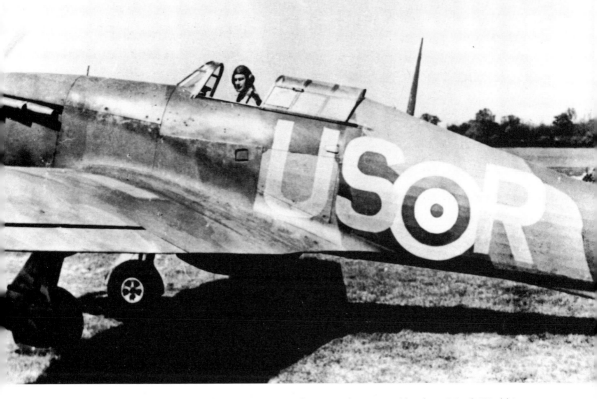

Battle of France veteran Pilot Officer Peter Down of 56 Squadron scrambles from North Weald in August 1940.

The other raiding formation successfully attacked Eastchurch, dropping over 100 bombs, but as this was not a fighter airfield the effort was wasted.

A second raid on Rochford fought its way up the Thames Estuary at 12.35 hours. Spitfires of 54 Squadron got tangled up with the escorting Me 109s, destroying one, but in a not uncommon incident of 'friendly fire', Flight Lieutenant Al Deere, a tough fighter ace from New Zealand, was shot down by another Spitfire and baled out.

The enemy then launched wave upon wave of fighter sweeps, which on the radar screens were interpreted as bombing raids heading for sector airfields. Among the embroiled RAF fighters was 85 Squadron, up from Croydon, commanded by Squadron Leader Peter Townsend, which destroyed six Me 109s for no loss, although Sergeant F.R. Walker-Smith's aircraft was damaged – an excellent result by a Hurricane squadron. At 16.25 hours, *Leutnant* H.H. Landry of *Stab* III/JG 3 was set upon by Sergeant Ronnie Hamlyn, a Spitfire pilot with 610 Squadron, and the Hurricane of 56 Squadron's Flight Lieutenant Percy Weaver. At the time, the British Prime Minister had just left Dover Castle, and saw the Me 109 diving, out of control. Ordering his driver to speed to the crash site at Church Farm, Church Whitfield. Striding up to the blazing and wrecked

Squadron Leader John Hill, Commanding Officer of 222 Squadron at Hornchurch. A popular leader, Hill survived the war but has since died.

enemy fighter, Churchill remarked, 'I hope to God it isn't a British plane.' Before leaving with a cartridge case as a souvenir, the Prime Minister was assured that it was a German aircraft; 'Thank God,' he replied. 'That's another less on a long list!' The pilot, *Leutnant* Landry, had baled out but was badly wounded and died in hospital on 23 September.

That afternoon saw Squadron Leader George Denholm's 603 Squadron, newly arrived at Hornchurch the previous day, in action over south-east England for the first time. At 16.45 hours, the Squadron was bounced by Me 109s high above Dover; again, it was a catastrophic baptism of fire: Flight Lieutenant J.L.G. Cunningham and Pilot Officer D.K. MacDonald were both missing, and Flying Officer I.S. Ritchie returned to base wounded, his Spitfire badly damaged. Sadly, Pilot Officer Noel 'Broody' Benson was shot down in flames and killed, his Spitfire crashing at Great Hay Farm, Appledore; only the previous day, this mere 19-year-old youth had enthused how he was 'going to show 'em' once the Squadron was operating from Hornchurch. Sergeant Jack Stokoe: 'On that day we flew four patrols, intercepting Me 109s on two of them. I claimed one damaged but the trimming wires of my own aircraft were shot away.'

Thursday 29 August The decimated 264 Squadron, having suffered grievous losses, was no longer operational and was relieved at Hornchurch by Squadron Leader John Hill's 222 Squadron Spitfires. As the unit's ORB put it, over the forthcoming days 222 Squadron would be 'very positively engaged in operations'.

The previous day, 11 Group's controllers had become lured into reacting to the enemy's otherwise relatively harmless fighter sweeps, and lost a number of aircraft and pilots as a result. Air Vice-Marshal Park was determined that this would not happen again. After a quiet morning, however, soon after 15.00 hours the Germans played their hand: the minimal number of bombers, being used as bait, droned across the Channel covered high above by the most enormous phalanx of fighters so far – a staggering 500 Me 109s and Me 110s. Squadron Leader Peter Townsend's 85 Squadron, patrolling nearby as the enemy appeared between Beachy Head and Hastings, was given permission to engage. The resulting combat, however, transpired to be the most successful fought by I/JG 26 so far: Sergeant Booth's Hurricane was severely damaged off Eastbourne, Sergeant Ellis was hit over the Channel and baled out, as did Sergeant F.R. Walker-Smith. In response, Squadron Leader Townsend shot down and killed *Oberfeldwebel* Hubert Graf von Treuburg, of 1/JG 26, over the Channel.

Sensibly, the 11 Group Controller refused to repeat the mistake of yesterday and kept the defending fighters leashed. In this way the Luftwaffe could send over thousands of fighters, if it chose, but if the defenders ignored them they were no threat. Further fighter sweeps continued throughout the evening, although few RAF fighters engaged: 151 Squadron's Pilot Officer A.G. Wainwright was shot down and baled out, and 501 Squadron were bounced again, losing two

Hurricanes: Flight Lieutenant John Gibson and Sergeant W.J. Green baling out safely.

That evening, Pilot Officer Richard Hillary, a Spitfire pilot of 603 Squadron, became separated from his Squadron, but instead of returning to base, he tacked himself on to the rear of 85 Squadron's Hurricanes, weaving to and fro behind them. Squadron Leader Peter Townsend:

> Our Hurricanes were in open, or search, line astern formation, covered by a section of three tail-end Charlies. The appearance of Hillary's Spitfire, which from the front looked not altogether dissimilar to the Me 109, caused us confusion in identifying the enemy when we were attacked over Winchelsea. Hillary might have known better. We lost Flight Lieutenant Hamilton, a Canadian and a superb flight commander, purely because the Me 109s were identified a fraction of a second too late.

Pilot Officer Hillary was also shot down, forced landing his Spitfire near Lympne; in his first-hand account *The Last Enemy*, Hillary, an auxiliary pilot, described the experience as 'the most amusing though painful'. He was the fourth 603 Squadron pilot to be shot down that day: one Spitfire was a write-off but all pilots were safe. Squadron Leader Harry Hogan:

> Some of the replacement pilots sent to 501 Squadron were straight from OTU, and these we tried to get into the air as soon as possible to provide a little extra experience, but we were just too tired to give them any dogfighting practice at all. They were all very green, youngsters who were completely bewildered and lost in action.

Sergeant Norman Ramsay: 'People missing or killed at that stage of the battle meant little to me. I had joined 222 from 610 Squadron at Biggin Hill, after we had lost 10, yes 10, pilots, so I was well used to disappearing faces. Having been shot down myself I had learned to survive, to get the experience necessary for survival.'

Sergeant Bernard 'Jimmy' Jennings: 'Casualties? Well, when it came to that sort of thing we just didn't talk about it much, didn't dwell upon that sort of thing. It was just a case of "Old so and so's copped it", and that was it.'

Friday 30 August Up with the lark, Major Adolf Galland's pilots of JG 26 flew an early *freie hunt* over Kent, which the defenders sensibly ignored. Another similar sweep was treated likewise, but it was obvious that this would be a day of high activity. At 11.00 hours forty He 111s and thirty Do 17s, escorted by nearly 100 fighters, were incoming over the Kentish coast. 151 Squadron was first to react to the threat, destroying two bombers but losing two Hurricanes and pilots; these included the Squadron's new CO, namely Squadron Leader Eric King, who, two weeks before, was up over Southampton with Flight Lieutenant Nicolson when the latter performed his 'signal act of valour'.

222 Squadron was patrolling over Gravesend, but the Spitfires were bounced by Me 109s. Sergeant Iain Hutchinson: 'It was the first time we had engaged the enemy since our arrival at Hornchurch only the previous day, and was the usual scenario: the Me 109s were higher and knew exactly what they were doing, while we were just learning the ropes. I didn't even see the one that hit me.' Fortunately Sergeant Hutchinson, who was unhurt, managed to crash land his Spitfire near Hornchurch. Sergeant Reg Johnson:

> In our first 48 hours at Hornchurch we lost 18 Spitfires and a number of pilots. We proceeded to go into action in the tight formation we had been trained to use, but consequently our losses were heavy. Eventually we evolved a 'Tail End Charlie' section which weaved about, above, below and to the rear of the Squadron (which was still in tight formation). It helped. I was made a permanent member of Green Section, with Pilot Officer Laurie Whitbread and one other, and we were given that job to do.

According to the 222 Squadron ORB, on 30 August 'the Squadron was very positively engaged in operations and flew three patrols during the day. Sergeant J.I. Johnson was killed, Flight Lieutenant Matheson and Sergeant Edridge were wounded.' During those three sorties, 222 Squadron lost a total of six Spitfires destroyed and three damaged in yet another example of a 'green' squadron being roughly handled while still adjusting to the completely different tempo of combat.

Another squadron, 603, fresh to south-east England was also in action, over Deal: the CO, Squadron Leader Denholm, was shot down and baled out, as was Sergeant Sarre later in the day. Sergeant Jack Stokoe: 'We made four interceptions throughout the day, during the course of which I was credited with having destroyed an Me 109 and damaged another.'

The Hurricanes of 253 Squadron were also new to Kenley, having arrived from Prestwick only the day before, and during the morning's fighting suffered three Hurricanes damaged and three destroyed. Two pilots were killed: Pilot Officer D.N.O. Jenkins was machine-gunned by German fighters while hanging beneath his parachute, and 19-year-old Pilot Officer Colin Francis was posted missing (the latter would not be found until forty-one years after the Battle of Britain, when his aircraft and remains were recovered from a field at Wrotham in Kent). That afternoon the Squadron lost another pilot killed and two more aircraft damaged.

Me 109s also gave the hapless 616 Squadron trouble again: over West Malling, Me 109s attacked the Squadron head-on, shooting down Pilot Officer Jack Bell, who was killed, and Sergeant Hopewell's Spitfire was damaged when he overshot the runway upon returning to Kenley.

As these raids withdrew, fresh waves of enemy fighters and bombers were incoming at twenty minutes intervals, provoking further combat. Indeed, the

In March 1941 Douglas Bader became Wing Commander (Flying) at Tangmere, where he is pictured with his Spitfire Mk VA in which he was brought down over France in an incident of 'friendly fire' on 9 August 1941.

scale of fighting was such that Air Vice-Marshal Leigh-Mallory, whose 19 and 310 Squadrons were patrolling over the 11 Group airfields of Debden and Biggin Hill, decided to send one of Coltishall's squadrons to Duxford, where it would remain at readiness. Squadron Leader Douglas Bader's 242 Squadron, therefore, flew south to Duxford, but while *en route* was for some unknown reason recalled. Bader, who had brooded, sulked and stormed about 12 Group's lack of action, was fuming. Upon return, he immediately harangued the Controller over the phone, who, a short while later, ordered 242 Squadron off again. Arriving at Duxford without further incident, Bader and his Canadians settled down to await the call for action that they were so desperate to receive.

At 16.00 hours, 300 plus enemy aircraft were reported over Kent and the Thames Estuary, the raiders splitting up to attack the airfields at Kenley, North Weald, Hornchurch, Debden, Lympne, Detling and Biggin Hill. At 16.20 hours, sixty He 111s of I/KG 1 and II/KG 53, escorted by Me 110s, crossed the coast north of the Thames. Doubtless anticipating an attack on the Sector Stations in that area, the 11 Group Controller requested reinforcements from 12 Group. At 16.23 hours, therefore, Wing Commander Woodhall scrambled 242 Squadron, Squadron Leader Bader leading fourteen Hurricanes off from Duxford with orders to patrol North Weald at 15,000 feet.

The enemy formation next showed its true intention, I/KG 1 heading for the Vauxhall Motor Works and aerodrome at Luton, while II/KG 53, being the larger of the two raiding parties, began to fight its way to the Handley Page aircraft factory at Radlett. At 16.25 hours, 56 Squadron was scrambled from North Weald, and 1 Squadron from Northolt. At 16.55 hours, two Spitfires of 222 Squadron were sent up from Hornchurch, while Squadron Leader Harry Hogan's 501 Squadron had already taken off from Gravesend. At 16.50 hours, while flying east over Chatham, 501 Squadron tally ho'd a large force of He 111s which sub-divided into *staffeln*, each in an arrowhead formation. According to the Squadron's combat report:

> The bombers were at 15,000 feet and flying west, south of the Thames Estuary towards London. Stepped up behind them were formations of Me 109s and 110s. The enemy aircraft turned north over Southend, and the Squadron circled around them, attacking the second vic head-on. This broke up, and one He 111 jettisoned its bombs. Another was pursued by two of our fighters and landed on the water near the *Girdler* lightship. Another crashed in Southend. Our aircraft were not attacked by fighters, which were some distance behind.

Shortly after take-off, 1 Squadron sighted six enemy aircraft 'north of London', which it prepared to attack, but fortunately recognized them as Blenheims before any gun buttons were thumbed. Upon breaking away, Squadron Leader Pemberton's pilots saw the enemy formation: 30–40 bombers protected by a similar number of fighters and in no standard formation from 12,000–25,000 feet. 1 Squadron's subsequent attack was carried out with each pilot acting independently; Sergeant Merchant:

> I was No 2 of Red Section and upon sighting enemy followed my Section Leader in line astern. After attacking a Do 17, which was in company with another E/A, an Me 110 dived on me from astern. Breaking away, I shook him off, and then saw ahead a single He 111K. Climbing and going ahead, I attacked from the beam. On the second attack the port engine stopped. At this moment a Hurricane from another squadron dived on the rear of the He 111 and got in a burst. Again attacking from the front I got in a long burst, and a man jumped by parachute. A further two parachutists jumped after about one minute, as I put in another burst. The aircraft dived down and crashed in the middle of a road near a cemetery to the east of Southend.

The He 111 claimed by Sergeant Marchant crashed at Lifstan Way, Southend; it was the same raider claimed by 501 Squadron, so this is a prime example of how one actual enemy loss became two, as it were, and so on. 1 Squadron's Pilot Officer Pat Hancock:

> I pursued the main body of enemy aircraft. One He 111 was lagging behind. I gained height and prepared to attack it. Before doing so, however, a Spitfire did an astern attack

An official German photograph showing the pilot and bombardier of an He 111 in flight.

of about five seconds duration. I then went in and fired several long bursts at each engine in turn. I observed smoke, oil and flames coming from each engine. I did not follow the aircraft to the ground as a vic of Me 110s appeared to be attacking me. I evaded them and returned to base.

Again, the He 111 attacked by Hancock is believed to have been that which came to grief at Lifstan Way. The Spitfire mentioned was no doubt one of the two 222 Squadron machines involved: Flying Officer Cutts and Sergeant Davis also claimed a He 111 'probable' in that area.

1 Squadron's Sergeant Clowes also claimed an He 111 that 'emitted smoke and some flames', reporting that on his second pass the bomber's 'perspex nose exploded', although this too was the Lifstan Way raider. Another shared kill was the 5/KG 53 He 111 that crashed at Colne Engaine, near Halstead: this bomber was first attacked and damaged by 1 Squadron's Pilot Officer Matthews before being finished off by 56 Squadron's Flight Lieutenant Gracie (interestingly, the North Weald Sector Commander, that indomitable Irishman Wing Commander Victor Beamish, was flying with 56 Squadron and claimed an Me 110 'probable' during this engagement). 1 Squadron's CO, Squadron Leader Pemberton, attacked an Me 110 'in company with a Hurricane of LE squadron', which was one of two 110s that crashed at Ponders End, to the east of Enfield. 'LE' were the code letters of Squadron Leader Bader's 242 Squadron.

Romantic and exaggerated accounts of this action claim that 242 Squadron was ordered to patrol North Weald at 15,000 feet but instead climbed to 19,000 feet, Bader flying twenty miles west of his allotted position so as to have the sun behind him. Consequently, attacking from the sun, 242 Squadron executed the perfect bounce. The 242 Squadron combat report, however, offers a slightly different view: 'Squadron 242 was ordered at 1623 hours from Duxford to patrol North Weald at 15,000 feet on a vector 190°, just north of North Weald. They received a vector of 340°. Three aircraft were noticed to the right of the formation, so the Squadron Leader detached Blue Section to investigate.'

These three aircraft were almost certainly some of the Blenheims reported by 1 Squadron, and the updated vector was in response to the enemy's changing course. The Coltishall Intelligence Officer, Flight Lieutenant Maybaum, continued his report:

Green Leader then drew attention to a large enemy formation on their left so the rest of the Squadron turned and saw a vast number of aeroplanes flying in an easterly direction. These were recognised to be from 70–100 E/A, twin-engined and in tight formation, stepped up at 12,000 feet, after which there was a gap of 1,000 feet, then another swarm of twin-engined machines stepped up from about 15,000 feet to 20,000 feet.

The foregoing report indicates that Squadron Leader Bader actually complied with instructions, his own report confirming this, adding that '242 Squadron had the height advantage on the lower group and as it was obviously impossible to attack all the enemy it was decided to attack down sun on the lower group.' Maybaum's report continued:

> Green Section were ordered to attack the top of the lower formation; Red and Yellow Sections were ordered into line astern. It seemed impossible to order any formation attack. The Squadron Leader dived straight into the middle of the formation closely followed by Red Two and Red Three; the packed formation broke up and a dogfight ensued. Squadron Leader Bader saw three Me 110s do climbing turns to the left and three to the right. Their tactics appeared to be to climb in turns until they were nearly stalling above the tail of Squadron Leader Bader's aircraft. Squadron Leader Bader fired a short burst into the Me 110 at practically point blank range and the E/A burst into flames and disintegrated almost immediately. Squadron Leader Bader continued his zoom and saw another Me 110 below and so turned in behind it and got a very easy shot at about 100 to 150 yards range. After the E/A had received Squadron Leader Bader's first burst of from two to four seconds, the enemy pilot avoided further action by putting the stick violently forwards and backwards.
>
> Squadron Leader Bader got in another burst and saw pieces of the enemy's starboard wing fly off; then the whole starboard wing went on fire and the E/A went down burning in a spiral dive. Squadron Leader Bader then saw in his mirror another Me 110; he did a quick turn and noticed five or six white streams coming out of forward-firing guns; the E/A immediately put his nose down and was lost, but subsequently seen far below. Squadron Leader Bader saw nothing around him, called Duxford and was told to land.

Red Two, Pilot Officer Willie McKnight, went into attack with Squadron Leader Bader; he got behind an Me 110 and opened fire at 100 yards, the enemy aircraft bursting into flames and crashing. After a beam attack on a formation of He 111s, Red Two turned the tables on an Me 110, which had attacked him from behind, chasing the enemy machine from 10,000 to 1,000 feet. From just thirty yards, McKnight opened fire; the 110 crashed at Enfield Sewage Farm, Ponders End. After the initial Section attack, Red Three, Pilot Officer Denis Crowley-Milling, damaged an He 111, which Pilot Officer Hart confirmed having seen go down in flames. Yellow One, Flight Lieutenant Ball, emptied a third of his ammunition into an Me 110, which Pilot Officer Stansfeld also attacked, the 110 going down with both engines on fire, and so it went on, with many more claims by 242 Squadron's elated pilots.

This was what Squadron Leader Bader and 242 Squadron had been desperately waiting for: an opportunity to engage the enemy in numbers. As indicated by the foregoing, however, there were other squadrons involved in this combat, which also recorded victories. Due to the high numbers of engaging fighters, however, various pilots had independently attacked and claimed the same German aircraft, which became duplicated on the balance sheet. In the heat of the moment the relatively inexperienced 242 Squadron had been oblivious to the presence of other RAF fighters and so believed that 242, and 242 alone, was responsible for this successful interception. In total, 242 Squadron claimed seven Me 110s destroyed and three probables, and five He 111s destroyed. At the time, these claims were accepted unconditionally and without question, it being the result that not only Squadron Leader Bader craved but also the 12 Group commander, Air Vice-Marshal Leigh-Mallory, who signaled the Squadron: 'Heartiest congratulations on a first class show. Well done 242.' The Chief of the Air Staff (CAS) added his congratulations: 'Magnificent fighting. You are well on top of the enemy and obviously the fine Canadian traditions of the last war are safe in your hands.' The Under-Secretary of State for Air sent a similar message. Certainly the destruction of twelve enemy aircraft for no loss would have been remarkable – had it been accurate.

The romantic legend surrounding the story of Douglas Bader also claims that the raid in question was turned about by 242 Squadron before it reached the Handley Page factory. Neither is this true. The majority of RAF fighters, low on ammunition and fuel, actually disengaged some ten miles before the bombers reached their target where, hampered by accurate and heavy ack ack, the bombardiers' aim was poor; little damage was caused and work on the new Halifax bomber was unaffected (the other raiding force, however, hit the Vauxhall works hard, killing fifty-three people). Squadron Leader Douglas Bader:

> What happened was we got off a squadron, just 12 of us, and we had everything in our favour, height, I knew where the Germans were, and we had the sun. We shot down a few without any problems whatsoever. When we were writing out our combat reports afterwards, Leigh-Mallory rang me up and said, 'Congratulations, Bader, on the Squadron's performance today.' I said, 'Thank you very much, Sir, but if we'd had more aeroplanes then we would have shot down a whole lot more!' He asked what I meant and I explained that with more fighters our results would have been even better. He said, 'Look, I'd like to talk to you about this,' and so I flew over to Hucknall and told him what I thought.

And so it was that the seeds were sown for 12 Group operating, contrary to the System of Air Defence and the Commander-in-Chief's wishes, large formations of fighters. The evidence proves, however, that the whole theory was flawed from the outset, as it was not just the twelve Hurricanes of 242 Squadron in action against the Hatfield raiders, but around fifty RAF fighters – more than the so-called 'Big Wing' would ever comprise. Moreover, it is important to note that the Hatfield raid had not been escorted by lethal Me 109s, but by the inferior Me 110. The perceived success of 242 Squadron on 30 August, 1940, however, coupled with Squadron Leader Bader's theory, provided Air Vice-Marshal Leigh-Mallory with just the thing he needed to argue for and win a greater part in the fighting for 12 Group.

The fighting Poles of 303 'Kosciusko' Squadron won a reputation for fearlessness, savagely prosecuting their own private air war against Hitler in their Hurricanes out of Northolt. Pictured at that station during the Battle of Britain are Squadron Leader Ronald Kellett, the British CO (with forage cap), and Flight Lieutenant Witold Urbanowicz (behind Kellett), the Polish commander of 'B' Flight. Both men were highly successful fighter pilots in 1940, and decorated accordingly; they survived the war.

A Spitfire of 222 Squadron written off at Hornchurch by enemy bombing on 31 August 1940.

The day was also significant for the Poles of 303 Squadron, based at Northolt in 11 Group. At 16.15 hours, 'B' Flight had taken off from that Sector Station on a training flight, 'intercepting' some Blenheims (the aircraft referred to by 1 and 242 Squadron) over St Albans at 16.35 hours. While escorting the Blenheims back to Northolt, the Poles sighted the Hatfield raiding force, withdrawing and being 'attacked by an unknown number of our fighters'. Flying Officer Ludwik Paskiewicz, Green One, was for some reason unable to communicate with his formation leader by radio, so flew in front of him, waggling his wings before turning to attack the Germans. In his subsequent solo interception, Green One destroyed a Dornier, which crashed and exploded, chalking up the Squadron's first kill. Afterwards, the Poles were made operational; as Air Chief Marshal Dowding later said, 'We needed them. We needed them all.'

On this day, Fighter Command flew more sorties – 1,054 – than on any previous day's fighting. Altogether twenty-two squadrons had been engaged, most of them twice and some as many as four times. It would be the shape of things to come.

The German High Command issued operational orders to the 16th *Armee* for Operation *Seelöwe*. Clearly the enemy remained confident that the RAF would be defeated and that England would still be invaded.

Saturday 31 August Shortly before 08.00 hours, three waves of enemy aircraft were plotted incoming over the Thames Estuary, while a fourth approached Dover. The latter was identified as a fighter sweep and so 501 and

Left: Flight Lieutenant Percy 'Squeak' Weaver DFC, a professional pre-war airman with 56 Squadron. Having performed stalwart service, Weaver was reported missing on 31 August 1940. Later, a sock bearing a 'Weaver' nametape was found in the River Blackwater, near the Essex coast, so it is believed that his Hurricane crashed into the water.

Below: Graham 'Minnie' Manton was a pre-war regular officer and posted to command 56 Squadron at North Weald during the Battle of Britain. A successful fighter pilot, he is pictured here with a Spitfire Mk IX in Burma.

1 (Canadian) Squadrons were turned about by the Controller; although 501 Squadron escaped unscathed, Me 109s attacked the Canadians, destroying three Hurricanes.

The raids incoming along the Thames were bound for fighter airfields. 257 Squadron was scrambled from Martlesham, intercepting fifty Me 110s near Clacton but losing Pilot Officer Maffett, who was killed when his Hurricane crashed at Walton-on-the-Naze. 56 Squadron was scrambled from North Weald to engage a formation of Do 17s heading for Debden. Over the Essex coast, the Squadron was bounced by 7/JG 26, which destroyed four Hurricanes; sadly, Flight Lieutenant Percy Weaver was killed. Squadron Leader G.A.L. 'Minnie' Manton:

> From those hectic times I remember one particular incident, probably because it occurred shortly after I had taken over the Squadron following two-and-a-half years behind a desk at the Air Ministry. Every moment with 56 Squadron, therefore, was new and exciting for me. After only my first or second combat, I was returning to North Weald, trying desperately to gather my wits, when another 56 Squadron machine came alongside and formated on me. The pilot opened his hood, gave me a great grin, a thumbs up and then one finger to indicate that he had made a kill: it was 'Squeak' Weaver.
>
> Squeak went missing on the very day I left the Squadron on posting to command RAF Manston – or at least what was left of it! They rang me from North Weald the next day to tell me the news, such was Flight Lieutenant Weaver's standing in the Squadron.
>
> Whilst most eulogies tend to go overboard, my recollections of Squeak Weaver are all clear and sincere. Of all the boisterous, reckless young men in the Squadron he stood out. He was universally liked and because of his irrepressible good humour, enthusiasm for life and everything he did, and his fearless attitude to battle, he became an absolute lynchpin in the Squadron. His loss was, I know, felt most deeply at a time when we all tried to shrug off such things for obvious reasons.

Flight Lieutenant Weaver's Hurricane, V7373, crashed at Osea Island in the River Blackwater on the Essex coast. Although his body was never recovered, as a sock bearing a 'Weaver' nametape was later washed up it was assumed that he had perished. Only hours after 'Squeak' had been reported missing, 56 Squadron was notified that he had been awarded a DFC. As if to make this loss even more poignant, the following day 56 Squadron was withdrawn from North Weald, to Boscombe Down in 10 Group, where although there was action to be had, the tempo of battle was not as great as over south-east England.

Another raid now headed for the Duxford Sector, causing the Sector Controller, Wing Commander Woodhall, to request reinforcements. 11 Group responded by diverting 111 Squadron which made a spirited head-on attack, destroying two enemy machines for the loss of one Hurricane. It was insufficient, however, to prevent Fowlmere being bombed. Corporal Fred Roberts:

It was between 0800–0830 hours when the first bombs were dropped. We, the ground staff, were queuing for breakfast, our 19 Squadron's Spitfires being airborne. We heard the noise of what transpired to be Do 17s approaching. I dived into the nearest slit-trench and upon looking up could see the sun shining on little dots high in the sky. I could also see the first stick of bombs falling. Fortunately they were released too late and so only two fell on the airfield, one amongst the bell tents, making a crater four feet deep and five feet across. The earth blown out of the crater collapsed one of the other tents. There were two lads asleep inside who were partially buried, but neither were harmed. The second bomb exploded near the boundary fence, but the rest of that stick fell in the orchards and watercress beds beyond the airfield. Looking back now it makes me smile to think of us crouching in that trench holding enamel plates over our heads with cutlery and mugs in hand! I also recall that Flight Sergeant George 'Grumpy' Unwin's 'A' Flight Spitfire was up on trestles in the blister hangar when the air raid warning came. He came running along with the other pilots, but due to his aircraft being indisposed, was unable to take-off with the others. He was yelling and swearing for his plane, and I reckon that we broke a record for returning a Spitfire to serviceability! George was airborne and after the others just 10 minutes later, following a straight take-off from the hangar, across wind and with no engine warm-up. It certainly showed the man's courage and the faith he put in his groundcrew.

Fortunately, 19 Squadron was airborne before the raid hit: 'B' Flight had already been scrambled to intercept the attack on nearby Debden, but 'A' Flight was off duty and went up in a panic, intercepting the raid by II/KG 2's Do 17s, escorted by ZG 26's Me 110s. Sergeant David Cox:

We were caught on the hop! Most of us were still in bed as the Squadron was stood down! We got a panic message to scramble immediately. I put on my flying boots and jacket over my pyjamas. We took off at about 0800 hours and climbed south to 17,000 feet. It was jolly cold up there as the flying jacket only came down to my waist!

We soon came in sight of the enemy, about 30 Dorniers with a large number of Me 110s above and behind. I was No Three in Blue Section, which was led by Flying Officer Coward. We were above and behind the bombers but below the 110s. We were put into echelon starboard and dived onto a section of bombers. Before I could open fire I was attacked by the 110s, so I took evasive action, a very, very sharp left-hand climbing turn, after which I found myself alone and no longer in contact with the Squadron.

I then climbed to about 20,000 feet and flew south-east. Over Clacton I saw about 20–30 Me 110s milling around in a left-hand circle and about 2,000 feet below me. I dived down onto the circle and fired at one 110 that had become detached from the formation. My cannons operated perfectly as I was keeping a straight line with no turning. The 110 turned slightly to port and then dived away steeply with his port engine belching black smoke. I was then attacked by four other 110s and so, being out of ammunition, got the hell out of it!

Do 17s of KG 3 in flight
and heading for England.

Flying Officer James Coward:

We intercepted 15 Do 17s escorted by 80 Me 110s just south of Duxford. Flight
Lieutenant Clouston led us into a copybook Fighter Command No 1 Attack from dead
ahead, turning in three sections line astern, to come up in sections echeloned port behind
the enemy, who were in vics of three and in line astern. The fourth section, led by Flying
Officer Frank Brinsden, was detailed to climb up and intercept the fighters. I got a cannon
shell through the cockpit which shattered my left leg below the knee, also severing the
elevator controls, and I had to bale out. I put a tourniquet round my thigh, using my
helmet radio lead, and landed by parachute about four miles north of Duxford on the
Royston to Newmarket Road. I was admitted to Addenbrooke's Hospital in Cambridge
and was out of the battle from then on.

James Coward was actually bleeding to death from his leg wound while
descending by parachute, but was fortunately still wearing his leather flying
helmet, complete with radio lead, which he used to tie a tourniquet and therefore
save his own life. His left leg, however, was subsequently amputated below the
knee. Flying Officer Frank Brinsden:

At about 15,000 feet plus, whilst still climbing and with the controls therefore sluggish, I
was attacked from head-on and from up sun by a 110 which I then noticed was part of
a large formation. There then followed an almighty bang, loss of control and me over the
side pretty sharpish! I landed by parachute at Starling Green, near Saffron Walden, and
my Spitfire, R6958, crashed at Brent, Pelham. I was very lucky not to have caught fire
because I reeked of petrol. I was also violently ill during the descent, possibly caused by
the parachute's motion.

The two Spitfires had been shot down by *Oberleutnant* Hans Barschal,
Gruppenadjutant of *Stab* III/ZG 26, and *Oberleutnant* Sophus Baagoe of 8/ZG
26. Flying Officer Brinsden's Section, bounced while climbing, had been in a
particularly unfortunate tactical situation; had Me 109s been present the damage
would undoubtedly been worse.

Pilot Officer Ray Aeberhardt's Spitfire was damaged during the action, his
flaps unresponsive. Landing without them meant that his groundspeed was too
high, and the Spitfire crashed and turned over, the 19-year-old being killed in the
resulting fire. Sergeant David Cox:

When I got back to Fowlmere I landed over the blazing remains of Pilot Officer
Aeberhardt's Spitfire. I visited his grave several times after the war and at first it was
on its own with a large private headstone and always looked after. After about 20
years it became overgrown and obviously uncared for. I tried to tidy it up myself and
put some flowers on it. The last time I visited the grave it had been moved to be with
the other RAF graves and, like them, was carefully tended. I remember Pilot Officer

Aeberhardt as a pleasant young officer who would always have a few words with us NCO pilots.

While 19 Squadron was in action, at 08.25 hours 242 Squadron was sent from Coltishall to protect Duxford; 310 Squadron went up from Duxford at that time, but landed an hour later with a nil return. At lunchtime, 242 Squadron patrolled London, again without sighting the enemy. The Czechs, however, had more luck: as more raids came in to bomb Biggin Hill and Hornchurch, between 13.15 and 13.30 hours, 310 Squadron attacked a formation of Do 17s, escorted by Me 110s and Me 109s, east of Hornchurch. The Czechs destroyed four bombers and two Me 109s but lost two Hurricanes; Pilot Officer Sterbacek, who was presumed to have crashed into the Thames, remains missing to this day, the first Czech fighter pilot to lose his life during the Battle of Britain. Wing Commander 'Woody' Woodhall:

> I met the Czechs on their return to the airfield and spoke with Squadron Leader Sacha Hess; he had disabled a Do 17 over Epping Forest which made a wheels-up forced landing in a field. He followed it down with the intention of making certain that no-one got out of it alive. He saw three Germans climb out, who, when they realised Sacha was diving on them, held up their hands. To quote his own words: 'I hesitate, then it was too late, so I go round again to make sure I kill them – they wave something white – again I do not shoot – then (disgustedly) I think it is no use – I am become too bloody British!'

Hess had good reason to desire revenge that day: he had recently received notification that his wife and daughter had been killed by the Germans.

222 Squadron was also up, yet again that day, mixing it with Me 109s high over Sittingbourne in Kent. Pilot Officer Laurie Whitbread:

> I manoeuvered until the Me 109 appeared in my sights, the enemy aircraft climbing slowly away, not having seen me. I fired from about 400 yards and rapidly closed to within 50 yards, when I could see the bullets entering the fuselage from tail to cockpit. The 109 half rolled onto its back and remained in that attitude, flying quite slowly with a little white smoke issuing from it. It eventually nosed down slowly when I was obliged to lose sight of it having noticed an aircraft approaching my tail, which turned out to be a Spitfire.

This enemy fighter was probably one belonging to 1/JG 77, which crashed between Walderslade and Broxley at 13.20 hours. The pilot, *Unteroffizier* Keck, baled out and was captured. The Hurricanes of Squadron Leader Peter Townsend's battle hardened 85 Squadron then combined with 603 Squadron's Spitfires to harry the raiders back out over the Channel. Townsend himself was shot down, baling out with a cannon shell in his foot which later required amputation of his left big toe. With so many fighters, of both sides, cutting and thrusting within what must have appeared to those on the ground a crazy pattern

The caption to this official Luftwaffe photograph of an unknown He 111 unit reads 'Back from a flight over England'.

of white vapour trails, it is impossible to ascertain which unit fought which, and who shot down who; indeed, as the fighting intensified further still this scenario became increasingly common as the summer wore on. The Hornchurch Station ORB likewise chronicles the day's dramatic events at that Sector Station:

Mass raids continued to be made against our aerodromes, again starting early in the morning. The first two attacks were delivered at 0830 and 1030 hours respectively and were directed at Biggin Hill, Eastchurch and Debden. The third attack was delivered at Hornchurch, but although our squadrons engaged, they were unable to break the enemy bomber formation, and so about 30 Dorniers dropped some 100 bombs across the airfield. Damage, however, was slight, although a bomb fell on the new Airmen's Mess, which had almost been completed. The only vital damage, however, was too a power cable, which was cut. The emergency power equipment was brought into operation until repair was effected. Three men were killed and 11 wounded. 54 Squadron attempted to take off during the attack and ran through the bombs. Three aircraft were destroyed, one being blown from the middle of the landing field to outside the boundary, but all three pilots miraculously escaped with only slight injuries.

The ORB of 54 Squadron provides more detail:

A large formation of enemy bombers – a most impressive sight in vic formation at 15,000 feet – reached the aerodromes and dropped their bombs (probably 60 in all) in a line from our original dispersal pens to the petrol dump and beyond into Elm Park. Perimeter track, dispersal pens and barrack block windows suffered but no other damage to buildings was caused, and the aerodrome, in spite of its ploughed condition, remained serviceable. The Squadron was ordered off just as the first bombs were beginning to fall and eight of our machines safely cleared the ground; the remaining section, however, just became airborne as the bombs exploded. All three machines were wholly wrecked in the air, and the survival of the pilots is a complete miracle. Sergeant Davis, taking off towards the hangars was thrown back across the River Ingrebourne two fields away, scrambling out of his machine unharmed. Flight Lieutenant Deere had one wing and his prop torn off; climbing to about 100 feet, he turned over and, coming down, slid along the aerodrome for a hundred yards upside down. He was rescued from this unenviable position by Pilot Officer Edsall, the third member of the Section, who had suffered a similar fate except that he had landed the right way up. Dashing across the aerodrome with bombs still dropping, he extricated Deere from his machine. All three pilots were ready again for battle by the next morning.

The Hornchurch Station ORB continues:

The fourth attack of the day was also directed at Hornchurch, and, once again, despite strong fighter opposition and AA fire, the bombers penetrated our defences. This time, however, their aim was most inaccurate, and the line of bombs fell from then towards the edge of the aerodrome. Two Spitfires parked near the edge of the aerodrome were written off, and one airman was killed. Otherwise, apart from the damage to dispersal pens, the perimeter track and the aerodrome surface, the raid was abortive and the aerodrome remained serviceable. Our squadrons, which had a very heavy day, accounted for no less that 19 of the enemy and a further seven probably destroyed. 603 Squadron alone were responsible for the destruction of 14 enemy aircraft. Although we lost a total of nine aircraft, either in combat or on the ground, only one pilot was lost.

It was not until the day's last interception, in fact, that 603 Squadron suffered losses, when I/JG 3's Me 109s engaged the Spitfires over London: Flying Officer B.J.G. Carbury was wounded but returned to base, but Flying Officer R.M. Waterston was killed; Pilot Officer G.K. 'Sheep' Gilroy baled out, his Spitfire crashing into 14 Hereford Road, Wanstead, killing a dog. Gilroy baled out but upon landing was attacked by a baying mob, who presumably thought him to be an enemy airman.

Yet again the bar had been raised: 31 August represented the heaviest fighting seen so far. It was also the day on which Fighter Command suffered more losses than on any other day throughout the sixteen week battle: nine pilots killed or missing. Among the latter was Flying Officer Michael Duke Doulton, of the famous porcelain family, whose last resting place would be unknown until 1984, when amateur aviation archaeologists recovered his remains and aircraft from a depth of twenty-five feet from Wennington Marsh.

Sunday 1 September Following the last few days fighting, the situation was undoubtedly critical for Fighter Command. The pressure on the defenders was relentless. Biggin Hill, Hornchurch and Kenley had all been hit to varying degrees, with damage caused to installations and communications in addition to fatalities among personnel. More squadrons were rotated in and out of the combat zone; Fighter Command still had plenty of aircraft, but many experienced pilots had either been killed or incapacitated by wounds; those that had survived to date were exhausted.

At 10.55 hours, another huge enemy formation was incoming over the Kentish coast, the threat soon sub-dividing into two, then five, separate formations heading not only for the airfields at Biggin Hill, Detling and Eastchurch, but also London Docks. Escorting KG 76 to Kenley were the Me 109s of JG 26, led by Major Galland at full strength. The depleted but still fighting Hurricanes of 85 Squadron were led into the air from Croydon by Sergeant 'Sammy' Allard, engaging and destroying an Me 109 which was among a *schwarm* amusing itself shooting up the Dover balloon barrage. The Spitfires of 72 Squadron, also up from Croydon and freshly arrived from Acklington only the previous day were on their first operational sortie and typically bounced over the coast by JG 26: four Spitfires were shot down, Pilot Officer Oswald St John Pigg being killed. And so the day wore on. Pilot Officer Buck Casson: 'We of No 616 Squadron flew five sorties that day. I claimed an Me 109 probable and a Do 17 confirmed destroyed. I also had a hole blown in my port wing.'

At lunchtime, 85 Squadron was in action again, intercepting a large raid bound for Biggin Hill. Two Hurricanes subsequently forced-landed with combat damage, but four were destroyed: Flying Officer A.V. Gowers baled out badly burned, as did Sergeant G.B. Booth, whose parachute was actually on fire. Flying Officer Patrick Woods-Scawen also baled out but was killed when his parachute failed to open; Sergeant John Ellis was reported missing. The Squadron could no longer be classified as operational, so decimated and exhausted had it now become; two days later it was withdrawn to Church Fenton.

At tea time, more enemy fighters roved around over Kent, but Air Vice-Marshal Park refused to respond; in frustration the *jagdfliegern* even strafed certain airfields. Biggin Hill, however, was absolutely plastered by enemy bombers, destroying the crucial Sector Operations Room and cutting the aerodrome off from the outside world. There were many casualties, especially among the WAAF, although two of their number, Sergeant Helen Turner and Corporal Elspeth Henderson, were later awarded Military Medals for their courage under fire. Working furiously throughout the night, telephone engineers restored vital communications, the Sector Operations Room being moved to a local butcher's

Flight Lieutenant Ian 'Widge' Gleed DFC leads a flight of 87 Squadron Hurricanes from Exeter to Bibury, August 1940. The latter was a tiny airfield in the Cotswolds, from where a flight of 87 Squadron frequently operated to afford some protection to the docks at Bristol and Gloucester.

shop! Although Biggin Hill was back on line, Air Vice-Marshal Park must have had grave concerns regarding the Station's ability to maintain operations should the pressure be maintained – and he had every reason to believe that it would.

At North Weald, Squadron Leader Teddy Donaldson's 151 Squadron packed up and withdrew to Digby, in 12 Group, to rest and re-form. Having seen action during the Fall of France, 151 had barely any respite before being heavily engaged in the Battle of Britain – during which time the Squadron suffered eleven pilots killed.

Monday 2 September Across the Channel, the Luftwaffe was intent upon giving the defenders no respite. First to be attacked were the airfields at Biggin Hill, Rochford, Eastchurch and North Weald; 12 Group was up, but patrolling the airfields at Duxford and Debden. 603 Squadron was up from Hornchurch,

Sergeant John Gilders of 41 Squadron, pictured at Hornchurch. 'Gilly' destroyed four enemy aircraft, shared and probably destroyed several more during the Battle of Britain, but crashed and was killed, probably as the result of oxygen failure, in 1941. Reported missing, his remains were recovered by aviation archaeologists in 1994 in probably the most controversial excavation to date. Sergeant Gilders, however, was subsequently and at last laid to rest with full military honours at Brookwood.

and engaged as the enemy withdrew back to the coast. Sergeant Jack Stokoe: 'During the morning patrol my own aircraft was damaged by a cannon shell in the windscreen, and my hand was slightly cut by splinters.'

At lunchtime even more enemy aircraft crossed the Channel, but the raids were broken up by over seventy Spitfires and Hurricanes. At teatime another raid of 250 plus bandits was incoming. Among the intercepting RAF squadrons was 616 Squadron, on what would be its last engagement during this spell of duty at Kenley: Flight Lieutenant Denys Gillam was shot down but baled out unhurt. Kenley itself was unmolested. Pilot Officer Buck Casson: 'I was airborne four times that day, patrolling base, but no action because the raiders retreated.'

During the teatime action, 603 Squadron, engaged Me 109s high above Maidstone. Sergeant Jack Stokoe:

On September 2nd, I was involved with two more interceptions, during the course of one of which I damaged two enemy aircraft but was myself shot down in flames, fortunately baling out. On that occasion, as I was attacking an enemy aircraft, I remember machine-gun bullets, or maybe cannon shells, hitting my Spitfire, followed by flames in the cockpit as the petrol tank exploded. I thought 'Christ! I've got to get out of here and *quick*!' I undid the straps and opened the hood, but this turned the flames into a blowtorch. I was not wearing gloves, as during our hasty scramble I had forgotten them, but had to put my hands back in the fire to invert the Spitfire so that I could drop out (no ejector seats in those days!). I remember seeing sheets of skin peeling off the backs of my hands before I fell out of the aeroplane. I was then concerned whether the parachute would function or whether it had been damaged by fire, but I pulled the ripcord and fortunately it opened perfectly.

I landed in a field, but the Home Guard queried whether I was an enemy agent! A few choice words in English soon convinced them I was genuine, and thereafter I was rushed into the emergency hospital at Leeds Castle, suffering from shock and severe burns to my hands, neck and face.

At the time, 603 Squadron was suffering such heavy casualties that the administration got pretty chaotic. For four days after baling out, although safe in hospital, I was officially posted Missing in Action! I was in hospital for six weeks before returning to operational duties on October 22nd.

Squadron Leader George Denholm:

603 Squadron had to learn quickly. We rapidly determined not to allow ourselves to be bounced. I therefore decided to fly on a reciprocal of the course provided by the ground controller, until at 15,000 feet when the Squadron would turn about, climbing all the time. Flying in this way meant that we usually saw the enemy striking inland beneath us and were therefore better positioned to attack. We also ensured that pilots always flew in pairs, for mutual protection. After an action, though, the Squadron would come home

Flight Lieutenant Ian 'Widge' Gleed DFC *en route* from Exeter to Bibury, August 1940, in his faithful AL-K. Unusually this aircraft had a red propeller spinner and, in keeping with the Squadron's tradition of Disney nose-arts, had Figaro the cat painted on the starboard side.

individually, or in ones and twos at intervals of about two minutes. In addition to leading the Squadron in the air, my duties also included checking who was missing after each action, which I generally did an hour after the end of each patrol. In that time a call would often come in from a pilot who had baled out or landed elsewhere.

On this day, 46 Squadron arrived at Stapleford, in the North Weald Sector, and was immediately in action, claiming an Me 109 destroyed but losing a Hurricane in the process – a much better first result than many other squadrons enjoyed.

The day also saw a particularly tragic casualty: Pilot Officer Charles 'Tony' Woods-Scawen of Tangmere's 43 Squadron, whose Hurricane was shot down by an Me 109 over Kent. Although on fire, the pilot initially intended to crash land his aircraft at Ivychurch, but the flames increased, forcing him to bale out but unfortunately he was too low and was killed. Only the previous day, his brother, Flying Officer Patrick 'Wombat' Woods-Scawen of 85 Squadron had been killed when his parachute failed to open. Later, their proud father received his gallant sons' DFCs from the King at Buckingham Palace. Sergeant Reg Nutter: 'No 257 Squadron was patrolling off North Foreland and I managed to get some good burst at an Me 109 which had swung in front of me while attempting to attack us from the rear. He immediately dived, streaming coolant, but I lost sight of him in the thick haze.'

Tuesday 3 September In the fifteen days that 616 Squadron had operated from Kenley, eleven Spitfires had been destroyed and three damaged. Five pilots had been killed, six wounded and another captured. In response, the squadron had claimed ten enemy aircraft destroyed, three probably destroyed and six damaged; of the squadron 'bag', in fact, seven destroyed, two probables and three damaged were claimed by that highly experienced and professional fighter pilot Flight Lieutenant Denys Gillam – who received a well-earned DFC for this outstanding effort. Such losses of both men and machines, however, meant that 616 Squadron had ceased to exist as an effective fighting unit and was withdrawn from the front line. 66 Squadron, therefore, flew from Coltishall and relieved the decimated 'South Yorkshire' Squadron, which withdrew and re-built in 12 Group. Corporal Bob Morris:

> When we of No 66 Squadron arrived at Kenley it was an absolute shambles, there was hardly a building left standing. As we drove around the aerodrome to our assembly point, I saw a car park full of vehicles – but there was not one which hadn't been riddled by gunfire or shrapnel. There were shelters destroyed, buildings flattened. We knew that we would be in for a hard time.

At 08.30 hours, a huge German fighter sweep formed up over Calais and set course to England, but the 11 Group Controller ensured that no RAF squadrons engaged. Concurrently, fifty-four Do 17s, escorted by eighty Me 110s, flew west over the Thames Estuary at 20,000 feet, before turning north at Southend and heading for North Weald. Confused by the changing course, the defenders were surprised and North Weald was heavily bombed: two hangars were destroyed by fire, the operations building was hit, as were other installations. Although the runway was badly cratered, North Weald nonetheless remained operational. As the raiders headed for home, battle was joined.

Squadron Leader Phillip Pinkham was leading eight 19 Squadron Spitfires on a standing patrol of Duxford and Debden when he was vectored to North Weald. Arriving as the bombers were withdrawing, Pinkham's Spitfires attacked, flying in pairs and in line astern, from above and ahead. In the subsequent combat, Flying Officer 'Ace' Haines claimed the destruction of an Me 110, and both Sub-Lieutenant 'Admiral' Blake and Flight Sergeant 'Grumpy' Unwin the probable destruction of two more. Six of the eight Spitfire pilots involved, however, suffered cannon stoppages.

An enormous dogfight developed over the Thames Estuary, into which sallied forth 603 Squadron. Pilot Officer Richard Hillary:

> At about 12,000 feet we came up through the clouds; I looked down and saw them spread out below me like layers of whipped cream. The sun was brilliant and made it difficult to see the next plane when turning. I was peering anxiously ahead, for the Controller had warned us that at least 50 enemy fighters were approaching very high. When we sighted

So critical did the shortage of pilots become for Fighter Command during the Battle of Britain that an appeal went out for volunteers from other commands and services. One who answered the call was Sub-Lieutenant Giles Arthur Blake, a Fleet Air Arm pilot who flew Spitfires with 19 Squadron. A popular character, Blake became the unit's last pilot to die during the Battle of Britain when shot down by Me 109s over London on 29 October 1940.

them, nobody shouted, as I think we all saw them at the same moment. They must have been 500–1,000 feet above and coming straight on like a swarm of locusts. I remember cursing and going automatically into line astern; the next moment we were in among them and it was every man for himself. As soon as they saw us they spread·out and dived, and the next 10 minutes was a blur of twisting machines and tracer bullets. One Me 109 went down in a sheet of flame on my right, and a Spitfire hurtled past in a half roll; I was weaving and turning in a desperate attempt to gain height, with the machine literally hanging on the airscrew. Then, just below me and to my left, I saw what I had been praying for: a 109 climbing and away from the sun. I closed in to 200 yards and from slightly one side gave him a two second burst. Fabric ripped off the wing and black smoke poured from the engine, but he did not go down. Like a fool, I did not break away, but put in a three-second burst. Red flames shot upwards and he spiraled out of sight.

Pilot Officer Dudley Stewart-Clark, an Old Etonian and Volunteer Reservist who flew Spitfires with 603 Squadron during the Battle of Britain. Having shared in the destruction of several German bombers, on 3 September 1940, he was shot down by *Hauptmann* Erich Böde, *Kommodore* of II/JG 26, but baled out safely. Sadly he was killed in action, still flying Spitfires, over France in 1941.

At that moment, Hillary's Spitfire filled the Revi gunsight of *Hauptmann* Erich Bode, *Kommandeur* of II/JG 26. The German thumbed the cannon button on his joystick, simultaneously squeezing the machine-gun trigger, and the Spitfire became a flamer. Pilot Officer Richard Hillary:

> I felt a terrific explosion which knocked the control column from my hand, and the whole machine quivered like a stricken animal. In a second, the cockpit was a mass of flames; instinctively I reached up to open the hood. It would not move. I tore off my straps and managed to force it back; but this took time, and when I dropped back in the seat and reached for the stick in an effort to turn the plane on its back, the heat was so intense that I could feel myself going. I remember a second of sharp agony, thinking 'So this is it!' and putting both hands to my eyes. Then I passed out.

Miraculously Hillary was thrown clear of his blazing Spitfire, and in spite of horrendous burns managed to deploy his parachute, drifting down into the Channel where he was rescued by the Margate lifeboat.

Next, *Hauptmann* Bode shot down Pilot Officer Dudley Stewart-Clark, who was also wounded and baled out. In six days, 603 Squadron had lost fourteen Spitfires, four pilots killed and six wounded.

46 Squadron, which had arrived at Stapleford the previous day, was also in action, the outcome being catastrophic: Three Hurricanes were destroyed, and

three more damaged; three pilots were wounded and Sergeant Gerald Edworthy was missing, pilot and aircraft swallowed up by the River Crouch at Redwood Creek, where both remain entombed to this day.

The Hurricanes of 1 Squadron were also embroiled in the action over Kent, probably with the Me 109s of JG 51. Flying Officer Colin Birch:

> I was flying as the third member of Flight Lieutenant Hillcoat's Section. We were bounced by Me 109s with yellow-painted spiral motifs on their airscrew spinners. I stalled in a hefty 'g' turn, coming to at 8–10,000 feet with no other aircraft in sight. I never saw either Flight Lieutenant Hillcoat or Pilot Officer Shaw ever again.

The Squadron lost two pilots, both of whom were reported missing: Pilot Officer Robert Shaw and Flight Lieutenant Brian Hillcoat. On 29 September 1940, PC 265 Whyman of the Kent County Constabulary joined civilian contractors of A.V. Nicholls to investigate the crash site of a British fighter at Park House, Chart Sutton. The aircraft wreckage, however, had been recovered by an RAF squad three days previously and identified as Hurricane P3782 – Pilot Officer Shaw's aircraft. Although there is no evidence to confirm that the missing pilot remained buried at the site, local people marked the site with a cross and planted a memorial garden – at which a service is still held annually. Pilot Officer Pat Hancock: 'After so long, all I can say is that at the time I was convinced that I saw Robert Shaw in his parachute, drifting seawards, land in the sea and float in his Mae West. I thought that he must have succumbed to the cold water quickly.'

As the enemy withdrew on 3 September, and the day's fighting came to a close, tragedy struck for the Blenheims of 25 Squadron. Returning to North Weald, the Blenheims were mistaken for Ju 88s and attacked by the inexperienced Hurricanes of 46 Squadron, up again from Stapleford: one Blenheim was destroyed and two others damaged, with one pilot killed in yet another incident of 'friendly fire'.

Sergeant Reg Nutter:

> Whilst intercepting some bombers attacking North Weald, I foolishly allowed myself to watch the fall of their bombs on the aerodrome, instead of watching my tail. I was promptly pounced upon by an Me 110. Although my Hurricane had been quite badly shot up and leaked petrol all over me, and despite having received shrapnel wounds to my right side, I managed to make it back to Martlesham Heath.

For 19 Squadron, the morning's action, which saw six of eight pilots suffer cannon stoppages, had been exasperating, and had brought the matter to a head. Wing Commander 'Woody' Woodhall:

> This further failure of 19 Squadron's cannons was unacceptable, so I got on the phone to 'LM' and urgently requested that the Squadron should have its eight-gun Spitfires back.

The following afternoon the AOC-in-C, 'Stuffy' Dowding himself, landed at Duxford without warning. I greeted him and he gruffly said, 'I want to talk to the pilots of 19 Squadron,' so I drove him over to Fowlmere. There he met 'Sandy' Lane and other pilots. He listened to their complaints almost in silence, then I drove him back to his aircraft, which he was piloting personally. As he climbed into the aeroplane, he merely said, 'You'll get your eight-gun Spitfires back.' 'Stuffy' was a man of few words, but he had listened to us all, asked a few pertinent questions then made his decision. As a result, that evening the instructors from the OTU at Hawarden flew their eight-gun Spitfires to Fowlmere, returning with the cannon Spitfires.

Flight Sergeant George Unwin:

This was good news. We were absolutely fed up with the cannons. Being in 12 Group and playing a supporting role meant that we didn't get into action as often as we would have liked, and when we did it was only for the cannons to jam. We were much more confident with the machine-gun Spits, but they were clapped out old things from an OTU, although we realised that beggars can't be choosers!

Wednesday 4 September British aircraft factories were now also being targeted by day. While seventy plus German bombers, escorted by a staggering 200 Me 109s, headed for targets in Kent, twenty Me 110s of V/LG 1 swept in low, at 6,000 feet, to attack the Hawker factory at Brooklands. *En route*, the 110s were attacked by 253 Squadron, up from Kenley, which accurately claimed six enemy aircraft destroyed and one damaged for no loss. Although the 110s reached Brooklands, the Vickers factory was bombed by mistake, halting Wellington bomber production for at least four days and killing eighty-eight workers. While withdrawing, however, V/LG 1 was intercepted by more defending fighters, losing more aircraft in the process. Indeed, this was a bad day generally for the Me 110: responding to an assistance shout from 11 Group, the 10 Group Spitfires of 234 Squadron caught III/ZG 26 over the West Sussex coast at 13.15 hours; three 110s were subsequently destroyed, making the day's grand total fifteen *zerstörers* lost on operations over England.

By now, Kent had become a huge aerial battlefield, as nine RAF fighter squadrons intercepted the main raid, among them 222 Squadron, up from Hornchurch. Over West Malling, Sergeant John Ramshaw, who had joined the Squadron straight from training school only five days before, was shot down and killed by an Me 109; Pilot Officer 'Chips' Carpenter attacked a 109 but upon breaking away his Spitfire was hit by ack ack, blowing the pilot out of his cockpit. Pilot Officer Assheton claimed two Me 109s destroyed, and Sergeant Chipping another. One of the enemy pilots that fell foul of 222 Squadron, however, was an *experte*, *Hauptmann* Wilhelm Balthasar, the *Kommodore* of JG 3, who was wounded. Back at Hornchurch, 222 Squadron waited in vain for the return of Pilot Officer John Cutts, who was posted missing. Later, the remains

Pilot Officer W.P.H. 'Robin' Rafter, a 19-year-old shot down over the Thames Estuary on 5 September 1940, on his first operational sortie from Hornchurch with 603 Squadron. Having baled out with a head wound, he returned to operations in November, but on his first flight inexplicably crashed and was killed; he was nineteen years old. In this studio photograph, Rafter has his top button undone – an affectation peculiar to fighter pilots.

of a pilot were recovered from a Spitfire crash site at Amberfield Farm, Chart Sutton, Kent, and buried as 'unknown' at Bell Road Cemetery, Sittingbourne. Following detailed research in 1998, evidence presented to the Ministry of Defence by this author proved conclusively that this pilot was actually 20-year-old Pilot Officer John Wintringham Cutts, whose headstone was consequently named accordingly: forty-eight years after the Battle of Britain, one less pilot was missing, and a family had both a full stop and a headstone upon which to focus their grief.

Thursday 5 September Another bitterly contested day, which saw twenty-two separate raids on both 11 Group's airfields and the oil storage depot at Thameshaven.

At Hornchurch, 19-year-old Pilot Officer William Pearce Houghton Rafter, known as 'Robin' to his family and friends, anxiously awaited the call to scramble for the first time. From Harborne in Birmingham, Robin was the younger son of the late Sir Charles Rafter, a former Chief Constable, and his elder brother, Pilot Officer Charles Rafter, was flying Wellington bombers with 214 Squadron at Stradishall. The younger Rafter had been given a Short Service Commission, straight from Cheltenham College, on 26 June 1939. His flying

Squadron Leader H.R.L. 'Robin' Hood, Commanding Officer of 41 Squadron until his death in action on 5 September 1940. Note the pilot's canvas oxygen mask with integral radio telephone, and personal insignia.

training complete, on 7 May 1940, Pilot Officer Rafter joined 225 Squadron, an army co-operation squadron flying Westland Lysander communications aircraft, at Odiham. In August, however, Pilot Officer Rafter and Flying Officer Hallam answered Fighter Command's call for volunteers, leaving Odiham on 22 August, bound for 7 OTU at Hawarden where they were taught to fly Spitfires. Ian Hallam was an experienced airman, with over 500 flying hours on single-engined types already, including six on Spitfires. At Hawarden the student pilots recorded just fifteen hours flying on Spitfires. Upon conclusion of the course, the young and inexperienced Pilot Officer Rafter was posted to 603 Squadron at Hornchurch, while the comparatively infinitely more experienced Flying Officer Hallam was sent north, away from the combat zone, to fly Spitfires with 610 Squadron. Before Hallam was posted to 222 Squadron on 1 October, he would have recorded another 21.05 hours on Spitfires in his log book. Surely, however, it would have made more sense to send Rafter to 610 Squadron, where he could gain more essential and basic experience? Nonetheless, on 31 August, Pilot Officer Rafter, together with two other former army co-operation pilots, Flying Officer B.R. MacNamara and Pilot Officer F.J. MacPhail, had reported for duty at Hornchurch.

At 09.34 hours on this fine September morning, 603 Squadron was scrambled from Hornchurch, Pilot Officer Rafter making his first flight since having joined the Squadron five days previously. A minute later, a large formation of enemy aircraft crossed the coast at Dungeness, heading for various airfields in Kent. First to engage were Squadron Leader Harry Hogan's 501 Squadron Hurricanes, up from Gravesend and patrolling between Canterbury and the coast. The Squadron reported that thirty Do 17s were escorted by seventy Me 109s, and Hogan's pilots attacked the latter; Pilot Officer Stanislaw Skalski, a Pole, was shot down but baled out, slightly wounded. Over Maidstone the enemy separated into numerous smaller formations, the coherent progress of which the Observer Corps found difficult to track.

41 Squadron's Spitfires had already taken off from Hornchurch, at 09.15 hours, and vectored south. Flying at 27,000 feet, the Spitfires were, for once, above the enemy fighter screen: one flight bounced and mixed it with the Me 109s, while the other crashed through the escorts to attack the bombers. In the ensuing combat, Flight Lieutenant Ryder damaged a 109, Pilot Officer Bennions reported having hit another, which he last saw 'streaming glycol and going down eight miles south of Maidstone', and Sergeant Carr-Lewty destroyed a 109 which crashed into a wood near Canterbury. Flight Lieutenant Webster hit two other 109s, one in the engine and another which burst into flames, although neither were seen to crash; Webster then hit another 109 which rolled over and went in near Maidstone. Flying Officer Boyle caught a 109 attacking two Spitfires, and promptly set the enemy machine on fire, while Squadron Leader Hood and Pilot Officer Wallens managed to penetrate the escorts and damage Do 17s.

Seconds after 41 Squadron tally ho'd, 603 Squadron joined the fray. There were now over 100 fighters involved in a huge dogfight over Kent – which, considering that Pilot Officer Rafter's experience to date comprised dull army co-operation and a handful of training flights, must have been bewildering; the young pilot later described his experience in a letter to his mother, Lady Rafter:

Well I was over Kent at a little over 25,000 feet... when I sighted a huge formation of Jerries. I very nearly shot a Spitfire down by mistake, but then saw on my starboard side, underneath me, an Me 109. I got all fixed and started my dive on the 109 and was nearing it when I saw in my mirror a couple of 109s on my tail. Well, I took what evasive action I could, but found two a bit of a problem. I started to get away from them when my tail must have been damaged as all movement on the control column was to no avail, thus putting my machine out of control. By this time I had a little piece of shrapnel in my leg, and probably owe my life to the fact that my machine was out of control as the Jerries evidently found difficulty in getting their sights on me as my machine was going all over the place. Luckily I was very high up and it then occurred to me to bale out. My oxygen tube had already become detached, but I had great difficulty in undoing the pin of my harness to loosen myself out of my seat. I eventually got the pin out, but could not get out of the aircraft. By this time the Jerries had ceased firing at me, but I had no idea where I was over. The next part of my experience was rather a miracle. The machine's nose dropped violently, thus having the effect of throwing me forward, the force so great that I went through the canopy, thus injuring my head. You can't imagine my surprise! I was then at about 15,000 feet and floating about in the air rather like a cork. You will understand why when I explain that instead of diving at 400 mph, I had rapidly slowed down to about 180 mph as the human body never falls faster, that being the terminal velocity. I then felt so light that I had to look to ensure that I was wearing a parachute. Luckily I had given it an inspection that morning. I pulled the cord and the chute opened up and I breathed once more.

Now the most terrifying experience happened. I floated down, right through the aerial battle that was taking place. I came through it without a scratch, but then I noticed a 109 coming towards me, and you have no idea what a damned fool you feel suspended in mid-air with an enemy fighter buzzing around you.

Well he never fired at me, as a Spitfire came along and drove him off; whether he would have done or not cannot be said. Next worry was where I was going to land as there were a lot of trees near. I avoided them and landed in a nice field. My Spitfire, which was new, crashed into a ploughed field some way away. The LDV accosted me with a shotgun as I was wearing my RAF battledress which must have confused them a bit. I was treated by a local first aid post and then taken to hospital.

The Me 109 'buzzing' the defenceless Pilot Officer Rafter had been seen off by another Spitfire of 603 Squadron. Pilot Officer Jerry 'Stapme' Stapleton:

I was diving to attack the bombers when I was engaged by two Me 109s. When I fired at the first one I noticed glycol coming from his radiator. I did a No 2 attack and as I fired was hit by bullets from another 109. I broke off downwards and continued my dive. At 6,000 feet I saw a single-engined machine diving vertically with no tail unit (author's note: Rafter's Spitfire). I looked up and saw a parachutist coming down circled by an Me 109. I attacked him (the 109) from the low quarter; he dived vertically for the ground then flattened out at ground level. I then did a series of beam attacks from both sides, and the enemy aircraft turned into my attacks. He finally forced landed. He tried to set his radio on fire by taking off his jacket and setting fire to it and putting it into the cockpit. He was prevented by the LDV.

The Me 109 pilot concerned was *Oberleutnant* Franz von Werra, the *Gruppenadjutant* of II/JG 3, who was captured at Loves Farm, Winchett Hill, Marden. A flamboyant character who had recently appeared in the German press posing with his pet lion cub, 'Simba', Von Werra later achieved notoriety as the only German prisoner to escape from Allied custody. Returning to combat flying, von Werra scored further successes over Russia and promoted to command I/JG 53. On 25 October 1941, however, he was routinely patrolling off the Dutch coast and went to a watery grave in the North Sea following an engine failure.

After the action on 5 September, Pilot Officer Rafter was hospitalized due to his head injury. On 11 October, his elder brother, Charles, was sadly killed in a flying accident at Stradishall; Rafter returned to 603 Squadron at Hornchurch a week after the Battle of Britain was decreed to have ended, but, on his first subsequent flight, on 29 November, his Spitfire inexplicably fell out of formation and crashed at Sutton Vallence, Kent, killing the pilot. Squadron Leader George Denholm:

> After an action the Squadron never returned to base as a cohesive unit, but in ones and twos. Therefore the only witnesses to Rafter's crash would have been whoever happened to be flying with him, if anyone. We were not high enough to be using oxygen, so failure of that life-supporting system was not responsible for the crash.

Pilot Officer Peter Olver:

> I do remember Rafter, mostly I expect because of the horror I felt at him having flown into the deck for no apparent reason. In those days if a pilot failed to return, you could usually be 100% certain that an Me 109 had sneaked up unseen, but during this operation there had been no such enemy fighters in the area.

The most likely explanation for Pilot Officer Rafter's demise, his sister, Mrs Elizabeth Barwell, felt was that 'he was so keen generally, and wanted to avenge our brother's death, that he returned to operational duties far too soon. I strongly suspect that his head wound was insufficiently healed and that on the day he crashed and was killed Robin simply blacked out.' Lady Rafter never really recovered from the death of her sons in 1940; the Rafter brothers were buried with their father at Harborne church.

Returning to the action over Kent on 5 September 1940, while Air Vice-Marshal Park's fighters were engaged further forward, 12 Group was called upon to protect the sector stations north of the Thames. At 09.47 hours, therefore, Squadron Leader Phillip Pinkham led eleven Spitfires of his 19 Squadron up from Fowlmere, with orders to patrol Hornchurch at 15,000 feet. Over the patrol area, Sergeant Jennings tally ho'd forty Do 17s escorted by forty Me 109s, approaching from the east and over the Thames Estuary. As Jennings had the enemy in sight, he led the Squadron towards them, until Squadron Leader Pinkham had the Germans in sight, ordering 'A' Flight to attack the fighters and 'B' the bombers. As the latter climbed to attack from the rear and in pairs, Flying Officer Walter 'Farmer' Lawson, Blue Two, lost sight of Blue One, Squadron Leader Pinkham, in the sun's glare. Lawson attacked the rearmost vic of Do 17s, noting bits breaking off one of his targets; Blue Two was then hit from behind by cannon fire, an unseen assailant causing serious damage to Spitfire N3286. Fortunately Flying Officer Lawson managed to nurse his aircraft back to base, while Blue Three, Pilot Officer Arthur Vokes, chased an Me 110 out to sea.

Black Section also managed to attack the bombers before attracting the escorting fighters' attentions and mixing it with the 109s. Green Section's experience was similar, although Green One, Flying Officer Haines, turned sharply so that the Me 109s overtook him, enabling him to latch on to a 109's tail. Haines then pursued this enemy fighter at tree-top height across Kent. Over Ashford the 109 was fatally damaged, the pilot, *Unteroffizier* Franz Hotzelmann, climbing to 800 feet before baling out; his 1/JG 54 machine, white nine, crashed into the rear of 6 Hardy Street, Maidstone, burying itself deep beneath the lawn and exploding. Fortunately the occupants were sheltering in a cellar and so escaped unhurt. Hotzelmann, however, landed heavily in the grounds of Melbourne House, breaking both legs.

Flight Lieutenant Brian Lane had climbed 'A' Flight in line astern, desperately trying to reach the Me 109s, which were 5,000 feet above and already diving out of the sun to bounce 'B' Flight. Lane's Spitfires were climbing into the sun, however, and were blinded by the intense glare, losing sight of their quarry. In spite of searching over Kent for fifteen minutes, 'A' Flight's contact was over.

Squadron Leader Phillip Pinkham failed to return from this engagement. Later, his Spitfire, P9422, was identified as the British fighter down in remote countryside near the village of Birling in Kent. The Squadron was informed

The Polish Sergeant Josef Jeka, a Hurricane pilot with 238 Squadron, pictured in spring 1941. A successful fighter pilot, he was decorated with the DFM by the RAF and with both the Virtuti Militari and Cross of Valour by his own people.

that their CO had attempted to bale out, but, no doubt due to wounds to his chin, chest and hip, only managed to do so when too low for his parachute to deploy. The 25-year-old officer, who had already earned an AFC for his work with the Meteorological Flight, was buried at St Andrew's, Kingsbury, London. Air Vice-Marshal Leigh-Mallory wrote to the pilot's parents, commenting that, 'In him I feel that the service has lost an exceptionally promising young officer.'

At Fowlmere, there was sadness at Squadron Leader Pinkham's death but jubilation when the popular Brian Lane was promoted to squadron leader and given command of 19 Squadron. It was Brian Lane, of course, who had led the Squadron into action time and time again during the Dunkirk fighting, after Squadron Leader Stephenson had been shot down and captured during 19 Squadron's first engagement over the French coast, and this exceptional fighter pilot and leader had continued to do so after Squadron Leader Pinkham took command, the new CO being pre-occupied with evaluating the experimental cannon-armed Spitfires. Flying Officer Frank Brinsden:

> Many of us felt that Brian should have got the Squadron after Stephenson was shot down, but instead command was given to Pinkham, an outsider who had no combat experience whatsoever. This made no sense to us at all, but Brian, as ever, just got on with his job as commander of 'A' Flight and not once complained or indicated anything other than 100% support for the new CO. At that time, promotion was all about seniority in the air force list, not about actual experience. This is why officers from other commands were able to lead fighter squadrons in 1940. It was a stupid and short-sighted system which fortunately disappeared, by and large, as the war progressed. For my part, I expected to succeed Brian as commander of 'A' Flight, as I had been his deputy, but instead he selected 'Farmer' Lawson from 'B' Flight. I was bitterly disappointed and regret to say that this was evident in my attitude. The result was that I received a formal dressing down from Brian, but he delivered this in such a way as to enhance my respect for him.

On that day, three replacement pilots who had arrived at Fowlmere straight from OTU two days previously were posted elsewhere – 19 Squadron, now heavily involved in operational flying and combat, was just too busy to take on 'sprogs'. Instead they were sent to Coltishall, to join 616 Squadron, which was rebuilding after the disastrous spell at Kenley; among them was Pilot Officer James Edgar 'Johnnie' Johnson, who would end the war as the RAF's top scoring fighter pilot. Pilot Officer Johnnie Johnson:

> The phone rang and the adjutant picked up the receiver.
> 'They've found the CO. Probably dead when he crashed.'
> For a moment he brooded.
> 'Well, good luck with 616.'

The day saw an endless round of patrols for Fighter Command. Having already flown two sorties, 222 Squadron was re-fuelling when Hornchurch was attacked again that afternoon. Frantically scrambling, Pilot Officer Scott destroyed two Me 110s and Sergeant Chipping probably destroyed another before being shot down and killed over Dover, possibly by anti-aircraft fire.

10 Group had also been called upon to reinforce Air Vice-Marshal Park's fighters. Up from Middle Wallop, inland of Southampton, 234 Squadron's Spitfires found themselves in action some distance away from home, over the Isle of Sheppey. The Squadron arrived in time to attack seven Me 109s, which had pounced on a Hurricane squadron. Pilot Officer Bob Doe:

> I dived down and fired at the leading enemy aircraft, but my bullets went behind him. I saw them enter the second 109 and then the third burst into flames and blew up. I went right between the rest.
>
> I was then attacked by the remainder who left the Hurricanes. I did tight turns with three shooting at me and three above me who came down in their turn. I half-rolled down, round the edge of the balloons, went through a pall of smoke above the burning oil tanks at full boost and at nought feet, weaving up a river.

Short of fuel, Pilot Officer Doe landed at Kenley. The Me 109 he had destroyed was a machine belonging to 7/JG 53, which had also been shot up by Flight Lieutenant Pat Hughes, of the same Squadron, and two Hurricane pilots of 46 Squadron. Hughes and Pilot Officer Zurakowski pursued a 9/JG 53 Me 109 from Sheppey, south-west across Kent and into East Sussex, until forcing the enemy fighter to ditch in the Channel twelve miles off Hastings. Pilot Officer Michael Appleby:

> Throughout August and early September, we of 609 Squadron, operating from Warmwell in the Middle Wallop Sector of 10 Group, were usually patrolling Brooklands, Guildford and other areas west of London in support of 11 Group. We generally harried the stragglers who had dropped their bombs and were on the way home. Things do happen fast at 20,000 feet in the air, collision speeds at well over 600 mph, so it is not surprising that with all that space around you it was not always possible to locate the enemy. Even if you did, they might be so far away that by the time you caught them up something else had happened in between. Nonetheless, if we did catch them we attacked, and the Squadron had quite a lot of success.
>
> On the airfield, dispersal points not only split the aircraft up but enabled them to take-off a little more easily from three separate taxying points. The strain of waiting at dispersal was greatly emphasised by the field telephone; every time the phone rang everyone just stopped, until the operator answering would shout out 'Sergeant so and so required in Sick Quarters', at which point we all promptly relaxed. On the other hand, if it was a scramble, we all rushed to our aircraft, preceded by the fitter and rigger, popped into the aircraft, set our parachute harness and did up our safety harness, quite tight, too.

Having set the throttle mixture and airscrew pitch controls, the fitter operated the starter battery and the engine started. Whilst taxying out to the take-off point down wind, we adopted our position in the formation previously decided.

As I have mentioned, we did give back up to 11 Group over London, but we also patrolled Portsmouth, intercepting raids coming across the Channel. In this way, we managed to intercept six Do 215 bombers intending to cause damage in Portsmouth, so we chased them back across the sea. Since they were protected by fighters I led my Section off to one side, intending to do a beam attack, which would probably be safer than attacking from the rear where their rear gunners could concentrate their fire. It was therefore somewhat galling to find that, having pressed on to get in the best position, the two aircraft that should have been with me had already turned and were attacking the Dorniers. I managed to get into position and join them. We managed to bring two of them down, one of which turned back to land in England, realizing that without engines he wasn't going to get far across the Channel. On this occasion I was credited with 1/6th of an aircraft, the other section of three also having been involved in the action and it being impossible to sort out who did what.

Also, I must not forget the time when the invasion was supposed to be imminent, church bells ringing, and we were all sitting in our aircraft awaiting a mass attack; nothing happened!

Friday 6 September There were three major raids during the day. The first came in at 08.40 hours, aimed again at southern airfields but no significant damage was caused. Among the enemy's targets was the airfield at Farnborough, in Hampshire, again another indication that Luftwaffe intelligence was often wanting, given that this was not a Fighter Command aerodrome. Nonetheless, 10 Group's 234 Squadron intercepted the raid, which was escorted by the whole of JG 26, led by Major Adolf Galland. Two Spitfires were quickly dispatched: Sergeant W.H. Hornby baled out with facial burns, but Pilot Officer W.G. Gordon was killed. The Spitfires, however, bounced 7/JG 26, which lost three Me 109s: *Oberleutnant* Hans Christinecke was captured and *Gefreiters* Peter Holzapfel were killed.

The day's second raid, at 13.00 hours, also failed to cause substantial damage. The oil tanks at Thameshaven, bombed the previous day, were still ablaze and belching black smoke, however, attracting the third and final raid at 18.00 hours. The fires were stoked accordingly with high explosive, and continued to burn fiercely.

By now, the situation for Fighter Command was critical. Airfields in 11 Group were under constant attack; although none had been rendered non-operational for more than a few hours, runways were becoming increasingly cratered and general damage was increasing. Moreover, and most importantly, Fighter Command was stretched through having to provide constant standing patrols and responding to threats several times or more every day. Both pilots and aircraft were flying long hours, and both needed rest. Corporal Bob Morris:

On 6 September 1940, *Hauptmann* Hubertus von Bonin of 1/JG 54 damaged a Spitfire over
the Channel which subsequently forced-landed near Calais. Pilot Officer James Caistor of 603
Squadron was captured, and his Spitfire, X4260, was evaluated by the enemy. Here enemy airmen
inspect that Spitfire shortly after Caistor was brought down.

From a ground viewpoint we had to learn very quickly about air raids which were coming
in thick and fast. Once I looked up and saw five parachutes descending. We of No 66
Squadron were now dispersed around the edge of the aerodrome at Kenley, with plenty
of space to work between the aircraft. We could not put the aircraft either in a hangar
or in a group for fear of them being wiped out together. This meant that we had to work
on them out in the open, often without any cover when a raid came in. They had built
some blast pens at Kenley, but nowhere near enough, so you could be quarter of a mile
from a shelter. It is perhaps surprising but you got used to it, almost blasé about it, in
fact. We used to carry on working after the siren had gone, right up until the Germans
were practically overhead. If you then left your aircraft and lay down on the ground some
distance away from it, the chances of being killed by a bomb were remote. Strafing was a
bit more hazardous, but the greatest problem was bomb-blast, i.e. what it actually threw
into the air. If it exploded near a road, building or runway then huge slabs and chunks
of concrete and masonry could come falling down on you. You therefore tended to lie
there and keep your fingers crossed that when all the rubbish thrown up came down, it
didn't hit you.

Pilot Officer David Crook: 'Whilst aircraft losses were quickly made good, experienced pilots could never be replaced. You could only train the new ones as best you could, keep them out of trouble as much as possible in the air and hope that they would live long enough to gain some experience. Sometimes they did.'

Such things were at the forefront of Air Chief Marshal Dowding's mind, who organized a conference at his headquarters, Bentley Priory, to decide measures to be taken to 'go downhill' in the most economical manner, thus permitting a rapid climb back. Dowding's current policy was to concentrate strength in 11 Group, which was reinforced by 10 and 12 Group whenever appropriate. When losses decreed, individual squadrons in 11 Group were replaced by fresher units from other groups, but the scale of fighting and losses now meant that this process could not be maintained indefinitely: soon there would be no 'fresh' squadrons available, as all would have been rotated and suffered casualties accordingly, and of course the OTU fresh pilots had no combat experience.

Shockingly, Dowding's SASO, Air Vice-Marshal Evill, had provided figures indicating that in the four weeks ending 4 September, casualties totaled 338;

An oft-used and posed photograph of 41 Squadron, pictured at Hornchurch shortly after the Battle of Britain, although rarely are all pilots identified; they are, from left, standing on Spitfire: P/Os H.C. Baker, D.A. Adams & F.J. Aldridge, Sgt E.V. Darling, P/O J.N. MacKenzie & F/L A.D.J. Lovell; standing, from left: P/O D.E. Mileham, F/L E.N. Ryder, Sgt R.A. Angus, S/L D.O. Finlay, Sgts T.W.R. Healy & J.S. Gilders, and POs E.P. Wells & R.C. Ford.

in that same period, the OTUs had only produced 280 pilots. Air Vice-Marshal Park confirmed that the shortage of pilots was critical: 11 Group alone was now suffering 100 casualties a week. The DCAS, Air Vice-Marshal Sholto Douglas, however, always eager to oppose Dowding, stated that the Commander-in-Chief was being overly 'pessimistic', but 'Stuffy', ever forthright, insisted that the DCAS '*must* see that we *are* going *downhill*'. As ever it was Air Chief Marshal Dowding and Air Vice-Marshal Park who came up with the solution at this 'going downhill conference': the Stabilising Scheme.

This designated fighter squadrons either 'A', 'B' or 'C' units. 'A' squadrons were those in the front line and maintained with an establishment of sixteen operational and combat ready pilots; 'B' were those being rested but with six combat ready pilots among their total of sixteen, and which could therefore be called upon in emergencies; 'C' squadrons were those unlikely to be called upon since they were rebuilding to strength having suffered significant casualties in the combat zone, indeed, their quota of operational pilots was a mere three. The requirement for 'A' squadrons in 11 Group to have sixteen operational pilots, however, meant that when units were withdrawn to quieter sectors to rest and refit, any pilots who had only recently arrived on the Squadron were immediately re-posted to another of Air Vice-Marshal Park's units. Pilot Officer Richard Jones:

I was posted to 64 Squadron at Kenley straight from OTU in June 1940, meaning that I was fortunately able to gain more Spitfire experience before the Battle of Britain really got going. Squadron Leader MacDonnell tried to give us battle practice whenever time allowed. We were paired off with a battle-experienced pilot to practise dog-fighting and yet more dog-fighting, to give us both experience in battle conditions and confidence in the Spitfire. I was lucky. Had I been posted to 64 Squadron later in the summer of 1940, there would just not have been the time for this extra-curricular training.

I well remember my first operational engagement with the enemy. We were about nine Spitfires against 30–40 enemy fighters. Before meeting them I had butterflies in my stomach, wondering what to expect. When they were spotted we waded into them and once engaged all fear disappeared – we immediately realised it was them or us – all hell appeared to be let loose with aircraft everywhere. The next moment, as so often happened, we were alone and the sky was empty. In fact, in the panic of my first engagement I don't think I even fired a shot, as it appeared to take all of my concentration just to avoid a collision. I felt that it was the most valuable experience that I had ever received in my life. I returned to base a more mature individual and felt extremely lucky to have survived to tell the tale.

On August 19th, we were relieved at Kenley, operating thereafter from Leconfield, in 12 Group. A month later, however, some bright spark at the Air Ministry must have decided that I was still had my wits about me and didn't need a rest, so I was posted to 19 Squadron at Fowlmere, also in 12 Group, but which was still an 'A' squadron.

At 12 Group headquarters, at Hucknall in Nottinghamshire, Air Vice-Marshal Leigh-Mallory was also issuing orders to his fighters as to how the battle was to be conducted from here on. Essentially this concerned the report submitted by Squadron Leader Bader after 242 Squadron's combat over Hatfield on 30 August; the Group Commander agreed with Bader's theory that if 12 Group arrived in the combat area with a large number of fighters then more damage could be exacted upon the enemy. Bader had suggested that three fighter squadrons should operate from Duxford in concert, as a 'wing', and Air Vice-Marshal Leigh-Mallory, seeing this as an opportunity to get 12 Group more action, supported this idea. Consequently, on 6 September, orders were issued from Hucknall to the effect that 242 Squadron, although still based at Coltishall, would operate from Duxford on a daily basis and fly with 19 and 310 Squadrons, and so the so-called 'Big Wing' was born. Squadron Leader Douglas Blackwood:

> The Big Wing thing was all started by Douglas Bader who, of course, had a Cranwell background, and so he naturally became leader. He also had the support of the Duxford Sector Controller and Station Commander, Wing Commander Woodhall. Douglas was an extremely brave and inspirational chap; we are, of course, talking about a man without legs who not only flew fighters but played squash and had a very low golf handicap! His pilots of No 242 Squadron would have followed him anywhere. At Duxford in 1940, we never did any practice sorties as a Wing, we just went off on an operational patrol one day with Douglas leading.

It is important to appreciate that this so-called 'Duxford Wing' was really an experiment, more a case of patrolling in strength. Indeed, in 1940, the TR9 radio sets in use were so limited that communications were restricted to a single squadron operating on a given frequency and able to talk only to each other and sector control. It was not even possible, therefore, for Squadron Leader Bader to communicate in the air with all three squadrons. Nonetheless, the 12 Group squadrons welcomed this new initiative, and the Duxford Wing flew its first patrol on 6 September, when at 08.50 hours it was ordered to patrol Hornchurch and North Weald. The sortie was uneventful, as was an identical patrol a short while later. The ORB of 19 Squadron, however, recorded that being on patrol with so many friendly fighters was 'most comforting indeed'.

4

NEMESIS:
7 SEPTEMBER – 30 SEPTEMBER 1940

On Saturday 7 September, the Battle of Britain entered its penultimate and most critical phase – for both defender and attacker. In the previous phase, the Luftwaffe had concentrated on Fighter Command airfields in southern England and targets connected with the aircraft industry. Although success against the latter was negligible, this phase of battle had exhausted Fighter Command, for which the whole situation was becoming increasingly critical. Why, then, did Göring yet again change direction?

On the night of 24/25 August, German bombers intending to attack Rochester and Thameshaven unintentionally bombed central London. In his Karinhall memorandum of 19 August, Göring had reserved the personal right to exclusively order raids on London and Liverpool. The *Reichsmarschall* was furious when he learned that bombs had been dropped on the British capital without his authority, immediately requiring reports identifying the crews responsible, promising that each aircraft captain would be punished and 'posted to infantry regiments'. Churchill was determined to 'return the compliment… upon Berlin', and so that next night saw Bomber Command send fifty Hampdens and Wellingtons to Berlin. The target, however, was covered in cloud and bombs largely fell harmlessly in countryside south of the German capital. Two people were injured in a Berlin suburb and a chalet was destroyed. The effect on German morale was shocking: Göring had assured them that such a thing just would not happen, that it was just not possible for the RAF to bomb Germany; the people believed him, but now they were both stunned and disillusioned.

Hitler was furious. On 4 September, he addressed a gathering at the launch of the *Winterhilfe* campaign, held at the Sportspalast in Berlin-Schöneberg. RAF airmen, he said, had not the courage or tenacity required to fly across the North Sea and bomb Germany by daylight, but only did so by night, protected by a cloak of darkness, their bombs being dropped indiscriminately on residential areas, farmhouses and villages. The Führer continued:

Left: Pictured at Castletown in Scotland before 504 Squadron moved south, Sergeant Denis Helcke destroyed an He 111 on 7 September 1940, but was killed ten days later when his Hurricane spun out of control during practice attacks over Faversham.

Below: Flight Lieutenant Pat Hughes DFC, an Australian Spitfire pilot with 234 Squadron. During the Battle of Britain Hughes claimed the destruction of seven enemy aircraft before his death in action over London on 7 September 1940; he was a 23-year-old married man.

You will understand that we must now reply, night for night and with increasing force. And if the British air force drops two, three or four thousand kilos of bombs, then we will drop 150,000, 180,000, 230,000, 300,000 or 400,000 kilos, or more, in one night. If they declare that they will attack our cities on a large-scale, we will erase theirs! We will put a stop to the game of these night-pirates, as God is our witness.

At a stage in the Battle of Britain when the Luftwaffe was actually making significant progress, Hitler now ordered Göring to attack London itself. The Führer refused Göring's request to focus upon the airfields around London, demanding that the capital itself should now become the exclusive focus of the Luftwaffe's assault. Soon after the war, at the Nuremburg Trials, Göring wrote that:

I considered the attacks on London useless, and I told the Führer again and again that inasmuch as I knew the English people as well as I did my own people, I could never force them to their knees by attacking London. We might have been able to subdue the Dutch people by such measures, but never the British.

The *Luftwaffe War Diaries*, however, do not entirely support Göring's claim, and he, in fact, took personal control of the battle's direction from this point onwards. On 3 September, he had met with his *Luftflotten* commanders, *Feldmarschalls* Albert Kesselring and Hugo Sperrle, and 'pressed the view that the current tactical policy should now be abandoned in favour of a large-scale assault on the most important target – the English capital'. Sperrle, however, did not accept Göring's view that the enemy fighter force had become too weak to resist such an attack, and that the current pressure on Fighter Command's airfields should be maintained. Kesselring was unable to understand why Air Chief Marshal Dowding had not withdrawn his fighters north, beyond German fighter range, but believed that Fighter Command must have surely reached this point by now. However, it was clear that the RAF would not be destroyed on the ground, and so the enemy chiefs agreed that the only option was to 'force their last reserves of Spitfires and Hurricanes into the air'. London, it was felt, was the only target likely to provoke this required reaction.

Göring also remained frustrated with his fighter pilots, blaming them, and them alone, for the fact that Fighter Command remained undefeated. In fact, so cock-eyed was Luftwaffe intelligence regarding the disposition of Air Chief Marshal Dowding's order of battle, that the enemy Commander-in-Chief was even beginning to doubt his fighter pilots' combat claims (which were, in fact, infinitely more accurate, overall, than Fighter Command's). Shortly after his train's arrival in the Pas-de-Calais, the *Reichsmarschall* sent for *Oberst* Werner Mölders and Major Adolf Galland, haranguing and blaming them personally for the *jagdwaffe's* perceived failure to date. Upon conclusion of this forty minute tirade, Goring asked his two favourite *kommodoren* what he could do to improve the capability of their units. Mölders asked for the new DB 601N engine, which performed better at high altitude than the power plant currently fitted to the basic Me 109E-4. Galland, however, asked for his *jagdgeschwader* to be re-equipped with Spitfires! Göring was beside himself with rage, missing the point completely: because of a lower wing loading, the Spitfire could easily reduce speed and turn at low speed; the Me 109's advantage was flying straight and level, climbing and diving, meaning that the German fighter pilots were unable to turn tight enough at low speed to always see their charges. Galland's point was that the Spitfire was, therefore, much better suited to bomber escort work than the Me 109. From this point onwards, relations between the enemy Commander-in-Chief and his fighter arm deteriorated, not least because Göring now insisted that the fighters would remain closely shackled to the bombers at all times. Gone, so far as the *jagdfliegern* was concerned, was the advantage of initiative and surprise afforded by *freie hunten*, and they were now being forced to undertake a role alien to their psyche as hunters and contrary to the intended function of their machines. And so the Battle of Britain entered yet another phase.

Hurricane pilots of 43 Squadron pictured outside the Officers' Mess at Tangmere on 7 September 1940. From left, standing: P/Os H.C. Upton, A.E.A. van den Hove d'Ertsenrijk (Belgian) & D. Gorrie; seated, from left: P/O S. Carey (adjutant), F/L J.I. Kilmartin, S/L George Lott (who lost an eye in combat on 9 July 1940), F/L R.C. Reynell and S/L C.B. Hull DFC (South African). Just three hours later, Dick Reynell and Caesar Hull were both killed in action, and Albert van den Hove d'Ertsenrijk perished in combat on 15 September. David Gorrie was killed in a collision during 1941.

Saturday 7 September Fighter Command, of course, had no idea that the course of Göring's assault was about to change tack, and as dawn broke anticipated a continuation of the attacks against 11 Group's airfields.

Following the odd reconnaissance aircraft stooging about over various parts of the British Isles, the first attack came in at 11.00 hours, although this gave no indication of what lay ahead. Some seventy enemy aircraft crossed the coast at Folkestone and separated, one formation flying along the coast to Hastings, the remainder fanning out over East Kent. Dover and the forward fighter airfield at Hawkinge were dive-bombed: at 11.26 hours, two waves of bomb-carrying Me 109 *jabos* attacked Hawkinge, leaving behind them fifteen more craters near the Officers' Mess. The enemy withdrew, leaving the radar screens devoid of plots for six puzzling hours, and having given no indication whatsoever that the emphasis of attacks was about to drastically change.

At 15.54 hours the first plots appeared over the Pas-de-Calais, rapidly followed by an unprecedented number which made perfectly clear that this was the biggest challenge faced so far. On the cliffs at Cap Gris Nez, near Calais, *Reichsmarschall* Göring and his entourage watched excitedly as 348 bombers – five complete *kampfgeschwadern* in total – escorted by 617 fighters passed overhead. This massive formation of nearly 1,000 aircraft occupied a staggering twenty mile front, was stepped up a mile-and-a half high and spread out over 800 square miles, wave upon wave heading for London.

At 16.17 hours, eleven squadrons were scrambled in 11 Group, and by 16.30 hours all of Air Vice-Marshal Park's fighters were up. Assistance was called for from 10 and 12 Groups, the size of the enemy formation alone suggesting to Air Chief Marshal Dowding and Air Vice-Marshal Park that London was the target.

Pilot Officer Bob Doe: 'After 234 Squadron was scrambled from Middle Wallop, I climbed like mad in an attempt to avoid the trauma of the previous two raids where I had been at a disadvantage from the very start, and managed to reach London at a reasonable altitude where I could have a go at the bombers on my terms.'

Among the RAF fighters speeding to intercept this enormous *Valhalla*, was Squadron Leader Bader and the Duxford Wing, which had been scrambled from Duxford at 16.45 hours, vectored to Debden and North Weald at angels 10. Bader, however, climbed the twelve Duxford fighters to 15,000 feet, and over North Weald saw anti-aircraft fire to the east and a phalanx of enemy bombers 5,000 feet higher, their fighter escort being another 5,000 feet higher still. Having sighted this raid, which was attacking Thameshaven, Squadron Leader Bader informed Wing Commander Woodhall, the Duxford Sector Controller, and was given permission to engage. The Duxford Wing was in a most unfavourable tactical position, having to climb furiously. This factor alone prevented an attack in strength being pressed home, but as the Me 109s rained down upon them, 242 Squadron attacked the enemy bombers. 242 Squadron Combat Report:

Red One (S/Ldr DRS Bader) on sighting e/a opened full throttle and boost, and climbed and turned left to cut off enemy and arrived with Red Two (Sub-Lt R.J. Cork) only, on the beam slightly in front. S/Ldr Bader gave a very short beam burst at about 100 yards at e/a, which were then flying section of three in line astern in a large rectangle. Then, accompanied by Red Two, gave short bursts at the middle of e/a of back section. The e/a began smoking preparatory to catching fire. S/Ldr Bader did not notice the result, which was later confirmed by P/O Turner as diving down in flames from the back of the bomber formation. At the time of S/Ldr Bader's attack on the Me 110, a yellow-nosed Me 109 was noticed reflected in his mirror and he turned to avoid the e/a. Big bang was heard by him in the cockpit of his Hurricane. An explosive bullet came through the right-hand side of fuselage, touching map case, knocking corner of the undercarriage selector quadrant and finished up against the petrol priming pump. S/Ldr Bader executed a steep diving turn and found a lone Me 110 below him which he attacked from straight astern and above him, and saw e/a go into steepish straight dive finishing in flames in a field just north of railway line turning approximately East (West of Wickford, due North of Thameshaven).

Red Two (Sub-Lt Cork) sighted e/a to the East and above. He climbed to meet e/a and carried out a beam attack on the leading section of bombers, firing at a Do 215 on the tail-end of the formation. Port engine burst into flames after two short bursts and crashed vertically. Red Two was then attacked by e/a from rear and hit a starboard mainplane. He broke away downwards and backwards, nearly colliding head-on with an Me 110. Red Two gave short burst before pulling away and saw front cabin of Me 110 break up and machine go into vertical dive. Two of the crew baled out. Whilst Red Two was following the e/a down, e/a was stalling and diving. An Me 109 attacked Red Two from the rear, one shot from e/a going through Red Two's hood, hitting bottom of reflector sight and bullet proof windscreen. Red Two received a number of glass splinters in his eyes so broke away downwards with a half roll and lost sight of e/a.

The Me 110 destroyed by Bader and Cork crashed at Downham Hill, near Wickford; both crew members were killed. The Squadron's Combat Report continues:

Red Three, P/O Crowley-Milling, flying in vic formation sighted AA fire to East. He climbed to meet e/a and engaged flight of 20 bombers. He fired two second burst at left hand rear bomber and then observed Me 110 just behind the last bomber. He fired four second burst at Me 110, setting port engine on fire and starboard engine smoking. Red Three was then attacked by Me 109, receiving cannon shell in radiator, one in left aileron, and one behind pilot's seat.

Pilot Officer Denis Crowley-Milling:

What the official report doesn't mention is that my windscreen was also shattered by a cannon shell. Fortunately we had armoured glass, which was laminated, a couple of inches thick, which saved my life. I managed to put the Hurricane down at Stow Maries. It was all pretty traumatic but at least I was personally unscathed!

LAC David Evans: 'The 'Crow' was lucky. When we got the Hurricane back home we found a 7.9mm round jammed in the windscreen. The armoured glass, and armour plate, was something else Stuffy Dowding had argued for, many pilots must owe him their lives for this foresight.' The Me 110 that Pilot Officer Crowley-Milling accounted for, jointly with Green Four, Sub-Lieutenant R.E. Gardner, crashed at Little Burstead. Again, the Squadron Combat Report continues:

> Blue One (F/Lt Powell-Sheddon) climbed to 22,000 feet to engage e/a but did not engage for some 10 minutes. He finally chased an Me 109 which was itself chasing a Hurricane. Both swerved in front of Blue One, about 100 yards away. Blue One gave a quick deflection burst at e/a as it passed. E/a turned left and again crossed Blue One's path at same range. Blue One gave another burst and hit e/a's tail. Blue One then got a third burst from above and behind at a range of 50 yards, bullets hitting e/a from which pieces came off. Blue One got into e/a slipstream, ceased fire and got out slightly to one side and fired again at e/a which then hung in the air for a few seconds and then fell forward in a vertical dive, smoke pouring from the starboard wing and fuselage. E/a disappeared into black smoke over Thameshaven.

Meanwhile, as Squadron Leader Brian Lane climbed 19 Squadron's Spitfires, an Me 110, which was being attacked by two Hurricanes of 310 Squadron, flashed in front of 'A' Flight, which, with Lane leading, sped off in pursuit. All five pilots subsequently fired at the hapless 110, which crashed near a railway line, one mile east of Hornchurch. This aircraft belonged to *Stab* II/ZG 2, which was escorting He 111s of KG 53. One crew member was killed when his parachute failed, the other landed safely in a field only to be captured by two elderly women from a nearby house! After the combat, 'A' Flight was split up, so Squadron Leader Lane, Flight Lieutenant Lawson and Sergeant Jennings, having lost contact with the ongoing air battle, returned to Fowlmere.

The other pilots of 19 Squadron, however, were still engaged. Red Three, Pilot Officer Cunningham, blacked out after breaking off the pursuit of the Me 110 destroyed by 'A' Flight, came too and joined up with a squadron of Hurricanes heading south-eastwards. At 17.20 hours, these fighters executed a front-quarter attack on twenty He 111s at 20,000 feet. Pilot Officer Cunningham's Spitfire hurtled through the bombers, in an attempt to break their formation, before singling out a particular Heinkel which caught fire and lost height. After a further attack, Cunningham last saw the raider ten miles inland from Deal, but after only a short burst at another vic of He 111s his ammunition was expended.

After attacking the Me 110 with the rest of 'A' Flight, Flight Sergeant Unwin found himself alone at 4,000 feet. Climbing under full boost to 25,000 feet he

The enemy: *Hauptmann* Herman Kell (right) flying his 3/KG 4 He 111. Kell had participated in the round-the-clock bombing of East India Docks and London on 7 September 1940.

saw 'a Hurricane squadron going somewhere in a hurry' and followed them. Suddenly three separate enemy formations, comprising thirty bombers each, appeared with their inevitable close fighter escort. Flight Sergeant George 'Grumpy' Unwin:

> I was surrounded by Me 109s and ended up fighting a running battle between Ramsgate and west London. The usual fight ensued, during which I definitely hit at least five of them but only two were shot down, both in flames. I then climbed for a breather and shadowed the third enemy formation when I saw a fourth arriving. By this time two of the other three formations had turned north and the other went straight in a westerly direction. The leading formation turned east and I was at 25,000 feet and above them. As there did not appear to be any of their escorts left, I dived on the rear vic and gave them the rest of my ammunition, about 50 rounds in each gun, and from 450, closing to 50 yards range. The bomber at which I fired wobbled a bit but otherwise carried on. Without ammunition I returned to Fowlmere.

When Squadron Leader Bader tally ho'd and led 242 Squadron to attack the bombers, Squadron Leader Blackwood led 310 Squadron in a charge at the enemy fighters. After the initial Squadron attack in line astern, the Czechs were

Sergeant Thorogood of 87 Squadron at immediate readiness at Bibury in August 1940.

split up, acting independently or in pairs. Over Canterbury Sergeant Furst attacked a I/LG 2 Me 109, which, although the pilot managed to bale out, exploded in mid-air; the Czech then struck against an Me 110 of 6/ZG 2 which ditched in the Channel off Birchington.

Caught on the climb by escorting fighters, this had not been a resoundingly successful first engagement for the Duxford Wing. Back at Duxford Squadron Leader Bader fumed that his Wing had been scrambled too late, but research suggests that this is not true. Simple calculations concerning time, speed and distance indicate that there was sufficient time for the Wing to have achieved an appropriate altitude while *en route* to the interception. Pilot Officer 'Teddy' Morton:

> Squadron Leader Bader would frequently telephone Ops 'B' to get the 'form'. At Mess parties he would button-hole me to discuss tactics, the 'Hun in the sun' and all that, and demanded to know why the Wing wasn't scrambled by 11 Group sooner. Alternatively he would insist on speaking to 'Woody' to get scrambles effected.

Feeling that squadrons were scrambled too late was not peculiar to 12 Group, however. Flight Lieutenant Peter Brothers:

I flew Hurricanes with 32 Squadron, and during our time at the coastal aerodromes at Hawkinge and Manston, or even further inland at Biggin Hill, we were often scrambled late. The Controller obviously had to ensure that it was the real thing and not a 'spoof' to get us airborne and catch us whilst refueling. This was frustrating at forward bases as there was so little time anyway.

Squadron Leader Douglas Bader: 'It was windy work, let there be no mistake.'

The Duxford Wing, however, claimed a total of twenty enemy aircraft destroyed, five probables and six damaged, offset against one pilot killed, another badly burned, with two Hurricanes destroyed and two damaged. This was just the kind of statistic that the 'Big Wing' supporters required, and congratulatory telegrams were soon received from Air Vice-Marshal Leigh-Mallory and the Secretary-of-State for Air, Sir Archibald Sinclair. In reality, however, the Duxford Wing had definitely destroyed six enemy aircraft, the confusion being caused by so many pilots being simultaneously engaged. The Wing, therefore, overclaimed by 3:1; this would remain a typical feature of Wing combats, but one that only became apparent after the war when German loss returns were examined.

Air Vice-Marshal Leigh-Mallory accepted Squadron Leader Bader's explanation that the Wing had been caught at a height disadvantage, and both men looked forward to another opportunity for the Duxford Wing to show its mettle.

Air Vice-Marshal Park's squadrons were all engaged over the capital on what became known as 'Black Saturday'. Among them was 222 Squadron, up from Hornchurch. Pilot Officer Laurie Whitbread:

We engaged an enemy formation of Me 109s. I became separated from the rest of the Squadron so I climbed back to my original altitude and flew round looking for a target. I found one in a formation of 25–30 Do 215s, which appeared to have no fighter escort. Keeping in the sun, I dived down on the last aircraft which was straggling behind some 100 yards at the rear of the formation and flying at 20,000 feet. I carried out a quarter attack from the port side (formation was flying westwards along south bank of the Thames at Dartford). I opened fire at 300 yards, range closing rapidly. The starboard engine set on fire and I broke away, the return fire from the rear three gunners and my closing range making it advisable.

Sergeant Basil 'Mike' Bush:

We of 504 Squadron had flown our Hurricanes south from Catterick to Hendon in No 11 Group, arriving on September 5th. I recall that whenever we were at readiness, awaiting the call to scramble, our favourite number was, appropriately, Vera Lynn singing 'In Room Five-hundred-and-four'! On September 7th we intercepted the big raid on London, during which a cannon shell passed through my instrument panel and into the reserve petrol tank beyond. I was damned lucky not to catch fire as petrol splashed all over me. I forced-landed my Hurricane at Eastchurch but, due to repairs being carried out, did not

Personnel of 504 Squadron examine machine-guns from an Me 110 destroyed by the Squadron over the West Country in September 1940. In the pilots' hut at Filton are, from left: Pilot Officer Trevor Parsons, Flight Lieutenant Tony Rook, Sergeant 'Wag' Haw, and an unidentified airman who is probably the orderly clerk.

return to Hendon with my aircraft until September 9th. I was given the next week off and did not fly again until September 17th.

Among the 10 Group squadrons reinforcing 11 Group over London was 152 Squadron. Pilot Officer Roger Hall:

We saw our own fighters, the 11 Group squadrons and some from 12 Group in the Midlands, climbing up from the north. There seemed to be quite a number of us. They too were black dots, climbing in groups of 12, or 36 in wing formation. Most of them were Hurricanes. We were soon engaged with Me 109s, the combat lasting about 15 minutes. When it was over, we were scattered all over Kent. As London blazed, the smoke from the docks being visible for miles, I recalled for a moment Mr Baldwin's prophecy, not a sanguine one, made to the House of Commons some five years before when he said that the bomber would always get through. Now it was doing just that.

Pilot Officer David Crook: 'In the next week or two we (of 609 Squadron) flew up to London almost every day, sometimes twice a day, in order to give the overworked London squadrons a helping hand. They certainly needed it; the weight and intensity of these raids exceeded anything I had seen before.'

On that Saturday, Londoners had witnessed combat on a hitherto unseen scale throughout the short history of aerial warfare to date. Through sheer weight of numbers the Germans had reached their target, starting huge fires in the docklands and East End. Vast areas were devastated and nearly 1,800 Londoners lost their lives. Late that evening Air Vice-Marshal Park was airborne over the blazing capital in his personal Hurricane, 'OK1'. It was a sight that the tough New Zealander would vividly remember. Air Vice-Marshal Keith Park: 'It was burning all down the river. It was a horrid sight. But I looked down and said, 'Thank God for that,' because I knew that the Nazis had switched their attack from our fighter stations, thinking they were knocked out. They weren't, but they were pretty groggy.'

The day's action had cost the Luftwaffe forty aircraft, but Fighter Command had lost twenty-seven, with fourteen more pilots killed. Among the dead were more experienced and irreplaceable pilots, including Flight Lieutenant Richard Carew Reynell, the Hawker test pilot who flew as a flight commander in 43 Squadron, which also lost its CO, Squadron Leader Caesar Hull. Also among the dead was the Australian Flight Lieutenant Pat Hughes of 234 Squadron, who had only got married the previous month; 242 Squadron had a missing Canadian, Pilot Officer John Benzie, who was destined to lie undiscovered and buried with the wreckage of his Hurricane until 1980, as was 257 Squadron's Flight Lieutenant Hugh Beresford, who was entombed on the Isle of Sheppey until found by aviation archaeologists in 1979.

As the fires lit up the night sky, the enemy bombers came back, carrying out a massive attack which lasted from 20.10 hours to 04.30 hours the following morning. The bombers flew in shuttles, back and forth across the Channel, the fires burning so brightly that sophisticated navigation aids were not required. The RAF's nocturnal defences, however, were in their infancy: airborne interception radar had yet to be perfected and so the raiders were able to operate at night with impunity. By day the enemy assault had switched to London, and so too had the night blitz begun in earnest.

Sunday 8 September Following the previous day's exertions both sides were exhausted. Unsurprisingly, therefore, there was little action on this day, which enabled Air Chief Marshal Dowding to rotate his squadrons. 43 Squadron, leaderless and decimated, was pulled out of the line, being replaced at Tangmere by 607 Squadron. Pilot Officer Harry Welford:

I shall always remember September 8th, 1940, because it was the day after the evening that Betty Elise and I became engaged, but our move to Tangmere was confirmed that day. We were to relieve 43 Squadron, which had barely half the intended complement of pilots left capable of operational duties. Of course it was a tragedy so far as my fiancée was concerned and, though I felt the same, there was a war to be fought and we were trained

607 'County of Durham' Squadron of the Auxiliary Air Force flew south to Tangmere on 8 September 1940, relieving the battered remnants of 43 Squadron. Initially roughly handled by the enemy, as were so many squadrons during the period of adjustment to the increased tempo of combat, 607 ultimately gave a good account. 'A' Flight is pictured here at Tangmere; from left: Sgt Anderson & F/S Atkin (armourers), Sgts R.A. Spyer and W.G. Cunnington, Sgts Fort (engine fitter) & Ventham (rigger), F/L W.F. Blackadder (flight commander), F/O M.M. Irving, P/O Watson (Intelligence Officer) & P/O M.R. Ingle-Finch.

fighters. This was the beginning of the end, and, as we all climbed into our Hurricanes, having bid our adieus that fine Sunday morning, I wondered how many of us would see Usworth or Newcastle again. Strange as it may seem, dirty, smoky old Newcastle was suddenly a seventh heaven compared to the green fields of southern England.

We arrived at a completely blitzed aerodrome and were greeted by the remains of 43 Squadron, some on crutches, others with arms in slings, and yet another with his head swathed in bandages having had his face torn by an exploding enemy cannon shell. Though they had so many casualties it was amazing to see them walking about. Needless to say, they were very pleased to see us, having just been up on the third sortie of the day and waiting for news of their latest casualties. We only had time to refuel before being called upon to fly an operational patrol that evening. There was no interception and no casualties.

At night the enemy bombers returned to London, stoking further the huge docklands fires that had blazed unabated for hours now. By morning, twelve more fires had been started, and another 412 Londoners were dead. The survivors were not to know that they would have to endure a further fifty-five consecutive nights of such torment and anguish before the *nachtangriff* abated.

Monday 9 September The day dawned with a 9/10ths covering of cloud over southern England, the overcast remaining until the afternoon. During the late afternoon, a spate of raids attacked targets in the south London area, and combat once more erupted in the skies above Kent, Sussex and Surrey.

At 16.50 hours, the largest raid of the day was incoming: twenty-six He 111s of II/KG 1, escorted by twenty Me 110s and sixty Me 109s. Apparently tasked with attacking Farnborough, the enemy formation turned west, south of London, passing through the Kenley, Biggin Hill and Northolt Sectors – a gauntlet to run indeed! Nine squadrons were scrambled, eight of which – some ninety Spitfires and Hurricanes – attacked in concert, a formidable and crushing sight for the German aircrew involved, to whom Göring still insisted that Fighter Command was on its knees. Other enemy formations were also on the board, including forty Ju 88s of KG 30, together with the inevitable fighter escort.

Up from Biggin Hill were the Spitfires of 92 Squadron, which had arrived in Sector only the previous day from Pembrey in South Wales. Yet again this was another Squadron that was roughly handled on its first engagement over the 11 Group area. Over Biggin Hill, the Spitfires were bounced by III/JG 26, three of their number being shot down by the *Kommandeur*, *Oberleutnant* Gerhard Schöpfel: two pilots were slightly wounded, the other badly burned; two Spitfires were damaged and one destroyed. 607 Squadron's Hurricanes, freshly arrived at Tangmere the day before, was also roughly handled by Me 109s. Pilot Officer Harry Welford:

The following day, much to my disappointment, I was not called upon to fly and inevitably the Squadron later went off. As it happened I was the most fortunate, as in this, the Squadron's first engagement since arriving in 11 Group, our Hurricanes were well and truly bounced by Me 109s: we lost six out of 12 aircraft; three NCOs were wounded and three officers killed. Amongst the latter were my best friends, Stuart Parnall and Scotty Lenahan, and as no more was ever heard of young George Drake, his death was presumed. We were shocked, we just couldn't take it all in. No-one talked of it but we all hoped for news of the missing from some pub or hospital. No news came and so we bit back our tears and sorrow. It was 'You heard about Stuart and Scotty? Rotten luck, wasn't it?' and someone would add, 'And young George Drake, bloody good blokes, all of them.' After that epitaph the matter would be dismissed with the ordering of another round of drinks to avoid any further evidence of sentiment. The truth of it, though, still hurts me to think of it even now.

After the Battle of France, we had received a number of replacement pilots, straight from OTU; amongst them was Pilot Officer George Drake, a 19 year old South African. He had such a boyish face that I always thought he was too young to be pitched into battle, but then so were many others. He was very inquisitive, always interested in how we 'Brits' thought and lived. No bad thing that, as I daresay he expected to be amongst us for some time. Sadly he wasn't.

Pilot Officer Drake was destined to be the first of the Few reported missing during the Battle of Britain to be recovered by aviation archaeologists after the war. In 1972, thirty-two years after he was shot down, George Drake's human remains were found with his aircraft, Hurricane P2728, at Goudhurst in Kent. The pilot's brother, Arthur, was traced by the authorities and provides a little detail regarding his long lost brother's life:

> Our family lived at Kroonstad, in the province of Pretoria, where our father was Stationmaster. George matriculated at Paarl Boys' High School in 1938, and was a member of the Paarl branch of the St John Ambulance Association. He always wanted to fly but was rejected by our own air force for being colour blind. Appreciating that in the event of war Great Britain would desperately need pilots, he then successfully applied for the RAF. To his younger brothers, Eric and myself, George was very much the hero; our father was secretly very proud but mother was naturally much concerned for her eldest son. George worked his passage to England and achieved his ambition to become a fighter pilot. Joining the RAF to fight for Britain was George's only ambition. He went out to the fighting knowing that the odds were against him and his friends. He was very proud of what he was doing and we have always been proud of him down the years.

Pilot Officer George Drake was buried with full military honours at Brookwood Military Cemetery on 22 November 1972. In the same action that claimed the life of young George Drake, the experienced Spitfire pilots of 222 Squadron were also engaged. Pilot Officer Laurie Whitbread:

> Whilst on patrol over East Kent we sighted a formation of enemy bombers flying west at 20,000 feet, above cloud. It had an escort of Me 109s, flying above and behind at 26,000 feet, and also another formation of fighters flying to one side, at the same height as the bombers. The fighters were engaged. I had a combat with an Me 109. A burst of roughly four seconds from my guns appeared to shoot off the starboard aileron when the 109 went into a spin. It continued to spin downwards into the cloud layer when it disappeared from view. My flight leader stated that he observed the 109 spin down and the pilot bale out.

In his diary, the young Ludlovian wrote: 'One Me 109 claim, confirmed by Van Mentz.' The enemy fighter belonged to 6/JG 27 and crashed at Mounts Farm, Benenden, at 18.15 hours. The pilot, *Unteroffizier* Rauwolf, was captured.

On this occasion, 12 Group had been requested immediately. At 16.50 hours, as the first large formation crossed the south coast, Squadron Leader Jimmy McComb's 611 Squadron was scrambled from Fowlmere to patrol the North Weald line. At 17.00 hours, the Duxford Wing was scrambled. The two Hurricane

A section of 222 Squadron Spitfire pilots at readiness, Kirton, 1940; from left: Sergeant John Burgess, Flying Officer Brian van Mentz (South African) and Pilot Officer Hillary Edridge. Van Mentz was killed in an air raid during 1941; Edridge was shot down by Me 109s and killed on 30 October 1940.

squadrons, 242 and 310, took off from Duxford, Squadron Leader Bader leading at the head of his Canadians and setting course for North Weald. The Spitfires of 19 Squadron took off from nearby Fowlmere and hastened after the Hurricanes, which they easily caught given the Spitfire's superior performance.

Over North Weald, a large formation of enemy bombers was sighted, approaching from the south-east. It had been decided that 19 Squadron would attack the enemy fighters, enabling the Hurricanes to go for the bombers. Consequently the Spitfires mixed it with the escorting Me 109s and 110s: Flight Lieutenant Clouston set a 109 ablaze before hitting another, which 'glided down in apparent distress'. Sub-Lieutenant 'Admiral' Blake followed the enemy back out to sea where he attacked a straggling He 111, leaving it on fire and losing height. The armoured glass windscreen of his fighter, however, was pierced by a 7.9mm round, which eventually lodged in his self-sealing fuel tank. Pilot Officer Cunningham attacked an Me 109, which he left 'enveloped in flames', and Sergeant Cox sent another diving vertically and on fire.

Squadron Leader Bader led 242 and 310 Squadrons to attack the bombers, the CO of 242 leaving the enemy leader 'in flames'. In total, 242 Squadron claimed ten enemy aircraft destroyed in this engagement, but lost two Hurricanes: Pilot Officer Sclanders was killed and Sergeant Lonsdale baled out. 310 Squadron's Czechs claimed three bombers destroyed, but Flight Lieutenant Gordon Sinclair collided with Flying Officer John Boulton, who was killed. Flight Lieutenant Gordon Sinclair:

Our formation was too tight, and as I prepared to attack a Dornier my wing collided with Johnnie's. Whose fault it was we will never know, but sadly Johnnie Boulton was killed. I then collided with the Dornier and had to get out. I took to my parachute, and sprained my ankle when I landed in Coulsdon High Street. Then a detachment of guardsmen appeared from nearby Caterham, and the lieutenant in charge was an old school chum of mine! He said, 'Good God, Gordon, what are you doing lying there?'

In total, the Duxford Wing claimed twenty enemy aircraft destroyed, six probables and two damaged, leading to another congratulatory signal from Air Vice-Marshal Leigh-Mallory and the CAS. Only four of these claims can be confirmed, however, representing an over claiming factor of 5:1. Nonetheless, 12 Group was now well and truly in the battle.

At night the bombers returned to London, and by daybreak the following day another 370 Londoners were dead and 1,400 injured.

Tuesday 10 September Adverse weather conditions dictated that no major attacks were mounted by the Luftwaffe.

Squadron Leader Bader flew from Coltishall to 12 Group headquarters at Hucknall, where he discussed the Duxford Wing's progress to date, and future possibilities, with Air Vice-Marshal Leigh-Mallory.

The main Fighter Command casualties on this day were three Spitfires of 602 Squadron at Tangmere which were damaged during night flying training accidents, although the pilots involved were unhurt. The Spitfire was not intended as a nocturnal fighter and nor, for a variety of reasons, was it a good one when pressed into such service. But desperate indeed was the hour, as the enemy bombers again returned to London that night.

Due to the auspices of Air Chief Marshal Dowding's Stabilising Scheme, on this day two Polish fighter pilots reported for duty with 607 Squadron at Tangmere, namely Pilot Officers Franek Surma and Jan Orzechowski. These pilots had flown Hurricanes with 151 Squadron at North Weald since 25 August, seeing action: on 30 August, Pilot Officer Surma claimed an He 111 probably destroyed, and the following day Pilot Officer Orzechwski was shot up by an Me 109, crash landing at Foulness. On 1 September, 151 Squadron was withdrawn to Digby, but the Poles were considered sufficiently fresh to be returned to 11 Group. Pilot Officer Harry Welford:

I recollect a short, stocky, rather serious man who would have been Jan Orzechowski. He smoked cigarettes incessantly and used a cigarette holder. The Polish officers tried to strike a pose, I imagine, to keep their end up with us rather casual Brits. They were extremely good pilots, but quite mad and totally fearless. Franek Surma, who was with me in 'B' Flight, was a bit more relaxed and met us half way, probably because he spoke more English than the others.

Corporal Bob Morris:

Flying Officer Rafael 'Watty' Watson, a pre-war regular pilot who flew Hurricanes with 87 Squadron during the Battle of Britain. A veteran of the Battle of France, Watson survived the war and died in 1986.

On this day, we of 66 Squadron moved from Kenley to Gravesend, which was no more than a civilian flying club airfield. We were the only squadron there, at what was Biggin Hill's satellite. At Gravesend we looked down the River Thames, opposite Tilbury, and I remember bombs hitting large floating oil tanks in the river there. I always admired the sailors of the little boats, tugs and the like that used to pull out these tanks, which were on fire, to stop the flames spreading. Unlike at Kenley, however, we were not bombed at Gravesend. There was only one hangar there, our dining room, a small hut for flying control and a pilots' crew room. Without much to hit on a grass airfield we would have been difficult to put out of action anyway.

We had half a day off every 10 days, which we used to spend fast asleep. We were exhausted, working dawn to dusk. As we had lost so many pilots at Kenley we began receiving replacements at Gravesend, one of which, an American volunteer called Pilot Officer Reilly, I got to know quite well. Sadly he was shot down and killed, and I was later part of the honour guard at his funeral.

At Gravesend we used to watch the German aircraft coming in, heading for London or elsewhere, the trails in the sky, and how relieved we were when they passed overhead and went straight on! Being close to the river there would often be a ground mist, which could last all day, meaning that no aircraft could take off, but at least the Germans couldn't see us. On such days we always used to get our work done by early afternoon when, inevitably, a football would appear and a game would start on the edge of the aerodrome. We never used to pick a side, you just joined in with whichever side seemed to be winning, and that was the way you kicked! On one occasion we were busy playing when we heard these German aircraft circling around overhead, looking for something to bomb. Suddenly, right through the fog, came a parachute flare which landed on our football pitch – someone kicked some dirt onto it and we just carried on playing. No-one ran for shelter, that was how used we had become to it all.

You never heard anyone talk about defeat. Of course we were not conversant with all the facts, though occasionally we would get some air force 'big wing' come and give us a pep talk. Our entertainment was to walk to Rochester or Strood, to the pictures, then walk back again. We also went to dances at the Co-op Hall in Gravesend. Life went on.

Wednesday 11 September Poor weather in the morning once more dictated that the enemy's main assault was delayed until afternoon. At 15.00 hours, the He 111s of I & II/KG 26 left their French bases, bound for England. After rendezvousing with their 200 fighter escort, the bombers headed up the Thames Estuary to London. From 15.30 hours onwards Fighter Command squadrons attacked the enemy formation but was unable to reach the bombers until after their deadly cargoes had started exploding in the docklands below. The Me 110 escorts withdrew southwards, where they formed a defensive circle over Croydon, covering the bombers' shortest exit route – out over the coast between Dover and Dungeness. Inaccurate routing on the approach, however, led to the Me 109s expending too much fuel and a substantial number of the escorting fighters had to break off and return to France. This left the Heinkels with little protection, and unsurprisingly they suffered heavy loses: ten were shot down and twelve more damaged.

Major Adolf Galland's JG 26, however, had remained over Kent, the *Kommodore* shooting down a Hurricane north-west of Dungeness. In her diary, Miss Homewood of Wills Farm, Romney Marsh, wrote: 'He 111 made a crash landing at Burmarsh, crew set fire to plane. Hurricane crashed at Newchurch, burying itself deep in the ground.' That Hurricane is believed to have been Galland's victim, but the aircraft was not identified until disturbed by aviation archaeologists in 1971; the aircraft was P3770, and personal effects confirmed the pilot to have been Pilot Officer Arthur Clarke of 504 Squadron. Cutting a long story short, Pilot Officer Clarke's remains were not recovered, his family deciding that they should remain at the crash site, where the pilot is still at rest today. At the adjacent roadside, however, a memorial to this missing pilot can be seen, fresh flowers often being left as a personal tribute to one of the Few.

Sergeant Tony Pickering:

No 501 Squadron was based at Kenley by this time, having moved there from Gravesend. On September 11th, Squadron Leader Hogan ordered a head-on attack against a formation of enemy bombers over London. We dived down on the Huns and I just pressed the gun button and shut my eyes! One of the nose gunners gave me a squirt and hit the sump, I started smoking but managed to spiral down away from the fight. It was a lovely day and I could see Kenley below quite clearly. As there was no-one about I thought that I would just come down and make a normal landing. At about 3,000 feet, however, the petrol caught fire and I was over the side pretty sharpish! My Hurricane went down and crashed, and I landed by parachute in a Guards Depot, where I was given a couple of whiskies. I was wearing ordinary uniform trousers, shoes, an open neck shirt with no tie as it was hot, and that was it. I hadn't even had a shave that morning and I remember being a bit singed around the face and hair but was otherwise uninjured.

At 15.30 hours, Squadron Leader Brian Lane had led eight Spitfires of his own 19 Squadron, together with six of 266, off from Fowlmere as the lead unit in an all-Spitfire wing, the other squadrons being Squadron Leader 'Sailor' Malan's 74 Squadron and Squadron Leader Jimmy McComb's 611. Lane's instructions were to patrol in a southerly direction towards the Thames Estuary. At about 15.50 hours, while flying at 20,000 feet over south-east London, the Spitfires sighted 100 enemy aircraft approaching them from the south. 74 and 611 Squadrons executed a left-hand turn, attacking on the beam of the enemy formation. Squadron Leader Lane led 19 Squadron in a head-on charge against the He 111s. Sergeant Bernard 'Jimmy' Jennings fired at an He 111 during Lane's initial charge, but later attacked the rearmost machine of fifteen Me 110s. The Spitfire pilot reported that 'this one fell back from the rest of the formation with smoke pouring out of his starboard engine. I did another attack from above and behind and he crashed in a wood, south of the Ashford railway line between Sittingbourne and Maidstone.' Flight Sergeant George 'Grumpy' Unwin:

I was at about 20,000 feet, flying my usual Spitfire, P9546, QV-H, and I suddenly saw this lone Dornier. How he was on his own I'll never know, but he was off home. So I went after him. Now the drill against a Dornier was he had a dustbin rear gunner, a dustbin hanging down below the fuselage and so you had to fix him first before closing in for the aircraft. This I did, very cleverly of course. I could see him shooting at me and so closed in and gave him a burst and shot him up. At least I thought I had, I'll never know to this day whether I did or didn't, or whether someone took his place. Because as I closed right in on him and started shooting I saw his rear gunner shooting back at me, the little red sparks you could see. I didn't pay much attention to it, thinking that after a quick spray from the spread of my guns he would stop. I carried on firing for quite a while, when suddenly I was covered in smoke. To my horror a hole appeared in my windscreen – I was leaning forward of course, one did to peer through the gunsight which was fortunately in the middle of a piece of armour plated, bullet resistant glass about an inch and a half. A hole appeared in front of my face. I thought, 'Good God I must be dead, or something' – no blood, no nothing, but I'm covered in smoke, I thought I was on fire. So I whipped the hood back, undid my straps and started to get out.

During the Battle of Britain. Air Chief Marshal Dowding skilfully rotated his squadrons in and out of the combat zone; 501 Squadron, however, was in the front line throughout. Here a group of pilots from that squadron, operating from Gravesend, are seen at readiness in August 1940; from left: Sgts T.G. Pickering & R.J.K. Gent, F/S P.F. Morfill, Sgts P.C.P. Farnes, A. Glowacki (Polish), unknown, W.B. Henn, S.A.H. Whitehouse, J.H. Lacey & P/O R.C. Dafforn. Behind them is the Squadron Operations Caravan and two Hawker Hurricanes.

By this time I'd broken away, I was going downhill. I was halfway out of the cockpit when I suddenly saw that the smoke was coming from the top of the engine through the engine cowling which is where the glycol pipe is, the coolant pipe. The smoke was a really browny colour, it wasn't black smoke. I could smell it too, it was glycol. So I got back in and strapped myself in again, leaving the hood open, still going downhill in case somebody was following me. Then I started looking for a field, finding one to land in near Brentwood in Essex. In those days you were supposed to get it down without hurting the aircraft. So I waited until I'd found my field and got down to about a thousand feet, dropped the undercarriage and did a forced landing in this field which had a few cows in it. Quite a big field, it was. No trouble at all.

I hadn't even got out of the cockpit before a jeep with a young subaltern and two soldiers with fixed bayonets came roaring through the gate. As soon as they saw it was one of ours they changed their attitude. I got a screwdriver from one of the soldiers and we took the top off, and there it was – a bullet had gone through the glycol pipe. As I had first served in the RAF as an engineering apprentice at Halton before the war, my technical knowledge was good, and so I knew what needed to be done to get me airborne again. The soldiers took me to North Weald, where I got help from a fitter plus spares and repaired the aircraft, which I flew back to Duxford two days later. The windscreen, however, could not be repaired on station and so P9546 was sent of to a Maintenance Unit (MU).

The forced-landing was much commended in the 19 Squadron ORB: 'Flight Sergeant Unwin made a wizard forced-landing with undercarriage down!!!!'

In what was 611 Squadron's first engagement of a massed formation, Squadron Leader McComb's pilots had also been in the battle's midst: Sergeant 'Sandy' Levenson attacked several enemy aircraft, including a 'Ju 88' which he actually flew alongside as the raider lost height. As he did so, his Spitfire was hit by AA fire and as black smoke poured from beneath the instrument panel he broke off to forced-land near Kenley. A nearby searchlight post then informed Levenson that the bomber concerned had crashed in flames a few miles south of Kenley. This actually was an He 111 of 3/KG 26 which came down at Lingfield; the Heinkel also featured in the combat reports of at least eight other RAF fighter pilots! 611 Squadron's Sergeant F.E.R. Shepherd, however, baled out over Croydon with his parachute in flames and was killed, his Spitfire crashing onto an air raid shelter, killing two civilians. 266 Squadron made no combat claims but lost a Spitfire, Pilot Officer Roach baling out safely over Billericay.

There was also action over 10 Group, when a heavily escorted raid got through to Portsmouth and Southampton, although little damage was caused. While airborne over Sussex, some of Air Vice-Marshal Brand's squadrons were called upon to reinforce 11 Group over London, among them 238 Squadron, which was freshly returned to battle following a two month sojourn at St Eval. Typically, this Squadron's first sortie in the combat zone was traumatic: three Hurricanes were lost, two pilots being killed, the other wounded. By the Battle of Britain's end, 238 Squadron would lose eight more pilots killed, five of them fighting over London. Sergeant Gordon Batt:

When we of 238 Squadron returned to Middle Wallop in September, the size of the German formations had increased: the bomber formation was usually 50–60 strong, in an oblong block and close formation, and above them were Me 110s, and Me 109s higher still. To counter this we often flew accompanied by one of Wallop's Spitfire squadrons. Our CO was the senior squadron commander and so we usually led, our Hurricanes attacking the bombers whilst the Spitfires held off the escort. It certainly did my morale a lot of good, God and Hitler know what it did to theirs! The only snag was that as 238 was first to attack, I never had the opportunity to look back – there must have been chaos!

Towards the end of August and throughout September, we were frequently called to the west of the London area. The Controller would give us a commentary regarding what was going on generally, and whilst holding off at 20,000 feet, we could hear him directing 11 Group's squadrons into action. From our position west of London, we could see ack-ack bursting over the capital, and condensation trails of the Spitfires, Hurricanes and Me 109s. the boys of 11 Group were obviously holding their own and we were sensibly being held in reserve. When we were vectored, the Controller would say something like: '25 Bandits, Angels 20, heading straight for you, they're all yours!' It really was slick control... All of the sorties, though, were quite frightening and fraught with danger!

Squadron Leader Duncan MacDonald:

On September 11th, one of my flight commanders in 238 Squadron, Flight Lieutenant Jackie Sing, was shot down over the sea and rescued by an American oil tanker. You can imagine his feelings when informed by the Captain that the cargo consisted of 100 octane aviation fuel for Fighter Command! The tanker made landfall at Shoreham, Sussex, and I motored down from Tangmere in the early evening to recover this valuable member of my Squadron who was a bit shaken but fortunately uninjured. He was in the air again next day and none the worse for this most frightening experience.

Across the Channel, at Caffiers near Calais, III/JG 26 had cause to celebrate: their *Kommandeur, Hauptmann* Gerhard Schöpfel, had been awarded the *Ritterkreuz*, the Knight's Cross, having achieved the necessary total of twenty aerial victories. This was only the second award of this coveted decoration throughout the whole of JG 26 and was richly deserved. On 18 August, Schöpfel had performed an unprecedented feat of arms when he destroyed four Hurricanes over Canterbury, and only two days before his award had shot down three Spitfires in a single action. Without a doubt, Gerhard Schöpfel was among the most experienced and dangerous *experten* on the *Kanalfront*, as many more Allied fighter pilots would discover to their cost.

Thursday 12 September Poor weather saw a day of vastly reduced aerial activity, although enemy reconnaissance bombers remained active over England. Squadron Leader Harry Fenton:

We of my 238 Squadron had a daily routine: rise before first light, at about 0330 hours, have a coffee and then go to dispersal, spending the day there and being scrambled in either section or squadron strength. We shared Middle Wallop with 609 Squadron, with whom we took it in turns to spend every third day down at Warmwell, undertaking convoy protection patrols. That was during the early days, but I was shot down and wounded on August 8th, returning to the Squadron on September 12th. By that time 238 had been back at Middle Wallop for two days but had already lost two pilots, both missing from action over 11 Group: David Hughes, and able flight commander, and Duszynski, a Pole whom I had not even met. The tempo of combat had completely changed.

Fighter Command suffered a sad loss on this day: Wing Commander Johnnie Dewar, CO of 87 Squadron at Exeter, failed to arrive at Tangmere on what was simply a routine flight. At thirty-three, Dewar was older than most operational fighter pilots, but nonetheless was among the first four officers to receive the double award of both DSO and DFC. During the Fall of France Dewar became an 'ace', destroying five enemy aircraft, adding 3½ more during the Battle of Britain. Clearly a most capable officer destined for great things, it is believed that Wing Commander Dewar, flying alone along the south coast, was picked off by a German fighter; his body was washed ashore on 30 September.

Friday 13 September Further poor flying weather saw another day with little activity. Over Maidstone, Sergeant James 'Ginger' Lacey of 501 Squadron, destined to become one of Fighter Command's top scoring fighter pilots in the Battle of Britain, destroyed an He 111 but was shot down himself by return fire. Taking to his parachute, the Hurricane pilot suffered slight burns, but fortunately survived the experience.

Pilot Officer Richard Jones:

When we returned from a sortie, anyone who had been successful in shooting down an enemy aircraft might do a victory roll over the airfield, but these were not encouraged because you didn't know whether your aircraft had some unseen damage to the flying controls. Immediately we landed the Intelligence Officer took full details from each pilots regarding what had happened, whilst the groundcrew, who were absolutely marvelous, did a fantastic job of rapidly preparing the aircraft for another immediate take-off.

Sergeant Tony Pickering:

One day I came across a lone Ju 88 somewhere over Kent, heading back to sea. I thought that it would be no problem to catch up the Hun, press the gun button and that would be it. Suddenly he just pulled away from me, just left me standing, had at least an extra 50 mph on me, and that was the last I saw of him. The Hurricane just wasn't fast enough. We even used to bend the throttle levers in flight, trying to squeeze a bit more boost out of the Merlin. A Spitfire would have caught that Ju 88. In the Hurricane's favour was that it could take a terrific amount of punishment but still keep flying, whereas the Spitfire couldn't take quite as much.

I was 18 during the Battle of Britain. I came from a small village where everyone knew everyone else, we went to school, did our homework in the evenings and went to church on Sundays. We were innocents, really, the RAF was a bit of a shock, all these chaps who were going around nightclubs and girls, it was something to touch a girl's arm at a dance in those days, not like it is now!

Saturday 14 September Thick cloud prevented twenty He 111s of KG 4 from finding their London targets, although bombs fell in Kingston and Wimbledon, killing forty-nine civilians. KG 1's Ju 88s bombed radar stations on the south coast; little damage was caused but new enemy electronic counter measures was causing troublesome interference.

At 15.50 hours, Squadron Leader Bader led his Duxford Wing over London, the formation now including the Polish Hurricanes of 302 Squadron. During the evening, the Wing went off on another uneventful patrol, but, astonishingly and in complete contravention of orders, Bader led the 12 Group fighters on a fighter sweep of Kent and, according to the 19 Squadron ORB, 'almost France'. Pilots putting themselves at unnecessary risk by flying over the sea had already

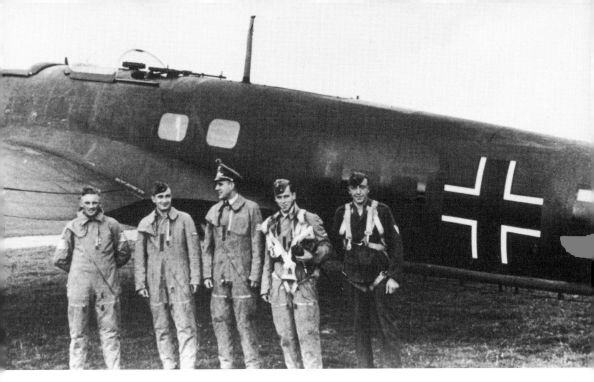

On the night of 13 September *Hauptmann* Hermann Kell of 3/KG 4, attempted a solo attack in bad weather on Victoria Station. His He 111, however, was shot down over England by night-fighter ace Pilot Officer Michael Herrick, a New Zealander of 25 Squadron. Kell was among three crew members who were captured, but two others were killed. Kell, centre, is pictured with his aircraft and crew in France during the Battle of Britain.

been the subject of a memo from Air Vice-Marshal Park, and what would have happened if a raid had come in from the east while Bader was swanning around over the Channel?

Pilot Officer 'Teddy' Morten:

> On one of the many occasions Bader tackled me in the Mess regarding the 'Hun in the sun' etc, he said, 'Morty, you know that yesterday you told the Wing to patrol North Weald at Angels 20?'
>
> 'Yes,' I said.
>
> 'Well, d'ya know where we were upon reaching required height?'
>
> 'No,' I said.
>
> 'Over *Reading*! We were looking down on the patrol area, up sun and all eyes skinned!'
>
> I thought that this was a bit too buccanerish and bound to cause trouble eventually.

Nonetheless, on this day Squadron Leader Bader was awarded the DSO. The story of the legless fighter pilot was, of course, a great propaganda coup and a tremendous morale booster which personified the nation's determined spirit.

At Hornchurch, 222 Squadron's Pilot Officer Laurie Whitbread wrote to his mother, giving no indication of the danger he faced on a daily basis:

Dear Mother,

Thank you for your letter, received this morning. How nice to have Rex and Doris and Colin at home together. I am disappointed that I won't be there too. Fancy Ludlow having some bombs!

Everything is going fine down here. We get far less to do now that the weather has broken. There is no sign of leaving this station yet, so I doubt that I will get any leave until things quieten down again.

I am keeping fit – except that I got a touch of frostbite in the left hand last week. Its better now, except for a large blister on the thumb.

Mother, would you see if I've left my RAF navy blue blazer at home. I don't want it but can't find it here. Please tell me in the next letter, I do hope that I haven't lost it.

Love to all, Cheerio, Laurie.

Prophetically, the 19 Squadron ORB commented on the current lack of activity, observing that the enemy must be 'Saving up for "der Tag", evidently.'

Sunday 15 September In the enemy camp, frustrations were mounting: the invasion fleet was due to sail for England on 20 September, and yet Fighter Command showed no sign whatsoever of throwing in the towel. Indeed, there was no evidence whatsoever to confirm Göring's insistence that the RAF was 'down to its last 50 Hurricanes and Spitfires'. Hitler was clearly losing confidence

Spitfire pilots: Pilot Officers David Crook (left) and Geoffrey Gaunt of 609 Squadron, pictured at Warmwell. Gaunt, a cousin of Hollywood star James Mason, was shot down in flames over London and killed on 15 September 1940.

in the Luftwaffe's ability to achieve the necessary supremacy of the skies, even purely over the proposed landing area. *Reichsmarschall* Göring was determined to prevail, however, and so unleashed another day of massive air attacks against London. The day would, he hoped, end decisively in his favour.

According to the HQ Fighter Command Intelligence Officer, the day dawned fair, becoming 'fair to cloudy during the morning with some showers mainly in the North and West and with cloud at 2,000 to 3,000 feet lowering to 1,000 to 2,000 feet and showers'. From first light onwards, standing patrols of RAF fighters were up over the coast between Land's End and Harwich. In addition, each Sector Station kept at least one squadron at readiness, to scramble at a moment's notice. Between 10.00 and 11.00 hours there were 'extensive enemy patrols in the Straits of Dover'. By 10.50 hours, the RDF screens were indicating a large raid moving out across the Channel, and five minutes later, all of 11 Group's squadrons were at readiness. The size of the raid fast approaching indicated that reinforcements from neighbouring groups would be necessary: at 11.30 hours the Duxford Wing, comprising 19, 242, 302 and 310 Squadrons, was scrambled; 611 Squadron, which was flying in from Digby, joined the Wing over Duxford a minute later.

At 11.33 hours, an enemy formation crossed the coast between Dover and Folkestone, being followed three minutes later by two further formations which flew in over Dover and the South Foreland. The enemy then flew a 'dog leg' course, first northwards towards the Thames Estuary, then turning south or south-west before reaching the north coast of Kent, then west to Maidstone before finally spreading out to fly over the entire London area. The raiders' selected targets were gasworks and other industrial targets, and docks in the London area. To meet this attack, twenty squadrons from 11 Group had been scrambled in addition to the Duxford Wing's five, and 10 Group's 609 Squadron – some 312 Spitfires and Hurricanes in all.

At 12.09 hours, twenty-four Do 17s of KG 76 were at 16,000 feet over Brixton; the Duxford Wing was 3,000 feet above and up-sun, with an elapsed time of thirty-eight minutes from scramble. The Dorniers were first subjected to a head-on charge by two 11 Group squadrons, 257 and 504. Squadron Leader Douglas Bader:

> This time, for a change, we outnumbered the Hun, and, believe me, no more than eight got home from that party. At one time you could see planes going down on fire all over the place, and the sky seemed full of parachutes. It was sudden death that morning, for our fighters shot them to blazes.
>
> One unfortunate German rear-gunner baled out of the Do 17 I attacked, but his parachute caught on the tail. There he was, swinging helplessly, with the aircraft swooping and diving and staggering all over the sky, being pulled about by the man hanging by his parachute from the tail. That bomber went crashing into the Thames Estuary, with the swinging gunner still there.

Sergeant Ray Holmes, a Hurricane pilot with 504 Squadron. On 15 September 1940, Holmes was among those RAF fighter pilots who shared the destruction of the Battle's most famous German casualty: the Do 17 that bombed Buckingham Palace and crashed on Victoria Station. Holmes delivered the *coup de grace* but his Hurricane was badly damaged by debris as the bomber broke up. Holmes baled out, landing in High Street, Chelsea, from where his Hurricane was recently recovered by aviation archaeologists.

Just about the same time, one of my boys saw a similar thing in another Do 17, though this time the gunner who tried to bale out had his parachute caught before it opened. It caught in the hood, and our pilot saw the other two members of the crew crawl up to set him free. He was swinging from his packed parachute until they pushed him clear. Then they jumped after him, and their plane went into the water with a terrific smack. I've always thought it was a pretty stout effort on the part of those two Huns who refused to leave their pal fastened to the doomed aircraft.

One of KG 76's Dorniers was flown by *Feldwebel* Wilhelm Raab, a veteran of the campaigns in both Poland and France, in addition to numerous sorties over England. High above Brixton, Raab's bomber was attacked by numerous RAF fighter pilots: first Sergeant Tyrer of 46 Squadron, then Flight Lieutenant Rimmer of 229 Squadron, and both Flight Lieutenant Peter Brothers and Pilot

Officer Mortimer of 257 Squadron. As the Dornier dived for cloud cover, Flight Lieutenant Powell-Sheddon and Pilot Officer Tamblyn of 242 Squadron attacked next. The CO of 19 Squadron, Squadron Leader Brian Lane, then also saw and attacked the Dornier, at first unaware of the attack in progress by the Hurricanes; realising that he had 'jumped the queue', he followed the Hurricanes and took his turn to fire. Lane was unable to tell, however, whether he or the two 242 Squadron Hurricanes were responsible for the hits he could see on Raab's aircraft. Descending at 100 feet per minute, the Dornier dropped out of the cloud and, after being attacked by even more fighters, Raab ordered his crew to bale out before tumbling into space himself. At 12.30 hours, Squadron Leader Lane watched the pilotless bomber narrowly miss a house and explode on impact at Underriver, south of Scvenoaks in Kent. Raab's fate certainly confirms the 310 Squadron statement that on this day 'no individual pilot could claim one bird as his own'. Squadron Leader Bob Stanford Tuck:

> This was the first time that I took my 257 'Burma' Squadron into action. We found a big bunch of mixed bombers, flying in formations of anything from 30 to 60, with escorting fighters above them. As I led my new Squadron in, I saw three of these parties nearing London. As the boys waded into the bombers, I went for some of the fighters. I picked off an Me 110 which I shot down over Barking, and one of his pals nearly got his own back when he put a bullet through my windscreen a few inches from my head. The Squadron had a bag of five in that first outing, and there was quite a party of the Mess that night.

KG 76 had certainly suffered at the hands of Fighter Command, six of their number crashing on English soil. Among these was probably the most famous German casualty of the whole battle, the Dornier which crashed on Victoria Station having been attacked by numerous fighters. The enemy pilot, *Oberleutnant* Zehbe, landed by parachute at Kennington; he was roughly handled by a civilian mob and later died from injuries received.

Some of 19 Squadron's Spitfires managed to engage the Me 109s, as had been planned: at 12.10 hours over Westerham, Flight Sergeant Unwin engaged 3/JG 53's *Staffelkapitän, Oberleutnant* Haase, in a dogfight:

> I was Red Three with Flight Lieutenant Lawson. We sighted the enemy aircraft which were flying in vics of three. The escorts dived singly onto us and I engaged an Me 109 with a yellow nose. I gave one burst of six seconds and it burst into flames. The pilot baled out and the enemy aircraft crashed between Redhill and Westerham.

Haase was killed as his parachute failed to open. As other Me 109s dived on 19 Squadron, Sergeant David Cox climbed and flew south. A few minutes later he found six 109s of 2/JG 27 flying in the same direction. Simultaneously the Germans saw the Spitfire, and so Green One attacked from astern. Cox's target immediately half-rolled and dived away. Four of the fighters then broke off and continued south, no doubt low on fuel, but the sixth attacked Cox head-on. As his assailant reared up to pass over the fleeting Spitfire, Cox climbed and turned sharply, attacking from below. The 109 dived through cloud, pursued by the VR Spitfire pilot who, upon emerging , saw his victim's wreckage burning in a field. This was at Lodge Wood, near Uckfield, and the pilot, *Unteroffizier* Walburger, was captured unhurt.

611 Squadron's ORB provides a dramatic account of the action:

611 Squadron joined Wing of Hurricanes over Duxford at 15,000 feet at 1131 hours then climbed to 27.000 feet to the left and above the Wing which was at 22.000 feet. When SW of London, 50 enemy bombers and 30 Me 109s escorting above were sighted coming from south. The Wing went into attack the bombers and escort turning south-east. 611 Squadron kept beside the Me 109s which were to the west and above. After the Wing attack had broken up bomber formation, the Me 109s did not come down. After waiting for about seven minutes, S/Ldr McComb informed Wing Leader that he was coming down, and gave order echelon port. The Squadron proceeding at the time south-east and up sun of the enemy. The Squadron in line astern, three sections of four aircraft executed a head-on attack down onto a formation of about 10 Do 215s and Do 17s. Then flying at 18,000 feet in a south easterly direction. S/Ldr McComb attacked Do 215 head on, hits observed, no results. Pulling up he made a beam attack on an Me 110 which turned in its back and went down. The Squadron formation then broke up. S/Ldr McComb chased an Me 109 which was in a dogfight with a Hurricane, but could not catch up with them as he was too far behind. He then proceeded to the coast in the hope of attacking homing lame ducks before returning to base. P/O Williams after making his attack with the Squadron but without any observed results, saw a Do 215 attacked by six fighters crash into a wood near BISHOPSBOURNE, KENT. Two of the crew baling out. P/O Lund dived into initial attack but enemy aircraft passed through his sights before he could fire. P/O O'Neill attacked six or seven times a Do 215 which had fallen behind the enemy formation. Four Hurricanes also attacked at same time. He chased this enemy aircraft as far as DUNGENESS where three other Spitfires carried on the attack. He then returned to base, being short of petrol and ammunition. F/Lt Leather carried out a head on attack on three Do 215s. No results observed. He then attacked a Do 215 at rear of large formation using up remainder of his ammunition. The port engine exploded and stopped. A number of other fighters also attacked this enemy aircraft and Red 2 reports seeing two crew bale out and machine crashed near BISHOPSBOURNE, KENT.

So far, Raab's Dornier had also appeared in the combat reports of two pilots from 611 Squadron; how many others it featured in is anyone's guess. The 611 Squadron report continues:

P/O Pollard, after firing a short burst in the initial dive attack, chased, in company with one other Spitfire and a Hurricane, a Do 215. Between Rochester and Herne Bay, enemy aircraft lost height, smoke coming from port engine. Crew of two baled out and aircraft crashed on edge of a wood about four miles south of Herne Bay. He landed at Detling at 1305 hours having lost his bearings, later returned to Gl.

This was a 3/KG 76 Do 17Z which was also engaged by Pilot Officer Meaker of 249 Squadron, and both Flight Lieutenant Ken Gillies and Pilot Officer 'Bogle' Bodie of 66 Squadron. The Dornier crashed in flames and exploded at Slurry. The very detailed 611 Squadron account continues:

Yellow Three, P/O Brown after initial dive attack on pulling out saw no enemy aircraft. After circling for about 10 minutes he returned to home base. P/O Walker after initial dive attack on pulling out saw no enemy aircraft. He developed engine trouble and had to force land at West Mailing at 1235 hours. F/Lt Stoddart fired one quick burst in initial dive attack, and then had to take evasive action in order to avoid attack from Me 109s. He circled for some time and then returned to base. F/Sgt Sadler after initial dive saw 12 Do 215s going south east so executed two frontal attacks on leader. Enemy aircraft believed hit but no results were seen. Abandoned chase at Lympne being short of ammunition and petrol. P/O Dewey fired a short burst at a Do 215 but observed no results. After circling for some time returned base. Sgt Levenson broke formation to attack an Me 109 but enemy aircraft got away. He then flew towards large formation of Do 215s flying at 18,000 feet. After sighting one Do 215 by itself at 14,000 feet he rolled over and carried out an old astern attack diving onto the enemy. Got in a long burst and both enemy aircraft motors were smoking when he broke away. Climbing again, he carried out the same attack. He broke away when both engines and both mainplanes immediately behind them were on fire.

For the overworked Luftwaffe, the presence of so many RAF fighters, which had harried them constantly from crossing the English coast to leaving it some while later, was at the very least alarming. The crushing effect that the arrival of fifty odd 12 Group fighters had on the Germans' morale cannot be underestimated. The combined success of Fighter Command and other defences during that morning's action had resulted in few casualties and little damage being caused. Two bombs had fallen on Buckingham Palace, however, thus showing the King and Queen to be in the fight alongside humble Eastenders.

The Prime Minister, Winston Churchill, had chosen this particular morning to visit the 11 Group Operations Room at Uxbridge. As he watched squadrons being flung into battle, the Prime Minister asked Air Vice-Marshal Park what reserves he had: 'None, Sir,' the commander of 11 Group replied, but to put that statement into context, he meant, of course, that all of *his* Group's squadrons were airborne. Certainly all of the Command's 'A' squadrons were committed to battle on this day, but those aircraft represented less than half of the total available. It is likely, however, that Air Vice-Marshal Park had been so bold as to commit his entire force during this action owing to the protective cloud layer which covered his airfields and thus concealed them from high altitude attack while his fighters were being 'turned around'.

Soon, the RDF screens indicated further formations moving out from Calais. Between 14.10 and 14.35 hours, eight or more formations of German bombers and their escorts crossed the English coastline between Rye and Dover, heading for London. As Squadron Leader Brian Lane later wrote, that the Wing 'ran into the whole Luftwaffe over London. Wave after wave of bombers covered by several hundred fighters.' Unfortunately, the 'whole Luftwaffe' was some 4,000 feet above the Wing, however. As the Duxford fighters climbed, the inevitable 109s plunged down and, as Bader yelled 'Break up!' the Wing scattered. A typically confused and extremely violent combat then took place between the opposing fighters, but few individual combats lasted more than twenty seconds – with so many fighters filling the sky, any pilot who concentrated on his target for longer ran a great risk of collision; again the 611 Squadron ORB provides a stirring account of a Spitfire squadron in action:

611 Squadron ran into several formations of bombers before sufficient height could be reached so ignored them, attempting to get height in Westerly direction to keep Me 109s off Wing. The squadron consisted of 8 aircraft in three sections flying line astern. It was not possible to out climb the Me 109s and the Wing appeared to be both attacking and being attacked. When at 20,000 feet over West London, the Squadron Leader sighted a formation of 25 Do 17s proceeding South unmolested and being by then separated from the Wing, gave the order Sections Echelon Right. The Squadron dived down on the formation, coming out of the sun. At the end of the general attack, Me 110s came down. S/Ldr McComb attacked rear E/A. Rear gunner ceased firing and smoke appeared from port engine. He then pulled up into a loop and dived again in inverted position. Guns worked perfectly in this position and E/A went down in flames. Result of attack is confirmed by Yellow Two and Yellow Leader. S/Ldr McComb then blacked out badly and came to in the clouds. After looking around and seeing nothing he returned to base. P/O Williams carried out a No 3 FC attack on an He 111. A second burst at 80 yards was given but no result observed. E/A returned machine-gun fire. He was unable then to return to Squadron which had now broken up, but observing two enemy formations, he made an astern attack on No 3 of the last section of the formation of Do 215. The formation turned north but Red 2's target fell out, losing height. He then carried out another attack finishing his ammunition. E/A descended into the clouds, one engine stopped, Red Two following. Cloud was 2,000 feet thick and on emerging no E/A was visible but two minutes later he saw enemy airman descending by parachute. Latter landed on edge of wood corner of Hawkhurst Golf Club about 15 miles North of Hastings.

F/Lt Leather followed Red Leader into attack astern and took machine next to his as his target was already aflame. He fired all ammunition and when broke away the Do 17 was in flames. He then was forced to land at Croydon at 1540 hours and later flew to Gl rejoining the Squadron.

P/O Brown had first to evade enemy fighters and then put one short burst into the Do 215 already attacked by Red Leader which had one engine out of action. Oil or glycol from E/A covered up windscreen and so he had to break away. Then he attacked one E/A which broke away from formation using deflection. E/A went into a steep spiral dive with escape hatch over pilot's seat open. No further results seen as large formation of Me 110s appeared and Yellow Two escaped into cloud.

P/O Lund attacked a Do 215 which was also being attacked by several other aircraft. He saw flashes of fire and smoke coming from E/A. While climbing back to main formation of bombers, one Me 110 came down on him so he fired one short burst before turning away and down. As the E/A passed his port side, black smoke was pouring from engine. No more E/A seen after this so he returned to base.

F/Sgt Sadler after attacking with Squadron, saw a Do 215 break away and begin losing height. He made two attacks on this E/A, his second attack being made at 50 yards. A Hurricane also attacked after him and the E/A apparently badly disabled disappeared below cloud.

P/O D.H. O'Neill lost touch with Blue Leader but after circling for about 6 minutes had to evade 8 Me 110s into cloud. Up again out of cloud saw Me 109s attacking one Hurricane and attacked one of these over Faversham without observing result although E/A took evasive action. After being attacked by another Me 109, he returned to base landing, however, by mistake first at Debden.

Sgt Levenson after attacking without visible result an Me 109 and a crippled Do 215 found himself at 10,000 feet over Brooklands aerodrome. He then saw about 50 Do 215s guarded by two Me 109s overhead. He climbed to 1,000 feet below formation and delivered a quarter frontal attack opening fire first at 100 yards, developing this into normal quarter attack at about 200 yards when all his ammunition was exhausted. He observed ammunition hitting leading E/A and the leading vic of 4 A/C broke away to port, smoke coming from engines of No.1 and No.2. No further result was seen but he assumed that No 1 was out of action. F/Lt Stoddart and P/O Dewey, owing to refueling, took off 15 minutes after the squadron. The weather above cloud was perfect with visibility good.

Squadron Leader Brian Lane:

At approximately 1440 hours AA fire was sighted to the south and at the same time a formation of about 30 Do 215s was seen. I climbed up astern of the enemy aircraft to engage the fighter escort which could be seen above the bombers at about 30,000 feet. Three Me 109s dived on our formation and I turned to starboard. A loose dogfight ensued with more Me 109s coming down. I could not get near to any enemy aircraft so I climbed up and engaged a formation of Me 110s without result. I then sighted 10 Me 109s just above me and attacked one of them. I got on his tail and fired several bursts of about two seconds. The enemy aircraft was taking violent evasive action and made for cloud level. I managed to get in another burst of about five seconds before it flicked over inverted and entered cloud in a shallow dive, apparently out of control. I then flew south and attacked two further formations of about 30 Do 215s from astern and head-on. The

Squadron Leader Brian Lane DFC, CO of 19 Squadron, de-briefs at Fowlmere following a combat over London in September 1940; at left is Flight Lieutenant Walter 'Farmer' Lawson DFC, and right is Flight Sergeant George 'Grumpy' Unwin DFM. While all three were successful fighter pilots, Lane and Unwin were exceptional. Sadly, Lawson and Lane shared the same fate: both were reported missing in action after the Battle of Britain. Unwin served in the post war RAF, winning a DSO in the Malayan Emergency, and died in 2006, aged ninety-two.

enemy aircraft did not appear to like the head on attack as they jumped about a bit as I passed through. I observed no result from these attacks. Fire from the rear of the enemy aircraft was opened at 1,000 yards. Me 110s opened fire at similar range but appeared to have no idea of deflection shooting.

Squadron Leader Lane's combat represented the only protracted dogfight between the opposing fighters on this day. Flight Sergeant Unwin was Lane's Red Three, and reported sighting 'thousands of 109s'. When the Wing was attacked, at close range 'Grumpy' fired a three second burst at a 109 which half-rolled and dived steeply into the clouds. Although the Spitfire pilot pursued his prey, he lost the 109 at 6,000 feet when his windscreen froze up. Climbing back up to 25,000 feet, a *Rotte* of 109s appeared above him, flying south. Unwin gave chase and caught both over Lydd. The first consequently burst into flames and went down vertically, and the second crashed into the sea. It is likely that these two 109s were from I/JG 77: *Oberleutnant* Kunze, of the *Geschwaderstabschwarm*, was killed when his aircraft crashed at Lympne; *Unteroffizier* Meixner also lost his life when his 109 crashed into the sea off Dungeness at about 14.55 hours. This brought Flight Sergeant Unwin's total of Me 109s definitely destroyed this day to three.

As the Me 109s once more rained down on 19 Squadron, Green One, Flying Officer Alan 'Ace' Haines, attacked a 3/LG 2 machine flown by *Unteroffizier* Klick. The enemy machine's radiator was badly damaged so Klick had no option but to make a forced-landing at Shellness where he was captured. Haines went on to engage an Me 110 which he also claimed as destroyed when he saw it crash on a French beach. Green Section's other two pilots, Flight Sergeant Harry Steere and Pilot Officer Arthur Vokes, were also successful; the latter wrote in his log book:

'B' Flight attacked 6 Do 17s, one breaking away chased by F/Sgt Steere and self. One Jerry baled out. One Me 110 surprised me and bored a hole in starboard wing. After two or three turns I got on his tail and gave him everything. Dived vertically into cloud, starboard engine smoking. One probable Me 110. Hundreds of Jerries!

Sub-Lieutenant 'Admiral' Blake noted the number of enemy aircraft engaged as 'innumerable', but nonetheless dived to attack six Dorniers which had become detached from the main formation. He then attacked the 109s, which came down from above, firing at one particular machine twice, after which the 109 'burst into flames'. Blake next joined a queue of fighters attacking an He 111, but was forced to land at Rochford as his Spitfire had been hit and was smoking badly. Pilot Officer Wallace 'Jock' Cunningham shot down a 7/JG 51 Me 109, which crashed at St Margaret's-at-Cliff, near Dover. The pilot, *Leutnant* Bildau, baled out and was captured. Sergeant Jack Potter, however, ill advisedly chased the enemy far out across the Channel, being shot down off Calais by *Feldwebel* Luders of 6/JG 26; the British pilot was captured.

Everywhere there were twisting, turning, fighters, those with RAF roundels from 10, 11 and 12 Groups. The *Kommodore* of JG 26, Major Adolf Galland, singled out the Hurricane of 310 Squadron's Sergeant Hubacek:

With the *Stabstaffel* I attacked two Hurricanes, which were about 800 metres below us. Maintaining surprise, I closed on the wingman and opened fire from 120 metres, as he was in a gentle turn to the left. The enemy plane reeled as my rounds struck the nose from below, and pieces fell from the left wing and fuselage. The left side of the fuselage burst into flame.

Galland's *Katchmarek*, *Oberleutnant* Horten, had shot down the CO of 310 Squadron. Squadron Leader Sacha Hess: 'I had the impression that there was machine-gun fire behind me. I looked back several times but saw nothing. I re-trimmed the aircraft but at that moment I was hit – I do not know by what.' Hess baled out, landing at Billericay 'little worse except for bruises'.

The action was not just over the capital, however. So urgent was the call, all but two of 10 Group's squadrons had reinforced Air Vice-Marshal Park's fighters. 'B' Flight of 152 Squadron, up from Warmwell, intercepted twenty-seven

III/KG 55 He 111s attacking Portland, destroying one of the bombers. Later, the Me 110s of *Erprobungsgruppe* 210 headed across the Channel to attack the Supermarine Spitfire factory at Woolston, Southampton, but fortunately they were so heavily engaged by anti-aircraft fire over the Solent that the raid was aborted. As the enemy withdrew back to Cherbourg, so ended the great assault of 15 September.

For Fighter Command, the day had undoubtedly been a great victory, and Göring's huge effort to force the British fighters into the air for destruction *en masse* had failed. The British press proclaimed that the RAF had destroyed a total of 185 enemy machines, for the loss of only thirty fighters and ten pilots. In reality, the Luftwaffe had suffered fifty-six aircraft destroyed, less, in fact than on 15 August (seventy-five) and 18 August (sixty-nine). Nonetheless, this day's fighting, still celebrated annually as 'Battle of Britain Day', represented, as the defenders so clearly sensed, a major turning point. Across the Channel it must by now have been becoming increasingly clear that Göring was unable to deliver.

Monday 16 September After the previous day's massive effort, both sides were no doubt relieved that the day was overcast and stormy. The only drama was played out off the east coast, when 616 Squadron's Flying Officer MacFie and Pilot Officer Leckrone intercepted and destroyed a Ju 88 attacking a convoy. The third member of their Section, Sergeant Iveson, ran out of petrol and ditched in the sea twenty miles off Cromer; fortunately he was rescued by an RAF launch.

Tuesday 17 September Göring remained insistent that the RAF would be destroyed in 'four or five days', ordering a return to attacks on Fighter Command installations and aircraft factories. In another effort to force the RAF fighters up, *Luftflotte* 2 launched a huge *freie hunt*, coming in over Dover and Folkestone at 15.00 hours. Each wave comprised two gruppen of Me 109s, which were incoming until 16.00 hours. Sensibly, Air Vice-Marshal Park largely ignored these incursions, although 501 Squadron was bounced by elements of JG 53 over Ashford, losing Sergeant Eddie Egan. Sergeant Tony Pickering:

I was flying with Sergeant Eddie Egan when he was killed. I didn't know Eddie terribly well, but I suppose I could count him as a friend. We were flying along, just the two of us, looking out all the time for trouble, and I saw four Spitfires, or what we thought were Spitfires, behind us. We were talking to each other on the R/T, monitoring the movements of these fighters. Suddenly one of them zoomed forward, just left the others standing, shooting Eddie down. I turned towards Eddie's assailant but the old Hurricane was just too slow. The Hun just shot Eddie down and flew off with the others, they just climbed high and left us. I looked over the side and saw Eddie going down, the aircraft in flames. Eddie crashed in a wood outside Ashford in Kent. After landing I filed a report on the location, and six months later had to see the Air Ministry and pin-point the site as Eddie had not been found. The next I ever heard of Eddie Egan was when I happened to read a newspaper article about his bones having been found by an aviation archaeology group – at the very spot I had told the authorities about in 1940. I got in touch but was not called as a witness by the resulting inquest, which was rather surprising given that I had actually seen Eddie go in!

The Hurricanes of 607 Squadron were up from Tangmere, having scrambled in flights, 'A' Flight first, followed by 'B' at 15.05 hours – it was the Squadron's fourth patrol of the day. 'B' Flight patrolled the Biggin Hill–Gravesend line at 17,000 feet, an arguably suicidal height given that 11 Group were reacting to a fighter sweep which were almost always flown at 20,000 feet or higher. Pilot Officer Harry Welford:

When attacked we were warned to break formation. I broke and took evasive action as a result of which I lost the Squadron. As we had instructions to reform rather than fly alone, I saw a group of fighters ahead and intended joining up with them when I saw that they were Me 109s! I took a quick burst but then an unseen 109 fired a cannon shell which hit my air intake. I did a quick flick roll which dropped me below cloud. Again no 109s about and just a lone Hurricane which guarded my tail as I forced landed. The engine had seized and looking down I saw a field into which I thought I could land. As I made the approach glycol and smoke streamed from the engine and when I opened the hood the fumes were sucked through the cockpit and impaired my vision. The field was smaller than I thought but there was a wattle fence which acted like an arrester wire and the plane skidded across the second field, and was brought to an abrupt stop by a tree at the far end, making me crack my head on the reflector sight and blood poured from my face. Thinking that the plane might catch fire, I undid my belt and jumped out only to fall flat on my face because my leg, which had been injured by shrapnel, collapsed on me. Two farm workers rushed over and picked me up and put me on a wattle fence telling me that there was a German plane down in the next field with the pilot in it, very dead. I regret now that I declined their offer to show me, but at the time I felt pretty dicky. I gave my report to Flight Lieutenant Jim Bazin in hospital and he acknowledged that I had shot down the German aircraft in the field next to mine. I was consequently in hospital with 'Tubby' Badger, 43 Squadron's former CO. He was very brave, always laughing, but sadly ultimately succumbed to his injuries.

Pilot Officer Welford had been shot down by *Hauptmann* Edu Neumann, the *Kommandeur* of I/JG 27, the British pilot not returning to his Squadron until 20 October.

The day's fighting ended in a draw, both sides losing three aircraft, although all three enemy pilots were either missing or killed. At Fowlmere, 19 Squadron was celebrating the award of a DFM to Flight Sergeant George Unwin, whose score now stood at ten enemy aircraft destroyed. 'Grumpy' had been the first NCO in the service to ever fly a Spitfire and was therefore a most experienced pilot. He was also among the most aggressive, finishing the battle as Fighter Command's fourteenth top scoring pilot. In reality, however, given that the majority of Unwin's claims tally with actual enemy losses, he is significantly

Sergeant Eddy Egan, a Volunteer Reservist flying Hurricanes with 501 Squadron. On patrol from Kenley on 17 September 1940, Sergeants Egan and Pickering were bounced by Me 109s; Egan was shot down and reported missing. His aircraft and remains were not found until 1976, when his aircraft and remains were recovered by aviation archaeologists from a wood near Bethersden, Kent. Sergeant Egan was subsequently buried with full military honours at Brookwood.

higher up that list. For a pilot of 12 Group who was not engaged as often as those in 11 Group, and given that 19 Squadron was frustrated by their cannons jamming throughout the first half of the Battle of Britain, this represents an admirable achievement reflecting Unwin's great skill and personal courage.

Wednesday 18 September The first incoming raids were more waves of fighters, sixty in all, which were engaged, unusually, by around the same number of Spitfires and Hurricanes from 11 Group; two Me 109s were destroyed but five Spitfires were lost (one pilot killed).

The next raid, at 12.30 hours, saw a small formation of Ju 88s, escorted by 100 Me 109s, attack Chatham and Rochester. Over the latter, the JG 26 *Stabsschwarm* bounced 46 Squadron, Major Galland himself shooting down three Hurricanes.

The day's final, and most significant, raid came in at 16.30 hours, when, incredibly, the unescorted Ju 88s of III/KG 77, a unit fresh to the battle over southern England, attacked Tilbury Docks. This was every fighter pilots' dream, and Air Vice-Marshal Park's reaction was swift and decisive: fourteen squadrons were scrambled and intercepted the bombers over the Thames Estuary. 12 Group had scrambled the Duxford Wing at 16.16 hours, and soon all of the airborne RAF fighters were engaged. When the fight was over, eight Ju 88s had been destroyed, for the loss of just one defending fighter destroyed (pilot safe) and two damaged. The Duxford Wing, however, which now comprised five squadrons, claimed a staggering twenty-four enemy aircraft destroyed; it has already been explained that claims are increased together with the number of aircraft involved, but such a claim by the 12 Group squadrons can only be considered 'exuberant', as Air Chief Marshal Dowding himself put it. The Big Wing did, however, have a hand in destroying at least six of the Ju 88s brought down, although so did pilots of 11 Group. Once more, however, the Wing's claims were accepted without question.

The Duxford Wing, given that operating fighters in numbers was contrary to the provisions of the system and the requirements of Air Chief Marshal Dowding, was clearly a controversial issue even at the time. The adjutant of 242 Squadron, Flight Lieutenant Peter MacDonald, was an MP, who, in an incredible example of disloyalty and insubordination to his Commander-in-Chief, spoke with the Prime Minister personally to complain about the tactical argument that was developing between the commanders of 11 and 12 Group. Producing as evidence what we now know were massively inaccurate combat claims made by the Duxford Wing, MacDonald persuaded Churchill that 12 Group had got it right, while Air Chief Marshal Dowding and Air Vice-Marshal Park had got it wrong. Churchill was convinced: with high level political support for Air Vice-Marshals Leigh-Mallory and Douglas, the writing was on the wall for Air Chief Marshal Dowding and Park who had looked not to curry favour or support from those in high places, but simply fought the Battle of Britain to the best of their respective and exceptional abilities.

It is interesting to consider what the actual Duxford Wing pilots thought of the tactic. Squadron Leader Douglas Blackwood:

> I suppose I would not be speaking unreasonably by saying that the Wing was eventually a failure in so much as there was never really time to get three or four squadrons off the ground and into some shape and form to attack the usual mass of enemy aircraft effectively. On one or two occasions I was detailed by Bader and the AOC to lead the formation, so I know something of the difficulty. But when we did attack a formation of enemy bombers, the Wing was extremely successful. I would say that the main reason for any loss of effectiveness was primarily due to a sort of jealousy between the AOCs of both 11 and 12 Groups. 11 Group felt that it was their responsibility to protect London without 12 Group interfering.

Sergeant Anton Markiewicz:

Whilst flying with the Big Wing in 1940 I was in favour of it. Destroying German aircraft before they reached the target, or forcing them to drop their bombs just anywhere would be a great achievement. But to use a large force to do that, left the industrial Midlands without adequate protection. It was rather risky. No doubt Fighter Command knew that, and did not want to take any chances. One thing I do remember is that if we missed the Germans Bader was very displeased, and let us know in simple language!

Flight Lieutenant Kenneth Stoddart:

We of 611 Squadron were stationed at Digby and for a period of time flew down to Fowlmere on a daily basis, returning home at dusk. The only views I may have had about Big Wings or anything else in those days would have been made in ignorance; apart from Dunkirk, they were the first days that the Squadron was truly involved in a big action.

Squadron Leader James Thomson:

The Big Wing was a wonderful operation to take part in as we felt that we were answering numbers with numbers. However, subsequent study suggested that Air Vice-Marshal Park's strategy may have been the sounder. He used smaller numbers to break up the attacking formations, so disrupting their concentration of force over the target area and the effectiveness of their attack. It also enabled him to retain some aircraft for the defence of their bases during that most vulnerable operation: refueling and re-arming. Furthermore, the Big Wing took some time to form up and reach the area under attack; occasionally it missed the boat.

The relative merits of the two methods were argued openly by the circulation of correspondence on the subject between the two Groups. Many of us felt that this was a diversion of mental effort from the main aim of defeating the Luftwaffe and was not entirely becoming of the authorities concerned.

Sergeant Ken Wilkinson:

Fighter Command's strategy of aerodrome locations was successful in that there were very few attempts in daylight of mass bombing raids over the east coast of England and Scotland, but the possibility always remained. The squadrons resting at Wittering, Kirton, Newcastle, Drem, Montrose, etc maintained the defence of the east coast. Most critics seem to forget that we had a lot to defend – this aspect may have had some bearing on the infrequent calls upon the Duxford Wing. If one can be satisfied that there was little or no likelihood of a major bomber offensive from the east, then the Duxford Wing was right. Seeing these large numbers of bombers and fighter escorts, and realising that 11 Group was continually taking a pasting, there had to be some help we could give; if 60 additional RAF fighters arrived from the north in time, chances were that the Luftwaffe could have been deterred earlier. Being the lowest of the low (i.e. a brand new RAFVR sergeant pilot), I had no idea about the arguments that we are now told were taking place regarding tactics, but my personal experience tells me that Fighter Command was dedicated to protecting our country and so I am loathe to believe that <u>one</u> Group AOC was pursuing selfish interests contrary to the common objective of defeating (or negating) the Luftwaffe.

Pilot Officer Vic Bergman:

In those heady days I was a mere pilot officer who loved flying, loved the Hurricane, and was able to point my guns at a German target. But my English was limited. I have always had the impression that the initial interception of the enemy was left to 11 Group. We were then to follow the raiders and damage or destroy as many as possible on their return journey. More than once, the Wing was released for lunch when Douglas Bader pegged into the dining room and called 'Come on boys, we are wanted!' That was followed by the clutter of cutlery on the unfinished plates – rush for the door, transport to dispersals, and in 15–20 minutes all 12 Hurricanes of 242 Squadron took off in formation on the grass airfield, immediately followed by ours of 310, and 19 Squadron's Spitfires from Fowlmere soon appeared overhead, their job being to protect us from the enemy fighters whilst we Hurricanes went for the bombers. It did not always work out like that, though. In mid-September our squadron was meeting a formation of Do 17s when we were jumped by a swarm of Me 109s: I was shot down.

Flight Sergeant George 'Grumpy' Unwin:

It didn't take Douglas Bader long to realise that sending a squadron of fighters to take on huge bomber raids was not the answer, especially as these raids were usually escorted by fighters. As he put it – if only we had three times the number of fighters as a unit we could shoot down three times the number of enemy aircraft. In my opinion there was a further factor that was behind his argument for the Big Wing; for the first five months of his return to the RAF he had been flying Spitfires: with 242 Squadron he was on Hurricanes, and no matter what the loyal Hurricane pilots may say, it was no match for the 109. Agreed, it could out-turn the Hun but obviously this is far outweighed if the target is leaving you by 30 mph. On the other hand, the Hurricane had it over the Spitfire as a gun platform, both from the steadiness of that platform and concentration of fire. In my opinion the Hurricane was capable of shooting down bombers more effectively provided it was not interfered with by the 109s. The Hurricane casualties at this time support this argument. Once we had the Big Wing operating it was very obviously the answer in that the Hurricane casualties dropped appreciably mid the number of German aircraft destroyed increased. The Wing started operating in the first week of September 1940, and was in action until November. In my opinion it was an unqualified success.

As for the argument as to the value of flying 60 fighters together, there really was no basis for this disagreement between the two AOCs, for the simple reason that it would not have been feasible to assemble such a large number of fighters from the aerodromes in 11 Group in time to intercept an incoming raid. We at Duxford and Fowlmere had a full 15 minutes of flying to arrive at the battle area (north of the Thames) and with our two aerodromes only a couple of miles apart we could easily assemble the Wing en route to London. I am convinced that the real trouble was caused by Keith Park steadfastly refusing to use the strength of Duxford to anywhere near its capabilities. Day after day we would sit at readiness without being called on to help out. When we were called out, quite often it was merely to patrol the 11 Group aerodromes whilst their squadrons were rearming and refueling. On other days we were too late on the scene. The most glaring example of this was when we were scrambled as a Wing and vectored to London area. After about seven minutes our Controller, using plain language, said, 'They are bombing North Weald, go there quickly!' This was the day that North Weald was very heavily damaged. When we arrived it was all over, we were too late, I suggest that 60 fighters could have considerably lessened that damage. The total flying time from Duxford to North Weald is six–seven minutes.

One other very important factor was the effect the Big Wing had on the German aircrews. They had been told that the RAF was just about finished and that all would soon be over. This was to boost their morale which by the time was pretty low – imagine their feelings when instead of being met by a depleted squadron, no less than 60 descended on them!

Pilot Officer Richard Jones:

Early in September 1940 I was transferred from 64 Squadron at Kenley in 11 Group to 19 Squadron at Fowlmere, a part of 12 Group. By then, the latter was a part of Douglas Barter's Big Wing. My immediate impression was the experience of flying with a Wing comprising five squadrons of both Spitfires and Hurricanes, instead of anything between 5–10 aircraft taking off from Kenley to intercept large numbers of enemy aircraft. To me this experience gave enormous confidence, looking around and seeing anything from 50 upwards of fighters keeping me company! The Big Wing must have had a great effect on the lowering of enemy morale, who, for the first time, encountered such a formidable opponent.

Flying Officer Frank Brinsden:

The constraints of Bader's ponderous formation was disaster in my opinion, a retrograde step. Nothing was achieved by arriving en masse because the Wing disintegrated almost immediately battle was joined. In fact time, and therefore advantage, was lost during assembly and this compounded the effect of scramble orders. These observations on tactics are, of course, in retrospect but I do recall at the time feeling some unease or dissatisfaction at 19 Squadron's inability to do better.

Thursday 19 September High winds, low cloud and heavy rain over England greatly reduced enemy air activity, which was largely confined to isolated raids by solitary aircraft, several of which were shot down.

Ludlow's Pilot Officer Laurie Whitbread poses with his 222 Squadron Spitfire at Kirton in June 1940. Blooded over Dunkirk, Whitbread destroyed an Me 109 in the Battle of Britain before being shot down and killed over Kent on 20 September 1940.

On this otherwise inauspicious day, British Intelligence intercepted and decoded a signal confirming that Hitler had postponed Operation *Seelöwe* 'indefinitely'.

Friday 20 September With the daylight bombing offensive having failed, the *Jagdwaffe* had resorted to flying *freie hunt* operations over southern England on a regular basis. While this was welcomed by the *Kanaljäger*, who for weeks had been frustrated by their close escort role, Göring had decided that one *staffel* in each *jagdgeschwader* would be converted into the *jabo* role. The operational value of the fighter-bomber was undeniable, but only presupposing a surplus of aircraft. The *jagdflieger* were furious that their new found freedom was to again be limited, especially as they had done everything possible to increase the performance of their aircraft to keep pace with a progressive enemy. The Me 109 could only carry one SC250 bomb, so even a complete *staffel* of *jabos* could cause little damage. The strategy, however, was that while Fighter Command could ignore fighter sweeps, it would be unable to do so if some aircraft within the formation carried bombs. The guinea pigs for this new idea were elements of *Erprobungsgruppe* 210. and *Lehrgeschwader* 2. In mid-September these units were moved into the Pas-de-Calais, largely to be escorted by Major Galland's JG 26. Within the fighter units, the leadership was bitterly criticised for this move which represented the first major crisis between the *Jagdwaffe* and the *Oberkommando der Wehrmacht* (OKW).

The first 'Tip n'run' raid, as they widely became known, occurred this day, when twenty-two II/LG 2 fighter-bombers, protected by numerous fighters, made a sortie to London. Not knowing of the enemy's new plan, the RAF controllers did not at first react, and were therefore surprised when II/LG2 swooped down and dropped bombs on the capital. The 11 Group Spitfire squadrons from Biggin Hill and Hornchurch were scrambled late, and the enemy fighter escort pounced on them over the Maidstone area.

222 and 603 Squadrons were scrambled from Hornchurch at 10.55 hours, but as they desperately clawed for height at full throttle over the Thames Estuary, the Me 109s fell on them. The first pilot of Fighter Command to fall that day was the former's Pilot Officer Laurie Whitbread. Sergeant Reg Johnson:

> My vivid memory is that this sortie was a 'B' Flight commitment only, led by Pilot Officer Broadhurst in Blue Section, followed by Pilot Officer Whitbread, myself and another in Green Section. We climbed to the suicidal height of 14,000 feet and stooged around in tight formation with only one pair of eyes available to scan the sky in front, perhaps over 200°. I do not think that we deserved to be jumped upon, but we certainly invited it. We were banking gently to the left, which allowed me at No 3 to look over the top of No 1, and I shouted the warning 'Bandits, 2 o' clock above – attacking!' I turned over and dived straight down. There is no way that Pilot Officer Whitbread could even have seen the enemy, formating as he was on the aircraft to his left and with three-quarters of his head and back to the attackers. When I left, it was his right side facing the 109s, which were already in firing range. I can only assume that having received my warning he too rolled to his right, exposing his left side to the enemy and was hit before he could commence his dive. It was a tragedy.

Pilot Officer Whitbread had been attacked by *Oberleutnant* Hans 'Assi' Hahn of II/JG 2 *Richthofen*. As Spitfire N3203 plunged earthwards, Hahn noted with satisfaction his nineteenth victory; four days later he would destroy his twentieth and receive the *Ritterkreuz*.

At 10.45 hours Flight Lieutenant Ted Graham of 72 Squadron had led off from Biggin Hill the Spitfires of Pilot Officers Lindsay, Males and Holland. At 10.25, Flight Lieutenant 'Pancho' Villa and Sergeant Rolls also entered the fray. At 11.20 hours over Canterbury, 23-year-old 'Dutch' Holland was blasted out of the sky. Although badly wounded he managed to bale out and was later admitted to hospital. Before he died, his last words to the doctor were, 'I'm all right, old pal, "Dutchy" can take it.' Pilot Officer Lindsay was also shot up, but although his Spitfire was seriously damaged the pilot was unhurt. Pilot Officer Robert Deacon-Elliot:

Johannes Seifert, a successful fighter pilot of JG 26, decorated with the Knight's Cross. Like many Germans who survived the Battle of Britain, *Hauptmann* Seifert was later killed opposing the American daylight bombing offensive.

I recall this date vividly. At the last moment before scramble, Operations HQ requested two pilots of 72 Squadron to proceed to Hawkingc and escort an Anson aircraft with army officers aboard who were spotting for shells landing on the French coast fired from big guns in the Dover/Folkestone area. Names were put into a hat and mine, together with Flying Officer Robson came out. At this point 'Dutch' Holland, a very close friend of mine, approached me. He was worried about the hazardous nature of the mission and volunteered to take my place. Naturally I said 'No', as my name had come out of the hat.

Whilst escorting the Anson at very low-level, reports from Operations warned us of enemy aircraft in the area, but at much greater heights. However, the Anson pilot decided to get back to Hawkinge quickly, yes, very quickly! We saw him push his nose down to sea level and beat it for base. He must have exceeded the Anson's speed limit because on seeing the aircraft at Hawkinge I noticed that the entire fuselage fabric was stripped to the extent that you could see through the aircraft. Mission accomplished, it was back to Biggin Hill. There I learned of 'Dutch's' death, which, at the time, was attributed to a direct hit by our own guns. A ghastly thought – had I accepted his offer to take my place we may both still be here today. I was also involved in a similar sortie three days later but on that occasion I was shot at and lost my tailplane and huge sections of my port wing. I crash landed at Detling having been escorted all the way down by Sergeant Norfolk. That was the end of Spitfire X4413, relegated to the scrap heap!

Over Maidstone at 11.30 hours, *Hauptmann* Johannes Seifert of I/JG 26, and *Oberfeldwebel* Heinrich Gottlob of II/JG 26 each picked off a 253 Squadron Hurricane. Sergeant R.A. Innes safely baled out but Pilot Officer Barton was wounded and later admitted to Ashford Hospital. *Oberleutnant* Erbo Graf von Kageneck of III/JG 27 fired at a Hurricane, possibly P5179 flown by Sergeant Kee. Pilot Officer John Greenwood:

> I remember being with Sergeant Kee and diving for our lives into cloud. As I recall he copped a little enemy fire and we landed together shortly afterwards having made no effort to locate the rest of the squadron. Kee's aircraft had a little fabric missing and a few holes. I think that I also stopped a .5 armour piercing bullet through my head armour, the core of the bullet lodging in my neck. It had only just penetrated but it was as sharp as a needle. I kept it as a souvenir for many years.

Also at 11.30 hours, in the south London area, *Gefreiter* Gruber of III/JG 27 attacked and damaged a Hurricane, possibly V6722 flown by Pilot Officer Glowacki of 605 Squadron. The squadron diary relates:

> A showery day with high winds. It appears that rough seas during the last few days have delayed German invasion plans. The moon is now well in the wane. Squadron did one patrol today and encountered only Me 109s which adopted different tactics to usual by flying alone in twos, threes or fours over a wide area which our pilots found very harassing, never knowing when they would swoop down on them. No losses, but Pilot Officer Glowacki's aircraft damaged Category II from cannon and machine-gun fire.

At 11.35 hours, *Hauptmann* Seifert struck again when he attacked Pilot Officer Edsall of 222 Squadron, seriously damaging his Spitfire which spiraled out of the fight to make a forced landing without flaps back at Hornchurch. Edsall subsequently overshot the airfield and crashed through the perimeter fence but was only slightly injured. At the same time, *Feldwebel* Heckman of II/JG 3 shot down 222 Squadron's Pilot Officer Assheton, who safely abandoned his aircraft high over Kent. At 11.34 and 11.35 hours, the German *Oberkannone*, Major Werner Mölders, destroyed two Spitfires of 92 Squadron over Dungeness: Pilot Officer Howard Hill, a 20-year-old New Zealander, was killed and Sergeant P.R. Eyles was never seen again. These two victories were numbers thirty-nine and forty for Major Mölders and earned for him the *Eichenlaub* (Oak Leaves) to his *Ritterkreuz*, making him only the second Luftwaffe officer to receive this coveted decoration. Flight Lieutenant Alan Wright:

The Polish Sergeant Anton Glowacki of 501 Squadron makes out a combat report at Kenley in September 1940. A successful fighter pilot, after the war Glowacki emigrated to New Zealand, where he died in 1980.

The squadron (92) was split in half due to oxygen failure. The first half were surprised by Me 109s. Howard and Eyles, both of Green Section, were lost. I have a vivid picture in my mind of me leading Green Section on that day. After the split, the front two sections, led by the CO, Squadron Leader Sanders, were left flying in a close formation of two vics in line astern. I happened to glance to my left and was amazed to see a 109 taking the place of the Spitfire that I expected to see there, a glance to the right showed another one! I immediately shouted 'BREAK!' and pulled up and around in a tight turn. The others probably reacted similarly. I noticed that we were immediately above a coastal town. I cannot remember what I did after the break, when flying at 200–300 mph one can, in just a few seconds, find oneself quite alone and unable to re-join the action.

At that time, many squadrons, including ours, would be vectored towards our targets in a close formation of nine, comprising three vics with two weavers criss-crossing overhead and safeguarding the blind area behind the formation. Its advantage was that the 11 aircraft as a whole were very manoeuverable. The danger was that if anything happened to the weavers and they were unable to use their R/T, the rest of the Squadron would be utterly vulnerable. On this occasion, in the rush to scramble, one or more of the rear pilots could have failed to switch on their oxygen, or it may not have been working properly, so that in the confusion the first half were left unaware that no-one was guarding their tails. No oxygen at the height of Everest could put you to sleep without you even realising it. Very sad, especially about Howard Hill who had flown with our Squadron since the previous October.

92 Squadron's Red Two, Pilot Officer T.S. 'Wimpey' Wade, attacked an Me 109 at 11.45 hours, 27,000 feet above Folkestone:

Ganic Squadron was split up due to attack by Me 109s. I got on the tail of one and after a short burst the enemy aircraft dived away steeply. At about 4,000 feet it pulled out and started evasive tactics. After two–three minutes it headed south-east at 5,000 feet. I fired a number of short bursts from astern at 100–150 yards range but was unable to close any further. After doing evasive medium turns for a short period he pulled up steeply into cloud at 2,000 feet, 15 miles from the French coast after which I lost him. I had seen my ammunition going into the wings but without the desired effect.

92 Squadron's CO, Squadron Leader P.J. 'Judy' Sanders, also attacked an Me 109 at 11.45, firing 2,450 rounds at it:

Flying Officer Alan Wright DFC poses with his groundcrew and 92 Squadron Spitfire at Pembrey in August 1940. Wright destroyed at least five enemy aircraft during the Battle of Britain, one of them being a rare nocturnal victory, an He 111 over Bristol. On 27 September while flying from Biggin Hill, his Spitfire was damaged in combat with Me 109s off Brighton; Wright forced-landed, slightly wounded. He survived the war but has since died.

As Squadron Leader patrolling Dungeness I knew that there were enemy aircraft about and was weaving. At 27,000 feet, Blue Section, behind me, was attacked, so I broke quickly to the left and saw an Me 109 also turning left behind me. I gave one short burst about 120 yards from above and from the right. The enemy aircraft at once half rolled to the right and dived steeply for about 10,000 feet. He then pulled up and I got a good deflection shot at him from above and slightly behind. He half rolled again and dived. I fired intermittently at him on the way down and he did not pull out. I came out of the dive at 500 feet and he crashed into the sea about five miles south of Dymchurch and disappeared. I tried to re-group the Squadron and received instructions to return to base and land.

Squadron Leader Sanders was also attacked during the combat and his Spitfire was damaged, possibly by *Leutnant* Altendorf of II/JG 53. He subsequently returned safely to Biggin Hill, although soaked in petrol from a ruptured fuel tank, only to burst into flames when he lit a cigarette shortly after landing. Fortunately he survived but was out of the battle from then on.

At 12.10 hours, 25–30,000 feet over the Ashford/Canterbury area, Biggin Hill's 72 Squadron Spitfires met fifty Me 109s. Afterwards, Sergeant Rolls submitted the following report:

I was Red Two in a section told to intercept the enemy fighters. We took off at 1040 and after having completed a patrol by ourselves were instructed to rejoin the rest of the Squadron as the leading Section. We did this and met the enemy near Canterbury. We were climbing up towards one batch of Me 109s when we were warned by our rearguard of another lot diving down on us. We kept climbing into the sun and the rest of the Squadron had used evasive action to get rid of the Me 109s. I soon found myself over Ashford and unable to see any of my Squadron near me. I was flying along at 22,000 feet when I saw what appeared to be a Spitfire or Hurricane diving down to 16–18,000 feet and then climbing again. I decided to have a look at it so I got into a position so that I had the sun behind me and could see the machine clearly. As it came up in the climb I saw plainly that it was actually an Me 109 with a yellow nose and fin. I let it climb up again and waited, thinking perhaps it would dive again. It did so and then I dived out of the sun onto its tail and waited for it to start to climb before I pressed the tit to fire. I let it have about three seconds fire and the 109 did a stall turn to starboard and I followed it. I saw a large black piece break away from the side of the cockpit on the port side. I got it in my sights again as it turned and let it have another four seconds burst. This time I saw smoke and what appeared to be oil and water coming from underneath it. It turned to dive and as it did I let him have a final burst when the whole back of the cockpit dropped away and the rest dropped down towards cloud. This was at about 12,000 feet. I flew through the cloud and made for the aerodrome as I had only 10 gallons of petrol left. I watched the spot where the machine went in and it was near Wye, between a wood and lake so far as I could make out from my own position. I landed back with three gallons of petrol and a leaky glycol seal.

Sergeant Rolls had shot down the only Me 109 to crash in England that day, an E-4, 2789, of 9/JG 27, which went in at Ospringe, Kent, killing the pilot, *Unteroffizier* Erich Clauser.

The skirmish over, the *Jagdwaffe* retired to their French bases leaving behind just Erich Clauser dead in the wreckage of his fighter. Fighter Command, however, had lost four pilots killed and several others wounded. Pilot Officer Geoff Wellum:

> On September 20th I flew two patrols with 92 Squadron in Spitfire K9998. After this length of time I can recall nothing of the action, but I do remember that during September and October 1940, Me 109s were always in the Biggin Hill Sector in numbers and caused problems. I recall that they were always above us as we never seemed to be scrambled in time to get enough height. Our climb was always a desperate, full throttle affair, but we never quite got up to them. I did manage to get a crack at two Me 109s on one patrol but although I saw strikes I could only claim them as damaged.

Although the surprise attack of 20 September 1940, had been successful, the Germans soon found, to their discomfort, that even the Hurricane could run rings around a bomb-laden Me 109. Eventually *Jagdführer* General Theo Osterkampf protested to Jeschonnek, chief of the Luftwaffe general staff, that it would not take long for the whole fighter arm to be grounded due to these 'senseless operations'. His protests helped. In November there were fewer such attacks and at the beginning of December they were halted altogether.

Saturday 21 September After the events of the previous day, Fighter Command could no longer ignore enemy fighter sweeps, not knowing whether the formations contained *jabos*. Responding to every single excursion, however, would be debilitatingly exhausting, and naturally Air Chief Marshal Dowding could not risk being unable to intercept a formation of German bombers, should one appear. To help give an earlier and clearer picture of what the enemy formations consisted of, two 'Jim Crow' flights were formed. Pilot Officer Keith Lawrence:

> It was at the Prime Minister's insistence, we were told, that 421 and 422 Flights were formed, operating from Gravesend. Our pilots had all fought in the Battle of Britain and our purpose was to fly singly or in pairs, reporting on the movement of ships or monitor the build up of Luftwaffe formations. I have always wondered whether this wasn't perhaps a ruse by Churchill and Dowding to conceal the fact that ULTRA was intercepting and de-coding Luftwaffe signals.

There was comparatively little action this day. At 16.30 hours, a single Spitfire of 611 Squadron, now based at Ternhill in Shropshire, was scrambled to intercept a 'bogey' at 20,000 feet over Liverpool; the enemy aircraft was a Do 215 of 2(F)/121 engaged on a reconnaissance sortie in preparation for the night's raid on that city. Pilot Officer Denis Adams:

Pilot Officer Keith Lawrence, a New Zealander who flew Spitfires with 234 Squadron during the Battle of Britain. Awarded a DFC for his efforts during summer 1940, in November 1940 he was shot down over the Channel by *Oberleutnant* Gustav 'Mickey' Sprick, *Staffelkapitän* of 8/JG 26. Baling out into the sea, Lawrence survived the experience and later fought with distinction over Malta.

The Do 215 was at about 30,000 feet when I caught up with it. I climbed a couple of hundred feet higher on the starboard side before attacking. When I did so my third and fourth starboard guns fired two rounds each before jamming. Apparently the armourers believed that the lubricant they used froze at such a great height. One thing omitted from my official combat report was that I tried to get the Dornier to land at either Hooton Park or Speke airfields. From that height the pilot could have made either easily, but he seemed pretty single-minded, flying a straight course but losing height all the time. I think he was pretty lucky to find a field to land in, North Wales is pretty rugged country!

The enemy aircraft crash landed at Trawfyndd. Unteroffizier Peizer was killed, but Leutnant Book, and Feldwebels Jansen and Kühl were captured.

Sunday 22 September Again Luftwaffe activity was vastly reduced, so much so, in fact, that Fighter Command flew less sorties on this than on any other day during the Battle of Britain. Again the only enemy aircraft brought down was a 4(F)/121 reconnaissance machine, which was shot down into the Channel by Spitfires of 234 Squadron.

Monday 23 September Another day of fighter sweeps, which took place between 09.30 and 10.45 hours when 200 enemy fighters roamed over Kent

Pilot Officer Dennis Adams (fifth from left) poses with other pilots of 41 Squadron, displaying a trophy from a Do 215 reconnaissance bomber destroyed by Adams over North Wales on 21 September 1940. The *balkankreuz* has been pressed into service as 41 Squadron's scoreboard.

in waves. Due to the presence of *jabos*, 11 Group had to intercept, losing eight aircraft with a pilot killed. In response, six Me 109s were shot down, one of them by Squadron Leader Bob Stanford Tuck of 257 Squadron just ten miles off Cap Gris Nez. Two 10 Group Spitfire pilots were also reported missing from routine patrols over the Channel.

Tuesday 24 September An early morning *freie hunt* saw the fighters of both sides clash once more over Kent. Over Rochester, Major Adolf Galland's JG 26 bounced 17 Squadron, shooting down two Hurricanes. One of these was the *Kommodore's* forty-first victim, for which he received the *Eichenlaub* to his *Ritterkreuz*.

Although London was still being hammered by the *kampfliegern* every night, it was definitely clear that the daylight emphasis had shifted away from attacks on the capital to another attempt to destroy Fighter Command in the air, and the factories supplying it. Once more the Supermarine factory at Woolston became the target for *Erprobungsgruppe* 210, which accurately dive-bombed the waterfront works. Although no serious damage was caused, ninety-eight employees were killed and forty wounded.

Wednesday 25 September The Bristol Aeroplane Company at Filton was accurately bombed by KG 55, confusing 10 Group's defences which assumed the enemy's target to be the Westland Aircraft Factory at Yeovil. The raid was intercepted after bombing their target, although 152 and 238 Squadrons destroyed five bombers during the subsequent interception. Later that day, the oil tanks at Portland and Plymouth were also bombed.

Interestingly, on this day *Luftflotte* 3's Me 109s, which had been moved up to the Pas-de-Calais in preparation for Operation *Seelöwe* and the major air assault on England, returned to their bases in Brittany and Normandy. It was also noted by British Intelligence that barges, concentrated around Calais, were also dispersing: it was clear that the immediate threat of invasion had passed. Sergeant Reg Nutter:

> The Battle of Britain is a kaleidoscope of memories: I recall trying to warn Pilot Officer Carl Capon that he was about to be attacked by an Me 109 but was unable to do so because my radio was u/s. I remember the Hon. David Coke returning from a battle over Portsmouth in which a German bullet had nicked him in the little finger of his throttle hand. Once I chased a lone Do 17 reconnaissance bomber in and out of clouds along the south coast whilst listening to American jazz music which was coming over the Squadron frequency!

Thursday 26 September The Luftwaffe's day started with reconnaissance flights over England, followed by raids on towns such as Whitby, Coventry and the area between Folkestone and Southampton. That afternoon saw large formations of German aircraft bound for Southampton, bent on the destruction of the Woolston works. As the German formation massed over northern France, consisting of over 100 fighters and bombers, the radar plotters and controllers of Fighter Command Operations Rooms in 11 Group anxiously monitored the progress of the raiders. Among the RAF defenders scrambled to intercept were the Hurricanes of 607, 229, 238 and 303 Squadrons, along with the Spitfires of 152, 602 and 609 . By 16.00 hours the raiders had reached their target and the Me 110 *zestörers* of ZG 76 carried out a fighter sweep in advance of KG 55's He 111s arriving over the factory. As the bombs came crashing down, the sky over the south coast rapidly became a grim killing ground. 607 Squadron ORB:

> Combats took place over the Isle of Wight and Portsmouth, at sea, 6 to 12 miles south of the Needles between 1550 and 1630 hours. Two Sections and one Flight took off at different times and eventually joined up as a Squadron to patrol base, Flt Lt Blackadder leading. They were vectored to Southampton where AA fire drew their attention to the presence of enemy aircraft. About 50 to 60 enemy aircraft in all, possibly Do 17s or Me 110s, were seen at 12,000–15,000 feet, flying in mass formation slightly below and to the right of the Hurricanes. Enemy aircraft were diving down on the various targets in and around Southampton. The Squadron went into sections line astern and made a head-on

diving attack, which developed into a beam quarter attack. Afterwards the Squadron was broken up and carried out a number of individual attacks on two separate enemy formations, one going out to sea and another coming inland. Each formation consisted of 40 bombers accompanied by fighters, positioned above and behind.

Our losses: Flying Officer Bowen baled out and returned to base from Kaylthorpe, Isle of Wight. Enemy losses: One Do 215 and one Me 109 destroyed in sea and one Ju 88 damaged.

Flight Lieutenant Francis Blackadder:

We were ordered to Southampton. Just as we reached it the Hun was diving down to bomb the Supermarine works. We came down on top of them in a head-on attack, some say right through the balloons, the Hun disappeared to the south towards Portsmouth and we were split up. Sergeant Cunnington and I spied another large formation of bombers, which we climbed up to meet. They had fighter escort and we were only able to carry out a rather stupid quarter attack, hose-piping the formation. I reported on their further movements to operations and they were eventually intercepted by fighters over Weymouth.

The Me 109 which had been claimed as destroyed by 607 Squadron had been shot down by Pilot Officer Surma, who, after the Squadron had been split up, had encountered twenty to thirty Ju 88s at 15,000 feet at 16.10 hours over the sea, fifteen to twenty miles south of St Catherine's Point. Below the bombers were their fighter escort of Me 109s, as the Polish pilot later reported:

I saw a bomber break away from the enemy formation and tried to overtake him. At the same moment I saw an Me 109 gliding down behind and above the Ju 88s. I followed the enemy aircraft for a considerable distance and, when several miles south of St Catherine's Point, I made two or three long bursts from 100 to 150 yards on the tail of the enemy aircraft, which immediately went into a dive and crashed into the sea.

At 16.20 hours, Flight Lieutenant Charles Bowen was shot down by Me 110s over the Isle of Wight. He parachuted to safety and his Hurricane crashed at Kaylthorpe, from where he made his way back to Tangmere.

The raid on the Spitfire factory was a complete success: the Supermarine works was gutted; thirty-six civilian workers were killed and sixty seriously injured. Aircraft production was completely halted, which caused a noticeable reduction in deliveries of new aircraft to squadrons over the next few weeks. During August, 149 Spitfires had been built at Woolston and, to the great credit of the Woolston work force, 139 were built in October. However, the attack had come too late in the Battle of Britain to have any effect on its eventual outcome. By this time, Lord Nuffield had opened the new Castle Bromwich Aircraft Factory (CBAF) in Birmingham, where the mass production methods of the automotive industry was being applied to Spitfire production. The new MK IIs were already rolling off the line, but production was not yet in full swing. Eventually, CBAF would take over as the main centre of Spitfire production, and clearly after the events of this day, which emphasized Woolston's vulnerability, that could not come too soon. Woolston was close enough to France to be bombed in daylight, whereas CBAF, which was far beyond the range of escorting fighters, was not. Surprisingly, however, the Luftwaffe never mounted a major nocturnal raid against CBAF, which again suggests that Luftwaffe intelligence was poor.

Pilot Officer Harry Welford:

We had a very intrepid and garrulous fighter pilot in Jim Bazin's Flight called Charles 'Chatty' Bowen, who seemed to have continued success in combat. Franek Surma envied 'Chatty's' success and wished that he could borrow some of Bowen's luck. 'Chatty' was known to carry a toy stuffed elephant as his mascot and Franek pleaded with, and cajoled 'Chatty' into lending it to him for a sortie. After much argument, and persuasion from other members of the flight, 'Chatty' agreed to lend Franek the mascot to fly with, on a sortie that he was not flying himself. Franek was instructed to return the mascot to Bowen's Hurricane the moment he landed. Later Surma returned jubilant as he had destroyed an Me 109. As promised he gave the mascot to the flight rigger, who returned it to the cockpit of Bowen's Hurricane. 'Chatty', however, could not find the mascot on his next trip and cursed Surma for not returning it. On that sortie Bowen was shot down and it was assumed that his change of luck was due to Surma not having returned the toy elephant. The twist to the tale is that when the salvage team recovered the wreckage of Bowen's Hurricane from the Isle of Wight, they discovered the elephant in the cockpit; it was believed that the mascot had fallen from the gun sight and jammed the rudder pedals.

The time that Franek and myself were in 'B' Flight together seems to have been extremely short, only six days – but the loss of life occurred so rapidly that the experiences of a lifetime could be crammed into a few days. Franek was the sort of person who immediately became popular and when we had a beer in the evening he would teach us how to say 'Nostravia', which means 'good health' in Polish. He impressed me. The story about the mascot I may have got second hand from some-one writing to me in Ashford Hospital after I had been shot down. The story is certainly true to the characters of both Frankie and 'Chatty', though. Before I was wounded, Frankie had certainly tried to borrow the mascot then. He used to call Bowen his 'lovelee boy', which infuriated 'Chatty' beyond all reason, as Bowen was a very senior pilot and Surma was junior even amongst his Polish comrades!

Friday 27 September At 08.15 hours, a large formation of Me 110s and Me 109s swept over southern England, and were engaged by 11 Group's squadrons. The enemy made no attempt to withdraw, however, milling about in an effort to ensure that when the next raid came in – directed at London – Air Vice-Marshal Park's fighters would be on the ground, being 'turned around'.

At mid-day, some 300 bandits crossed the Kentish coast between Dover and Lympne, heading for Chatham. The bombers, Ju 88s of I and II/KG 77, had been late arriving at the rendezvous with their escort, and were without fighter protection. Some 120 Spitfires and Hurricanes fell on them: eleven Ju 88s were lost. The frantic assistance calls from the enemy bomber crews brought numerous Me 109s and 110s rushing to the scene, and a huge dogfight developed over 'Hellfire Corner'.

At 11.55 hours, the Duxford Wing, now comprising 19, 242, 310 and 616 Squadrons, was scrambled to patrol the London area. Sensibly, Squadron Leader Bader, having learned valuable lessons during the last three weeks, climbed the Wing to 23,000 feet. Milling around between Canterbury and Dover the Duxford pilots saw a large formation of Me 109s; Bader led the Wing up-sun and, for once enjoying the advantage of both sun and height, bounced the enemy fighters. A typical cut and thrust fighter combat ensued, in which 242 Squadron's Pilot Officer Homer went down in flames. 310 Squadron's Sergeant Kaucky attacked an Me 109 but was indignant when 'a Spitfire dived on the same enemy aircraft and shot it down!' Sergeant Kominek sent another 109 down into the sea, the 9/JG 3 pilot being posted *vermisst*. Flight Lieutenant Gordon Sinclair:

I was attacked by an Me 109. The first burst destroyed my ailerons, the second set my Hurricane on fire. Because my ailerons had been shot away I was unable to invert my aircraft and drop out, and as the machine entered a steep dive I had some difficulty in extricating myself from the cockpit and getting over the side. I landed by parachute in the branches of a fir tree near Callam, from which some farm hands helped me down to mother earth. My Hurricane was practically burnt out before it crashed. This was the second time I had baled out during the Battle of Britain.

616 Squadron, having received many replacement pilots and now categorised a 'B' unit, was flying at 25,000 feet, above and behind the Spitfires of 19 Squadron, which was above the Wing's two Hurricane squadrons. There were Me 109s lurking higher still, however, which dived out of the sun, shooting down the weaver, Pilot Officer D.S. Smith, who crash landed but died from wounds in Faversham Cottage Hospital the following day. Pilot Officer Ken Holden claimed an Me 109 destroyed, and Sergeant Copeland a probable.

19 Squadron reported that the Wing had intercepted 'approximately 20 bombers and innumerable fighters', but Squadron Leader Lane's Spitfires were also hit by the high flying and unseen Me 109s. Sergeant Bernard 'Jimmy' Jennings:

I attacked the leader of a formation of five Me 109s and saw him turn to starboard with black smoke coming from his engine. As I followed him down I saw tracers pouring past me and found the other four 109s chasing me. I broke right and turned away. Pulling up, I

Flying Officer Ken Holden was a pre-war member of 616 'South Yorkshire' Squadron, an Auxiliary unit. Having scored over Dunkirk, Holden destroyed another Me 109 on 27 September 1940. The following year he commanded 145 Squadron, a part of Wing Commander Bader's Tangmere Wing, and survived the war.

saw a Spitfire or Hurricane in flames, spinning down; the pilot jumped out and I followed him down to the ground, he landed OK in a clearing near a big wood.

Sergeant David Cox:

Upon scramble I had jumped into the nearest Spitfire, QV-L, as mine would not start. This aircraft was nearly always flown by Sergeant Plzak, our 6' 6" Czech who had dubbed me 'Little Boy'. To save time I buckled on his parachute, which was already in the cockpit – more of that later!

We were top cover of the Duxford Wing but were attacked by a large number of Me 109s in the Dover area. After some hectic moments avoiding being shot down, I found myself more or less on my own between Ashford and Folkestone. I then saw towards Folkestone a Hurricane being attacked by four Me 109s. Before I could give any assistance, which was my intention having got within a few hundred yards of the scrap, the Hurricane went down in a vertical dive inland. (The Hurricane was probably Flight Lieutenant Sinclair's, which crashed at Godmersham, a few miles north of Wye).

The four Me 109s then turned their attentions to me. They knew their stuff as two got above me and two below. Naturally I had some hectic moments of turning this way and that as they came at me in attacks from all directions. I remember doing quite a lot of firing of my guns, but I think it was more in the hope of frightening them or raising my morale than in any real hope of shooting anything down!

All of a sudden there was a loud bang in the cockpit and for a second or two I was dazed. When I became normal again there was a lot of smoke about and my Spitfire was in a steep climb. As I lost flying speed I opened the hood, turned the aircraft over, undid my straps, and fell out, quickly pulling the ripcord of my parachute. When the canopy opened it gave me a severe jolt and several days later a lot of bruises showed on my chest and shoulders. Remember that the parachute harness was fitted for a man of 6' 6" – I was lucky not to fall out of it!

As I floated down a 109 came and had a look at me and then flew off. It was then that I felt a lot of pain in my right leg and saw lots of holes in my flying boots out of which blood was oozing. Ground observers said that I took about 15 minutes to come down as I was so high up – I know that it was jolly cold up there when I came out of the aeroplane. I landed in the corner of a ploughed field near a farm. By this time I was feeling rather rough and must have looked it as the farmer handed me a bottle of whisky, from which I took a large swig. I was later taken to hospital at Walsford where a surgeon from Folkestone Hospital extracted several large pieces of cannon shell from just below my knee cap down into my ankle. I was in hospital about six weeks and off flying until December 1940.

Pilot Officer Eric Burgoyne's 19 Squadron Spitfire was also hit by the 109s, but this pilot crashed and was killed at Coldred, just inland of Dover. Squadron Leader Lane himself had a lucky escape, but not at the hands of the enemy. Two days previously the squadron had begun re-equipping with Mk II Spitfires, one of which the CO was flying in this combat. After firing two short bursts, Lane's Spitfire became uncontrollable and skidded away, the pilot using all his strength to recover. This was only achieved at 3,000 feet, by which time Lane was considering baling out. Back at Fowlmere the aircraft was found to have a misshapen rudder and a wrongly adjusted trim tab which prevented one elevator functioning correctly. Flight Sergeant Unwin chased an Me 109 for ten minutes; dangerously near the French coast, a 30° deflection shot sent the enemy fighter into the Channel.

The Wing claimed to have destroyed thirteen enemy aircraft in this action, representing an over claiming factor of 3:1, offset against four aircraft lost, two pilots killed and another wounded.

There was also more action over 10 Group, when nineteen Me 110 *jabos* and thirty KG 55 were sent back to Filton. The German success of two days previously would not be repeated, however: 504 Squadron had wisely been moved from Hendon to Filton, and Air Vice-Marshal Brand's fighters were up and ready for the raiders. Only *Erprobungsgruppe* 210's *jabos* reached Filton, causing little damage but losing three Me 110s in the process. Simultaneously a large raid crossed the Kentish coast, bound for London, but this too was turned back by RAF fighters. Indeed, the Me 110s of V/LG 1 were virtually annihilated and had to be disbanded forty-eight hours later.

Two Hurricane pilots at readiness, 504 Squadron dispersal, Filton, September 1940: Pilot Officer Trevor Parsons (left) and Flight Lieutenant Tony Rook. Parsons was killed in action during 1942; Rook, who flew Hurricanes in Russia with other 504 Squadron pilots, survived the war.

609 Squadron had been engaged over the West Country, losing Pilot Officer R.F.G. 'Mike' Miller, whose Spitfire collided head-on with a 9/ZG 26 Me 110. Pilot Officer David Crook:

> I was flying just behind Mick and he turned slightly left to attack an Me 110 which was turning towards him. But the German was as determined as Mick and refused to give way or alter course to avoid this head-on attack. Their aggregate speed of closing was at least 600mph and an instant later they collided. There was a terrific explosion and a sheet of flame and black smoke seemed to hang in the air like a great ball of fire. Many little shattered fragments fluttered down, and that was all. Mick was killed instantly and so were his two German opponents; hardly any trace of them was ever found.

In a day of extremely heavy fighting, the Luftwaffe lost fifty-six aircraft destroyed and ten more damaged on offensive operations over England. Fighter Command lost twenty-eight fighters, with eleven pilots either killed or missing. Among the dead was 303 Squadron's Flying Officer Ludwik Paskiewicz, who had scored the unit's first kill on 30 August, and 603 Squadron's Pilot Officer Philip 'Pip' Cardell, whose Spitfire had been badly hit in combat over the Channel;

Two 504 Squadron Hurricanes on patrol from Filton, September 1940. Moved from Hendon due to raids against aircraft factories in the West Country, the Squadron saw much action and acquitted itself well.

unfortunately the pilot's parachute failed and he fell into the sea within sight of Folkestone. His friend, Pilot Officer Dexter, landed his Spitfire on Folkestone beach, commandeering a rowing boat and recovering Cardell's body. The 23-year-old pilot was taken home and buried at Great Paxton.

Saturday 28 September Smarting from the previous few days rough handling of their bombers, both *Luftflotte* 2 and 3 left their slower He 111s and Do 17s on the ground, sallying forth with small formations of faster Me 110 *jabos* and Ju 88s escorted by vast numbers of Me 109s – three entire *jagdgeschwader*. Flushed with recent success, the 11 Group Controller flung his fighter squadrons at the bombers, only to be dismayed when 200 Me 109s appeared. Although the bombers failed to reach their targets, Fighter Command's losses were heavy: fifteen aircraft were lost, nine pilots killed. Of the aircraft destroyed, eleven were Hurricanes, providing further evidence of the type's obsolescence. The *jagdwaffe* lost only three Me 109s and one pilot killed. Among the RAF squadrons engaged was 607, as the unit's diary recorded:

The Squadron patrolled areas between Beachy Head, Selsey Bill and Benbridge for about an hour, flying at about 12,000 feet. Three to four miles off Selsey the presence of about 40 enemy aircraft at 20,000 feet was reported by the Sector Controller. The Squadron climbed to investigate, and in doing so were attacked by a section of Me 110s, which had detached from the main enemy formation which was flying in circles and stepped up from 20,000–25,000 feet. The Hurricanes took evasive action and, although considerably damaged by cannon and machine gun fire, all but two returned to base. 'B' Flight was unable to climb fast enough to follow. The Squadron had climbed into the sun, and so patrolled Portsmouth until ordered to land. Whilst returning to base, two rear guard aircraft of 'A' Flight attacked a Do 215 flying at 5,000 feet over the sea, south of Selsey Bill, but without result. They were at once attacked by two Me 109s but took successful evasive action.

Two longstanding members of 607 Squadron were missing from this engagement, namely Flight Lieutenants William Gore and Maurice Irving.

In his log book entry for this day, Pilot Officer Richard Jones of 19 Squadron wrote, 'Shot down and crash landed at Hawkhurst, Kent. Killed three sheep. What a bloody mess!!!' Pilot Officer Richard Jones:

When patrolling the Tenterden area at 29,000 feet, the Controller informed us that as there were apparently no enemy aircraft in the vicinity we could return to 'Pancake'. I was 'Arse-End Charlie' and relaxed slightly as we dived to 20,000 feet. Suddenly about four feet of my starboard wing just peeled off – my initial thought was that it was a poor show on a new aircraft. Then a loud bang and hole appeared above the undercarriage. I was obviously the target of an enemy fighter up-sun. Immediately I took evasive action, simultaneously my engine cut for good and I was suddenly in a high speed stall and spin. My radio was u/s so I was unable to inform the squadron who returned to base blissfully unaware that I had been shot down.

I recovered from the spin at about 10,000 feet – the aircraft was not responding to the controls – I realised too that the hood was completely jammed. I subsequently crash-landed with a dead engine in one of only two suitable fields in a heavily wooded area just outside Hawkhurst. Unfortunately I did so amongst a flock of sheep and regret that several were killed. I was rescued by the army and first taken to the Hawkhurst doctor who treated a flesh wound to my leg, then to the Mess prior to returning safely to Fowlmere. My Spitfire had a broken propeller and radiator, a few holes and some missing parts, but was otherwise relatively intact.

Sunday 29 September There were no major engagements this day, although KG 55 sallied forth at 18.00 hours to bomb Liverpool. Instead of taking the direct route, making landfall over the Southampton area and flying due north, as the enemy bombers did after dark, in order to avoid 10 Group's day fighters, the Heinkels flew across the sea and along the Irish coast. Detected by radar, however, the He 111s were intercepted by the Hurricanes of 79 Squadron, which

Enemy airmen indicate bullet damage to the He 111 sustained over England. The mainstay of the enemy bomber force, by 30 September the He 111 units had suffered such heavy losses that the type was withdrawn to operate nocturnally.

was scrambled from Pembrey in South Wales. One bomber was destroyed and two others badly damaged, but three Hurricanes were lost with one pilot killed. Pilot Officer P.F. Mayhew forced landed at Enniscorthy, County Wexford, in neutral Eire. Although his aircraft was impounded, the pilot was subsequently repatriated.

Monday 30 September At dawn, most of England was shrouded in low-lying mist and swept by a light, generally north-easterly wind. The enemy had been active over the south-east coast since 06.35 hours, when lone reconnaissance aircraft probed inland as far as Farnborough and Worthing. At 09.00 hours came the first attack on Kent when twelve bombers and fifty fighters crossed the coast east and west of Dungeness respectively. Met by twelve British fighter squadrons, the raiders penetrated as far as the airfields at Biggin Hill and Kenley. Meanwhile, more German fighters patrolled Dungeness and others remained offshore at Dover. During the ensuing action, Northolt's 229 Squadron received rough treatment by the enemy: within eight minutes of combat four Hurricanes had been shot down, with three pilots wounded and one killed. At 10.10 hours, a further seventy-five enemy bombers and fighters crossed the coast at Dungeness and again made it to Biggin Hill and Kenley where the defenders broke up and scattered the enemy formations.

The next attack was to be launched against the West Country and undertaken by *Luftflotte* 3, involving the Me 109s of I and II/JG 2 with II/JG 53, and Me 110s of I and II/ZG 26. Together the raid comprised 100 enemy aircraft on a *freie hunt* which crossed the Dorset coast at St Alban's Head and penetrated to the Somerset border. 504 Squadron at Filton was scrambled to patrol Bristol, it being feared that the Bristol Aeroplane Works might again be the raiders' target. 238 Squadron's Hurricanes patrolled Bournemouth, meanwhile, but although they did not meet the enemy two Hurricanes collided and were lost. Pilot Officers Simmonds and Kings each baled out safely, although the latter was severely shaken as his parachute had ripped when it came into contact with his aircraft's tail. Pilot Officer Richard Covington landed his Hurricane in a field adjacent to where King landed, but later returned safely to base. 609 Squadron's Spitfires were scrambled from Warmwell, and at 11.00 hours 56 Squadron, which had earlier that morning flown down from Boscombe to operate out of Warmwell, was also scrambled to intercept the enemy raid.

56 Squadron's Hurricanes had been ordered to climb to 22,000 feet and patrol their airfield at Warmwell, but when at just 16,000 feet and still climbing, the enemy was sighted approaching from the south-east and out of the sun – Me

Exhaustion: Flight Sergeant 'Taffy' Higginson, a pre-war professional airman with 56 Squadron, snatches some 'kip' between sorties at North Weald.

110s flying at 22,000 feet and the Me 109s higher still. Pilot Officer Taffy Higginson was 'Baffin Leader' and he led the Hurricanes straight for the Me 110s in a head-on attack. As he later recorded in his log book, there were 'Fouzens of 'em'. At 11.25 hours, Higginson opened fire at the leading Me 110. As the two aircraft flashed by at a terrific closing speed, Baffin Leader immediately delivered a six second burst at an Me 109, but from 400 yards range his fire appeared ineffective. Red Three, Sergeant George Smythe, saw the Me 110 that Higginson had attacked break off and head for France with its port engine streaming smoke. Both crew members were in fact wounded, and the aircraft was subsequently written off when it crash landed in France.

Hauptmann Helmut Wick, *Kommandeur* of I/JG 2, and his *Stabschwarm* then pounced on 56 Squadron. Within seconds the German ace had added numbers thirty-two and thirty-three to his score. *Oberleutnant* Fiby, I/JG 2's adjutant, also claimed a British fighter destroyed. Fortunately for 56 Squadron, 609's Spitfires were just about to intervene. The Squadron was led on this occasion by Flight Lieutenant Frank Howell, who, upon sighting the enemy, had cleverly led his Spitfires out and up-sun over Weymouth Bay. 'Sorbo Leader' ordered sections line astern; just in the nick of time for the hopelessly outnumbered Hurricanes, 609 Squadron bounced the Germans from above and out of the sun over Weymouth. Howell led 'A' Flight off to attack from starboard, while Pilot Officer Michael Appleby led 'B' Flight off to port. Three Me 109s in line astern, and at the same height, passed Appleby's port side travelling in the same direction. At first the Spitfire pilot thought that the fighters were Hurricanes, and swung round to protect their rear, but soon realized his mistake; 'B' Flight then dived out of the sun, guns blazing. Appleby fired six two-second bursts onto the rearward Me 109, noting hits around the cockpit area, and flashes from within as the enemy aircraft dived down. Having followed the Me 109, Appleby broke off when another fighter appeared in his rear view mirror, although fortunately this proved to be a Spitfire.

In his dive after an Me 109, Pilot Officer David Crook's speed built up to 500mph, the sea rushing up at him. As he gingerly eased out of the dive, the strain was terrific and a black mist formed in front of his eyes. Upon levelling out, however, Crook attacked the Me 109 from below and astern as it too pulled out. The enemy fighter rolled over onto its back, burst into flames and dived straight into the sea off Swanage. Crook watched fascinated as the aircraft hit the water in a great cloud of white foam. The pilot did not get out. Sergeant Alan Feary had stuck with Crook and witnessed the German's demise. Crook then spotted a lone Me 109 going flat out for France. Crook dived again and easily caught the Me 109, at which he fired a 'good burst'. The cockpit canopy broke off, flashing by dangerously close to the pursuing Spitfire, and the Me 109 plunged towards the sea. To Crook's amazement, however, at sea-level the aircraft flattened out and climbed, streaming glycol. The Me 109 was still travelling at full speed for France, although badly hit. Crook poured the remainder of his ammunition into the enemy fighter from very close range. The Me 109 hurtled into the sea at great speed. Crook circled the spot but there was no trace of anything, just the waves of a neutral sea. The chase had actually taken him to just fifteen miles off Cherbourg, a very dangerous place indeed for a lone Spitfire to be. Having hastily returned to the English coast, elated at having destroyed two enemy aircraft in one sortie, Pilot Officer Crook approached the cliffs in Weymouth Bay at 300mph, just above the wave tops. At the last minute he pulled back on the stick, rocketing over the top 'to the very considerable amazement of some soldiers!'

Meanwhile, Howell's 'A' Flight were also getting stuck into the enemy. Pilot Officer John Bisdee, Yellow One, was flying in line astern on Sorbo Leader when three Me 109s made a beam attack on Yellow Section. Bisdee shouted 'Break Left!' and the enemy fire was avoided by a narrow margin. 'The Bish' then saw a lone Me 109 some 300 feet below him and diving south. The Spitfire pilot rolled over inverted, so as to prevent his engine from cutting, and in the process fired all his ammunition at the enemy aircraft. Pieces of tail unit broke off, and thick black smoke poured from the engine. Bisdee was then attacked from behind and immediately broke off. Red Three, Pilot Officer Michael Staples, got in a quick deflection shot at a fleeting Me 109 which emitted glycol as it dived seawards. Pilot Officer Keith Ogilvie: 'We ran into a swarm of Me 109s. I paired off with one and we commenced turning, I was pleased that the Spitfire was able to turn inside of the 109, but he suddenly flipped over and disappeared before I had fired a shot – a moral victory only!'

As quickly as it had begun the fight was over, the Germans heading back to France, and the Spitfires and Hurricanes retiring to their bases. Thanks to 609 Squadron's timely intervention, although still heavily outnumbered, for the loss of just two Hurricanes with both pilots safe, the RAF pilots had definitely destroyed four Me 109s in addition to Higginson's Me 110. Thus was the scene now set for a major battle over Wessex.

Earlier in the day KG 55's Operations Officer, Major Dr Ernst Kühl, had liaised with the *Wetterstelle* (meteorological office), and in the *Kartenstelle* (map room) had prepared an operational order for an attack on the Westland aircraft factory at Yeovil. The bombers were to assemble over Normandy before proceeding to Cherbourg where the forty-three He 111s would rendezvous with their fighter escort provided by *Jafü* 3, forty-seven Me 109s of JG 2, five of JG 53, and forty Me 110s of ZG 26. The entire formation was then to set course for Portland Bill before forging its way inland just over twenty miles to Yeovil.

The first RAF squadron to engage was 238, the Hurricanes of which made a head-on attack on the Heinkels as the approached Portland. Soon the party over Lyme Bay was joined by the Spitfires of 152 Squadron and the Hurricanes of 56 Squadron. Squadron Leader Herbert Pinfold:

I led 56 Squadron into attack, but I was hit by the bombers' combined firepower. With the cockpit full of glycol fumes do I bale out over the sea or land on it? I then saw a small 'hole' in the cloud to the north. I throttled right back, opened the cockpit hood and glided towards it, keeping an eye on the engine temperature which was slowly going up due to loss of coolant. When over the 'hole' I was delighted to see land, and even more so to see Warmwell airfield, where I executed a 'dead-stick' landing. Subsequent inspection revealed no damage to the aircraft or engine other than a few bullet holes in the fuselage and glycol tank which was just in front of the cockpit. Lucky me!

Sergeant Peter Fox:

I was 19 years of age, had flown Hurricanes for 20 hours but just couldn't believe it when I saw the enemy which I understood to be a 60+ mix of Heinkels and their fighter escort. I had never seen so many aircraft together before. As far as I knew, we of No 56 Squadron would be attacking the bombers whilst a Spitfire squadron engaged the enemy fighters. Tally Ho! My mouth felt very dirty tasting with apprehension. We gained height going out to sea, and then curved down and round into attack the Heinkels which were going towards the English coastline. One or more of ours went to attack the enemy leaders, and others the rear. I selected one of the latter, aimed firstly at one engine, pressed the gun button and sprayed across to the other. I did not see any return fire, but suddenly the Heinkel started to slow down and slowly peel off to port. I started to follow him down, still firing, when there was an explosion and I saw there was very little left of my instrument panel. I had been advised by an 'old-timer' to fly with my hood open when in action as bullets could damage it and prevent it sliding back. Luckily I had followed this advice otherwise my head would have been blown off as the shell hit the canopy. I broke to starboard, pulling upwards and away, with all controls seemingly working correctly. I got over land at about 3,000 feet and was wondering whether I would make Warmwell when I saw flames coming up between my legs. I don't think I even thought of my next action, but I had turned the kite upside down, released my harness and saw my feet way above me and the plane above my feet, presumably stalled. Where was the ripcord? I told myself to calm down, as I remembered a film where a German was shown dead on the ground with fingernail marks where he had clawed at his ripcord when his parachute had not opened. I also recall remembering that someone had told me that three or six, or some number, should be counted before pulling the cord. My hand went to the metal 'D' ring, all was forgotten about counting and I pulled! I had never pulled a ripcord before, never seen one pulled, never seen a parachute packed, and never had any instruction. The 'D' ring was flung into the air followed by some wire. Obviously I'd broken it. Whether my hands moved towards the parachute strapped to my backside or not I'll never know, but my thoughts were that I had to open the pack somehow, when I felt the small tug of the pilot chute, followed almost immediately by the full wrench of the main parachute. I was safe!

The next second I was aware of an 'enemy' racing down to shoot me, a pilot over his homeland who, if he survived, could fight again. A flaming plane – my Hurricane

Volunteer Reservist: Sergeant Peter Hutton Fox of 56 Squadron. Just eighteen years old during the Battle of Britain, Fox was shot down and baled out on his first engagement with the enemy. In 1995, Dilip Sarkar managed the recovery of this Hurricane's remains near Lyme Regis; an enthusiastic member of the team was Peter Fox himself, who subsequently became the only one of the Few to actually own his Battle of Britain fighter – even if in many pieces! Captured while flying Spitfires in 1941, Fox survived the war but died in tragic circumstances in 2005.

– then missed me literally by inches. The kite slowly screwed round, going into a steeper and steeper dive until almost vertical, aimed directly at the cross hedges of four fields to the NE of a wood towards which I was drifting. It hit the cross hedges spot on. A short, but noticeable pause and then a huge explosion followed by another pause before flames shot up to a great height. I'm glad that I wasn't in it! I was safe again, although I didn't feel so as the sea looked rather close and I didn't want to end up swimming. I then recalled the film about the German parachutist which had shown how, if you pulled the parachute cords on one side or the other, the direction was slipped off accordingly. I tried, but which side, as I could not see which way I was drifting. I certainly could not think aerodynamically at that moment. Leave well alone, I thought. I was safe again.

Blood! Trickling down my right leg. I tried to lift my leg to see, but couldn't. I'd met aircrew who had lost limbs but told me how they could still feel extremities which were no longer there. My leg had been shot off and would crumble under me when I landed. I was getting close to the ground, worried about my 'shot off leg', when I remembered the tale of a pilot being shot in the foot by the Home Guard. 'British!' I shouted at the top of my voice for the last few hundred feet. Oh Lord, I'm going straight into that wood. I grabbed the harness above my head to ease the bump of landing on my 'shot off leg' and pulled hard as my chute clipped a tree on the edge of the wood. I only fell over gently, when the wind pulled the chute sideways. I shouted 'British!' again, but as no-one came, started to roll up my parachute when a farm labourer climbed over a fence requesting confirmation that I was okay. My 'shot off leg' was not shot off. In fact it was a tiny wound about half an inch long on my knee where a small piece of shrapnel had entered, and another the same size also half an inch away where it had come out. A lady with a horse then came along and I draped my parachute over the animal, and off we went on foot until a van took me to Lyme Regis Police Station. I was entertained in a local pub to await Squadron transport back to Warmwell. Someone from Air Sea Rescue came in and I told him that I was pretty sure the Heinkel I had engaged with had gone down into the drink.

609 Squadron was also in action again. Pilot Officer Keith Ogilvie:

During the afternoon things happened on a much larger scale. We arrived in time to engage the He 111s. I did not see any results but found an He 111 and fired from his rear. The rear gunner returned my fire but then stopped. I began to pull in for a better target when there was an almighty bang behind me which destroyed my radio. A hole in the port wing told me that I had company! I was quick to break off, but never did see my attacker, nor indeed any other aircraft after that time. I made for home and landed gingerly but without incident with a flat tyre. As I recall we were so short of aircraft that I had to fly my plane to the Spitfire plant for repairs and returned to Middle Wallop with a serviceable example. It was an exciting day, but all I could claim in both engagements was experience.

By now the raid was approaching Yeovil, which was covered by cloud, concealing the target. Squadron Leader Peter Devitt:

> I was up with my 152 Squadron and poised to attack the bombers again when we saw bombs falling away from their bellies. On looking down to see what the target was, to my horror I saw the old Sherborne School Courts, which I knew so well, at that time I was just about to attack, which I did, but was molested by a pack of Me 109s. After that I could not see much of where the bombs fell, as I was too intent upon what was happening in my immediate vicinity, but I did see a great deal of smoke around my old school's buildings, and so knew that there were some hits and possibly casualties.

Due to the cloud covering, KG 55 had mistakenly bombed Sherborne instead of nearby Yeovil and the Westland Aircraft Factory.

High up, over 800 feet above sea-level, near the Chalk Pit on Pond Farm, 18-year-old Leslie Griffin was thatching a corn rick. Over the hill from a direction of Cerne Abbas the German formation appeared, travelling towards Yeovil:

> On spotting me they loosed off a burst of machine-gun fire. I slid off the roof as fast as possible. A few minutes later I returned to my work, watching those planes making their way, by which time the Yeovil barrage balloons had appeared and the Germans turned away. I could see everything. The Germans were en route for Sherborne, suddenly I heard and felt the shock of bombs as they were dropped on what had been, until then, a peaceful market town. A few minutes passed, then a pall of dust rose into the cloudy sky, and the sun shone through.

With the crash of the first bomb, picturesque Sherborne's idyll was shattered as its townsfolk experienced at first hand the true horror of war. When the siren wailed, warning people to take cover, the majority took heed, but none in the country town could have remotely suspected that soon Sherborne would actually be the target for two gruppen of He 111s. On what became known as Black Monday in Sherborne, the West Country was doing its best to enjoy the last of the summer sunshine. Monica Hutchings never expected anything to happen in the small town of 5,000, there being 'nothing worth bombing'. Furthermore, the town lay on the bombers' route to Bristol, a city already subjected to heavy attack, so when the siren sounded the young accounts clerk took little notice. As she made her way to take shelter at the Swan Hotel, Monica was momentarily petrified by the crash of exploding bombs – she threw herself down on the ground and lay in the centre of the main road. All around her flew masonry, and thick dust gathered in a great cloud. Next to her a man lay dying; he had forgotten the oft repeated instruction to lie flat.

For Sherborne, the raid was an absolute catastrophe. The bombs, 245 dropped by forty-three He 111s, extended in a distinct triple line from Bedmill Copse to Crackmore. The dead numbered eighteen, the injured thirty-two; thirty-one civilian properties were demolished, and 776 damaged. Percy Coaker, a well-known local character who ran a furniture shop in Cheap Street, put a sign on his door which typified the spirit prevalent throught Britain at the time: 'We have been bombed, buggered and bewildered, but business is as usual!'

As the raiders withdrew back to the coast, more 10 Group squadrons intercepted. Pilot Officer Roland 'Bee' Beaumont: 'After take-off from Exeter, I was leading 'B' Flight of 87 Squadron, the R/T told us to "Buster Portland, Angels 20, very many bandits heading south". Over Dorchester we briefly saw some Me 110s diving fast towards the coast, but we lost them in cloud. It was frustrating.'

At 16.00 hours, Squadron Leader Duncan MacDonald scrambled from Tangmere with his 213 Squadron to intercept a raid of 200 plus incoming over Kent. The 11 Group squadron, however, was soon vectored west, to reinforce 10 Group. Sergeant Geoffrey Stevens:

Quite abruptly and without warning we were ordered to turn 180° and told 'Buster'. R/T talk between our 'Bearskin Leader' and Ground Control elicited the information that it was a 60+ raid. We soon saw the enemy, first as dots which gradually developed into a mixture of He 111s and Me 110s, and some Me 109s which were, as usual, above us. We were at about the same height as the bombers and 110s. I initially went for one of the latter, but he evaded by executing a spiral dive. I did not follow as I wished to retain height, but then saw a formation of three He 111s below me, so I dived on them, selecting the left hand aircraft as my target. I got a fair amount of stick from all three gunners and opened with quite a long burst. However, I was travelling too fast and broke away left and downwards. I pulled back into a steep, almost vertical climb at full throttle, intending to come around again for another go, feeling quite sure that I had silenced the gunner in the aircraft I had fired at. At this point, near the top of the climb, the belly of an Me 110 slid into view going from right to left. I opened up and continued climbing. I saw strikes all along the underside, but I had reached the point of stall and at that moment ran out of ammunition. I fell out of the skies, as the saying goes, and as there was no point in returning to the fray I let the aircraft dive. This was very nearly my undoing, as I had built up too much speed and had great difficulty in getting out of the dive. The airscrew over-revved and sprayed oil all over the windscreen, but thankfully I made it by about 100 feet. Later the air frame fitter told me that several wooden slats which ran underside and aft of the cockpit had been stoved in by the pressure of my pull out.

213 Squadron had intercepted the enemy over Portland. For no loss, Squadron Leader MacDonald and Flying Officer Kellow each claimed an Me 110 destroyed. Sub-Lieutenant Jeram, a Fleet Air Arm pilot seconded to Fighter Command, claimed a further 110 as probably destroyed, while Sergeants Stevens and Barrow each claimed one damaged. Pilot Officer Atkinson claimed an Me 109 destroyed.

Just south of Portland, 504 Squadron eventually caught the enemy formation and Squadron Leader Sample led his Hurricanes into a quarter astern attack in sections on the rearmost German bombers, the Filton pilots scoring several successes but losing Pilot Officer John Hardacre, whose body was later washed up on the Isle of Wight. Sergeant Basil 'Mike' Bush:

After the interception I was unable to obtain radio contact with Filton. As it was getting dusk and I was lost somewhere south of Bristol I was fearful of getting caught in balloon cables, so decided to land in a field. I picked what I thought to be a long landing run in a particular field which I had spotted, but on the approach I came in low over a hedge and landed, only to discover that it was in a much shorter field than the one I had selected, and ahead I saw a brick wall. Having landed I could do nothing but jam on my brakes and switch off the engine. The action of applying the brakes – hard – resulted in tipping my Hurricane up on its nose. It then flipped over on to its back and I was left hanging by my harness upside down and several feet from the ground. Thankfully I was soon released by men of the Observer Corps from nearby Priddy village.

In fact, as the last aircraft of each side touched down at their respective aerodromes that fateful afternoon, so ended the final great daylight air battle of summer 1940. On 30 September 1940, the Luftwaffe had lost a total of forty-six aircraft destroyed, another twelve damaged, and two more written off in a flying accident. That afternoon, KG 55 had lost four He 111s, all shot down over the sea, all but four men of their crews perishing. The body of one, *Obergefreiter* Willi Schocke, was washed ashore at Horsesand Fort some two weeks later. Among those rescued by the *Seenotdienst*, albeit after thirty-six uncomfortable hours afloat in a dinghy, was Major *Doktor* Ernst Kühl, the remarkable *Geschwader* Operations Officer who had planned much of the raid himself. The crew of a 1(F)123 Ju 88 attacked by Pilot Officer Cock of 87 Squadron similarly crashed into the sea, its crew also being killed. 5/JG 2 had left *Unteroffizier* Alois Dollinger dead at Grimstone, his Me 109 burnt out at Sydling St Nicholas, Dorset.

Over the south-east, there had been further combat throughout the afternoon. Embroiled with Me 109s were the Spitfires of 41 Squadron. Sergeant Bob Beardsley: 'During this combat, in which I damaged an Me 109 and a Do 17, I had a hectic session with six 109s which chased me back to crash land on fire at Hawkinge. I got back to Hornchurch, carrying my heavy parachute, via the tube, arriving absolutely exhausted and to be asked where the bloody hell I had been!'

Fighter Command lost a total of twenty aircraft on this particular day. Eight had been lost over the West Country with two pilots killed and three wounded. A further eight aircraft were damaged.

After the events of this day, it was clear to the OKW that the Heinkel equipped *kampfgeschwadern* were unable to further sustain such heavy losses. Consequently the type was completely withdrawn from the daylight battle to operate over England at night. Another phase in the Battle of Britain had been fought to a close.

5

SURVIVAL:

1 OCTOBER – 31 OCTOBER 1940

With the failure of the enemy daylight bombing offensive, the Battle of Britain now moved into its fifth and final phase. In the main, the German bombing effort was shifted to nocturnal operations, chiefly to continue the progressive destruction of London, and secondly, and of much lower importance, to interfere with production in the great arms centres of the Midlands. During the day, Göring resorted mainly to using *jabos* at high altitude. As these were mixed in with ordinary fighters, the British controllers were unable to identify which enemy formations contained bomb-carrying aircraft and so were unable to prioritize, meaning that all had to be met. The volume of these raids, the majority against south-east England and London, stretched Fighter Command, already weakened by two months of bitter fighting, to the limit. 11 Group would have to mount standing patrols, of either one or two pairs of squadrons over the Maidstone Line. Immediately an approaching attack was detected, these units would be ordered to 30,000 feet, to contain the enemy fighters and provide top cover to other squadrons scrambled to meet the threat. The new enemy tactics required a much greater state of preparedness throughout 11 Group in particular, and the standing patrols greatly increased the hours of operational flying from 45–60 hours per squadron daily.

The OKW had also agreed that daylight bombing operations should continue to some extent, but only by either lone aircraft on occasions when weather conditions were suitable, or by Ju 88s of up to *gruppe* strength escorted by many fighters. Such bombing was clearly not preliminary to an invasion, but was considered by the enemy as an investment, showing small but growing damage to both industrial and domestic property. It was hoped that the proposed invasion would in the long term be assisted by such *störflug*, or harassing attacks, by hampering production and distribution, in addition to lowering public morale. The aircraft industry was still the main objective for such daylight raids: during October, thirty hits were recorded on aircraft factories against just eight between 7 and 30 September.

The wreckage of *Oberleutnant* Fiebig's Ju 88 (Stab I/KG 77), shot down by anti-aircraft fire while attacking the De Havilland works at Hatfield on 3 October 1940.

The 'Wizard Midget': Ian 'Widge' Gleed DFC (right) served as a flight commander with 87 Squadron during the Battle of Britain, destroying four enemy aircraft and a probable. He is pictured here as a squadron leader and CO of 87 Squadron with Wing Commander Victor Beamish AFC DSO DFC. Although the Station Commander of North Weald, the latter flew numerous operational sorties in the Battle of Britain, destroying two enemy aircraft and claiming numerous probables. Sadly Beamish was reported missing in 1942, and Gleed was killed in action over Tunisia the following year.

Sunday 1 October Portsmouth was the enemy's first target, being attacked by Me 110s which were intercepted by the Hurricanes of 238 Squadron; one raider was destroyed but two Hurricanes were lost and a pilot killed.

Freie hunten came in wave by wave over Kent, escorting *jabos*. Over Brighton, a lone Polish Hurricane of 303 Squadron bravely attacked II/JG 26 as the Me 109s withdrew, killing *Unteroffizier* Hans Bluder.

Among the missing was 607 Squadron's Flight Lieutenant Charles 'Chatty' Bowen, who had been shot down in combat with Me 110s over the Isle of Wight; the 'garrulous' flight commander would have no need of his elephant mascot now.

Monday 2 October Repeated attacks were made on both Biggin Hill and London from the high altitude of 30,000 feet. 603 Squadron clashed with 8/JG 3 over London, destroying three against the loss of a single Spitfire, the pilot of which baled out safely.

Tuesday 3 October The low cloud and rain that now enveloped the British Isles were perfect for the attacks against targets connected with the British aircraft industry carried out by lone Ju 88s. From mid-day onwards a fairly continuous succession of such raids crossed the south coast between 1,000–1,800 feet, bound for either London or the Midlands. Fighter Command flew countless patrols but failed to intercept any of the raiders due to the appalling weather. Bombs were dropped at Bedford, Kettering, Daventry, Stafford, Banbury, Crewe and Worcester. At the latter, the MECO factory was hit; much damage was caused, seven workers were killed and many more injured, before the Ju 88 responsible escaped back to France. The only raider accounted for by the defences was *Oberleutnant* Siegward Fiebig and his crew of *Stab* I/KG 77, who were captured when their Ju 88 was shot down by anti-aircraft fire attacking the De Havilland factory at Hatfield.

Wednesday 4 October The continuing bad weather saw enemy activity restricted to what were little more than reconnaissance sorties and nuisance attacks on shipping, East Anglia, Kent and Sussex. During the course of these futile operations, the Luftwaffe lost fifteen aircraft, and five more returned to their bases shot up. The only Fighter Command pilot lost that day, however, was a sad casualty: Flight Lieutenant Ken Gillies, a stalwart of 66 Squadron based at Gravesend, who was missing following combat with an He 111 off the east coast at 16.00 hours.

Thursday 5 October Although the weather remained poor, it had sufficiently improved for *Luftflotte* 2 to resume its high flying fighter sweeps and *jabo* attacks. 303 Squadron was positioned over Dungeness to intercept an incoming raid by *Erprobungsgruppe* 210, aimed at Beckton gasworks. The Poles hacked the Me 110s to pieces, destroying two and sending another pair back across the Channel and crash land.

Sunday 6 October Bad weather once more saw reduced enemy air activity, although 4/KG 30's Ju 88s bombed the Northolt Sector Station, blowing up a

Flight Lieutenant Ian 'Widge' Gleed DFC of 87 Squadron, unusually photographed by 'Rubber' Thorogood. Gleed was an exceptional fighter pilot, whose loss over Tunisia in 1943 was keenly felt.

taxying Hurricane, killing the Polish pilot. Seven German machines were brought down; Fighter Command lost no aircraft or pilots in aerial combat.

Monday 7 October Between 09.30–15.40 hours, *Luftflotte 2* mounted an endless stream of *freie hunten* and *jabo* attacks on south-east England. At 10.45 hours, a section of 41 Squadron Spitfires caught and destroyed an enemy reconnaissance bomber off Folkestone. Pilot Officer Denis Adams:

> I let the chaps think that I had been a clot and let the Dornier's rear gunner get me. In fact we had a new boy flying as my number three, and he was trying to get himself a squirt. As I turned to attack he let fly and took out my controls plus half the instruments, and also put bullets into my fuel tank! When I got back to Hornchurch in a commandeered car I was just sobering up, having met a very friendly farmer who insisted that I share a bottle of brandy with him. Oh boy, Kentish hospitality! Needless to say, I had quite a chat with the young man responsible next morning!

The main raid of the day, however, was again directed at the Westland Aircraft Factory at Yeovil. This time twenty Ju 88s of II/KG 51 were briefed to attack Westland, which had escaped damage a week earlier when KG 55 mistakenly bombed nearby Sherborne. The bombers were escorted by all three *gruppen* of ZG 26 and JG 2, and another seven Me 109s from JG 53. The raiding force was therefore substantial, numbering over 100 aircraft.

At 15.42 hours, the incoming raid was picked up on the radar screens and 10 Group began scrambling its fighter squadrons. Soon the Spitfires of 152 and 609 Squadrons, together with the Hurricanes of 238 Squadron, were engaged. Pilot Officer Richard Covington: 'I followed Bob Doe into attack, and I was going to have a go at this daisy chain of Me 110s that were milling about when an Me 109 got me from behind. I baled out – quickly!'

Pilot Officer Bob Doe:

> I attacked a Ju 88. My first burst stopped the starboard engine. Overtaking speed was very high so I half rolled upwards and attacked the enemy aircraft from above with a short burst from about 100 yards. I broke away and carried out a beam attack from the port side, from 300 yards. I broke away and started diving. As it dived a burst of fire appeared in front of the tail, which flew off. Three people baled out. The aircraft crashed in flames.

Pilot Officer John Bisdee of 609 Squadron also attacked the same bomber, which was flown by *Oberleutnant* Sigurd Hey of 5/KG 51:

> My starboard engine's radiator was hit. Though I dropped my bombs at once and switched the damaged motor to a feathered position, I could not hold my position in the Gruppe formation and fell behind. I then turned southwards, diving a couple of thousand feet, and tried to make the French coast on one engine. This time three fighters came up

Sergeant Denis Nichols of 56 Squadron. Like his friend Peter Fox, Nichols was shot down during his first combat flying from Boscombe Down, on 7 October 1940. Baling out and breaking his back, Nichols returned to operations and later flew as an airline pilot. In 1994, the author arranged recovery of 'Nick's' Hurricane from the crash site at Alton Pancras in Dorset, Nichols himself attending the subsequent excavation.

attacking from all different directions. First the controls were hit and I was only able to hold the aircraft horizontally by using the trimming system. Next the fuselage tank was hit which set the aircraft on fire. Then I gave the order to bale out, but received no reply as my crew had already left the aircraft unseen by me in the dense smoke. When the aircraft turned into a flat spin I was lucky to get out, but landed safely by parachute when I was taken prisoner by two old men armed with shotguns.

Pilot Officer John Bisdee: 'My most vivid memory of the entire Battle of Britain is coming right down to see that Ju 88 burning on the Downs with a crowd of yokels waving pitchforks and dancing around it! I did a victory roll over them and went back upstairs to see what was happening.'

At 15.30 hours, five 56 Squadron Hurricanes roared skywards from Warmwell. About ten minutes later, south-east of Yeovil, the 'Punjab' Squadron fighters entered the fray. Sergeant Dennis 'Nick' Nichols:

Like my friend Peter Fox, who had been shot down on the last big show, I was 19 years old and this was my first engagement. We took off from Warmwell being on detachment from our base at Boscombe Down. We took off in formation with me on the left of the leader, Flight Lieutenant Brooker, and I was 'Pip-squeak' man, the radio being blocked every 15 seconds. I can't remember hearing any R/T transmissions so perhaps the wireless was on the blink. I did not hear the 'Tally Ho'. Flying in tight formation the first I saw was tracer coming from one of our leader's guns. Quick glimpse and I saw a Ju 88 and fired my guns, still in formation, but had to break away to avoid collision with Flight Lieutenant Brooker. I then lost the squadron and pulled up, searching for the enemy. No sign of the bombers but some 110s in a defensive spiral well above. I pulled the 'tit' for maximum power and went to intercept. A Spitfire was attacking the top of the spiral so I went head-on for the bottom. I fired but, perhaps not surprisingly in view of their heavy forward-firing armament which I must have overlooked, was hit. Flames started coming from the nose of my aircraft and the windscreen was black with oil, so I broke away as I could not see out. I turned the aircraft on its back to bale out at 25,000 feet, first time a slow roll but I remained seated. Second time I tumbled out, spinning. I told myself not to panic and gave the ripcord a steady pull. When the parachute deployed, the lanyards on one side were twisted. I tried to untangle them without success but relaxed as at about 15,000 feet appeared to be coming down reasonably slowly. I did not see the ground coming up and crumpled in a heap upon landing. The Home Guard then appeared on the scene and told me to stick my hands up. They thought I was German but I just laughed at them between groans as I had actually broken my back. There was a Jerry parachutist stuck up a nearby tree, from the Ju 88, but the locals would not get him down until they had seen to me.

Sergeant Nichols had landed near the village of Alton Pancras, also on the Dorset Downs. At about 16.00 hours, Charlie Callaway was ploughing in the Vernall when he saw a parachute drifting towards Buckland Newton. He then saw the Hurricane 'coming down hard and well on fire!' His younger brother, Sam, was rabbiting nearby and he too saw the doomed British fighter 'descending at a shallow angle but all ablaze and travelling sharpish, like. It was so close that I could have reached out and touched it. There were several parachutes in the sky at the same time.' Villagers also recall cartridge cases from the combat overhead raining down on the cobbled streets.

At 15.55 hours, bombs began falling on Yeovil town centre. Not one bomb fell on the Westland works or airfield. Again, much civilian property was destroyed and sixteen people lost their lives, with many more injured.

As the enemy withdrew, the RAF fighters continually harassed them. Pilot Officer Roger Hall:

> I became separated from 152 Squadron, but saw what I thought were He 111s and got ahead of them near the Bristol Channel at a point which I think may have been Foreland Point. I did a head-on attack on the leader of the vic, opening at 1,000 yards – one long burst – and broke away above – half rolled and saw the left hand E/A drop from the formation with glycol pouring from him. He was going down fairly steeply. I then saw what I took to be two other He 111s flying NE. I chased them but caught up a Blenheim well inland past Yatesbury. Came down to 500 feet to pinpoint. Found five gallons in one tank only so put down in a field with wheels down, the engine having cut before I had completed my last turn in to approach the field. forced landed at Barton Stacey, but the Spitfire was a write-off.

At 16.30 hours Pilot Officer Herbert Ackroyd's 152 Squadron Spitfire was shot down, crashing at Shatcombe Farm, Wynford Eagle near Dorchester; the pilot baled out but had received fatal burns. The Dorset Constabulary noted the pilot's identity disc details and informed the RAF accordingly. Mrs Irene Akroyd was a WAAF at Warmwell and had watched her young husband's flaming Spitfire plunge from the heavens, not knowing, of course, the identity of the young pilot involved. Herbert Akroyd lingered on for a day in great pain before finding release in death on 8 October.

During this action, the Germans lost a Ju 88 and seven Me 110s destroyed. Fighter Command lost six fighters destroyed, one pilot killed with Pilot Officer Ackroyd expiring the following day.

Tuesday 8 October Four *jabo* attacks reached the capital throughout the day, protected by Me 109s at 32,000 feet, a massive height advantage. 66 Squadron lost two Spitfires over the Thames Estuary, both pilots being killed. A Defiant of 264 Squadron, engaged on a training flight, crashed at Marlow in Buckinghamshire, killing the crew, although the cause was unknown. Similarly, 303 Squadron lost a Hurricane which inexplicably crashed at Ewell, Surrey; the pilot, Sergeant Josef Frantisek, a Czech, was killed. With seventeen confirmed aerial victories, Frantisek would go down in history as the RAF's top scoring fighter pilot in the Battle of Britain, and his squadron, 303 Squadron, the top scoring unit. Sergeant Peter Fox: 'I remember well the greatest altitude I ever managed to achieve in a Hurricane: 32,800 feet. I really had to nurse the aircraft up the last few hundred feet and I kept falling out of the sky in stalls.'

Wednesday 9 October Squalls enabled small numbers of jabos to slip through Air Vice-Marshal Park's standing patrols and attack airfields in 11 Group, causing widespread damage. At 16.00 hours, Hornchurch's Spitfires clashed with II/JG 54 over the Thames Estuary. Flying Officer E.H. Thomas of 222 Squadron shot down *Feldwebel* F. Schweser of 7/JG 54, who forced landed and set his aircraft alight at Meridan Hunt Farm, near Hawkinge; the enemy pilot was captured by civilians. Also among the successful Spitfire pilots was 41 Squadron's Pilot Officer Eric Lock, who claimed two 109s destroyed over the Channel.

Eric Lock was a remarkable fighter pilot by any standards. A farmer's son from Bomere, near Shrewsbury, Lock had been brought up with a 12-bore and shooting game on the wing. His eyesight was exceptional, and his early mastering of deflection shooting gave him a clear advantage in the war torn skies of 1940. Fascinated by aircraft and inspired by the gliders of the famous Shropshire flying club at Long Mynd, in February 1939, aged nineteen, the young Eric joined the RAFVR and became a pilot. In June 1940, he was commissioned and posted to fly Spitfires with 41 Squadron at Catterick. On 26 July, the same month Pilot Officer Lock became a married man, the Squadron moved to Hornchurch. Between 15 August and 1 October, Eric Lock scored nine aerial victories, this feat being recognized by the award of a DFC. At first, however, Lock's stream of claims was treated with scepticism, but, as with 501 Squadron's Sergeant James 'Ginger' Lacey, post war research indicates that the Shropshireman's claims are all essentially accurate. By 3 August 1941, Lock was a flight commander with 611 Squadron, by which time he had been awarded a bar to his DFC and the DSO; his tally of enemy aircraft destroyed stood at twenty-six destroyed with eight probables. On the day in question, however, Flight Lieutenant Lock flew on a 'Rhubarb' with another Spitfire, and was last seen strafing German soldiers near Calais. Reported missing, even as late as 1983 the authorities were unable to provide the pilot's family with any information as to their loved one's fate. Research by this author in 1999, however, conclusively established that 'Sawn Off' Lock – so-called due to his slight stature – had been shot down off the French coast by *Oberleutnant* Johann Schmid of the JG 26 *Geschwaderstab* based at Audembert. On 6 November 1941, Schmid destroyed another Spitfire off Calais, bringing his score to forty-one victories in 137 combat sorties. While circling low over the point of impact, the wing of his Me 109F struck the sea and broke off. *Oberleutnant* Schmid, like Flight Lieutenant Lock, remains missing, emphasising the futility of war.

Thursday 10 October The pattern of small formations of high flying *jabos* continued. Fighter Command lost six aircraft, four pilots were killed and one wounded. The Luftwaffe lost seven aircraft. By now, both sides were suffering an increasing number of flying accidents, which under normal circumstances would be simply attributed to carelessness; these incidents, however, provide a

One of the most successful fighter pilots of the Battle of Britain was Pilot Officer Eric 'Sawn off' Lock, from Shrewsbury. Serving with 41 Squadron, between 15 August and 1 October 1940, Lock destroyed nine enemy aircraft, for which feat of arms he was awarded the DFC and Bar, a DSO following soon afterwards. His final score was twenty-six destroyed and eight probables, but the diminutive fighter ace was reported missing on 21 August 1941. Last seen strafing enemy troops near Calais, research by the author confirmed that Lock had been shot down into the Channel by *Oberleutnant* Johann Schmid of Stab JG 26. Lock is pictured here at Hornchurch with the station's mascot, 'Binder'.

firm indication that both sides were becoming exhausted. Sergeant Peter Fox: 'On this day, a Czech, Sergeant Hlavac, and myself were both weaving behind No 56 Squadron as "Tailend Charlies". Hlavac was shot down and killed, but I didn't even see him attacked, we all just flew on oblivious.'

Flight Sergeant Taffy Higginson:

The main recollection I have of serving with 56 Squadron at Boscombe Down and Warmwell is that we were a somewhat disorganised lot. As a result of the action that we had seen we needed to re-equip and receive replacement pilots. The Station Commander at Boscombe was a group captain who, I believe, later took a unit to Russia and was killed. He was a first class chap, good rugger player and liked by all. During the early part of our Boscombe sojourn I remember thinking that morale would perhaps be boosted if we had a Squadron mascot, so I went to the local town and bought a small monkey, which we named '109'. He was a great success and kept in a cage, on a lead. Anyway, the Station Commander gave a cocktail party for the Squadron and requested 109's presence. 109 went down very well, until, that is, he started to undertake enthusiastic sexual self-gratification! Morals being what they were in those days we had to remove him quickly!

Friday 11 October Yet more high-flying raids were incoming throughout the day, attacking targets in south-east England. It was a busy day for the enemy, the jabo pilots flying 115 sorties in total.

During the afternoon, German reconnaissance aircraft were most active all over England, gathering intelligence for the night's raids. Among them were two Do 17s of 1(K)/606 and another of 2(K)/606, which probed the Liverpool area. 611 Squadron, based at Digby, was operating a flight of Spitfires from Ternhill in Shropshire, to counter these incursions. At 17.30 hours, 'A' flight took off to patrol Anglesey, North Wales. At about 18.20 hours, while the flight was making a wide orbit at 17,000 feet in search formation line astern, Yellow Leader (Flying Officer D.H. Watkins) sighted the three enemy aircraft flying in a vic formation about twelve miles away and approaching from the south-west at 14,000 feet. After informing Red Leader (Flight Lieutenant Jack Leather), Yellow Leader ordered his section 'Echelon starboard, Go!', and attacked out of the sun. During the ensuing combat, two of the Dorniers were destroyed, while the third limped back to Brest badly damaged.

At 17.45 hours, 611 Squadron's Blue Section, Flying Officer Barrie Heath leading Sergeants Ken Pattison and Robert Angus, scrambled from Ternhill to patrol the Point of Ayr at 20,000 feet. Over Prestatyn, Blue Leader tally ho'd two Dorniers, approaching from the south-west, 500 feet below the Spitfires and quarter of a mile to port. Heath attacked one bomber, ordering Blue Two and Three to deal with the other. Over Denbigh, Blue Leader's damaged target disappeared into cloud, so the Spitfire pilot returned to base. Sergeant Angus also damaged the other enemy bomber, before it too disappeared, but Sergeant Pattison had disappeared.

It would appear that as Blue Section attacked, Blue Two somehow became disorientated and ultimately lost. In fading light and with no sophisticated navigational aids, the inexperienced Sergeant Pattison wandered across North Wales and Shropshire, then into north Worcestershire. With daylight fading fast, Harry Turner, the blacksmith at Cooksey Green, watched the Spitfire circling overhead with its landing lights on. The pilot selected a field adjacent to a farmhouse and was almost down safely when a herd of startled cows stampeded across the aircraft's projected landing path. Sergeant Pattison instinctively heaved the control column back, but inevitably the Spitfire stalled, crashing into a pear tree. Hitting the ground inverted and bouncing fifteen feet into the air, the aircraft then tore along the field until coming to rest against an ancient tree stump. Mr Turner, ran to the wreck, finding the pilot hanging upside down in his Sutton harness, which the blacksmith cut before releasing the trapped

Pilot Officer D.G. Williams of 92 Squadron, pictured with his Spitfire at Gatwick in April 1940. During the Battle of Britain Williams destroyed four enemy aircraft, shared two more and claimed a probable. On 10 October 1940, however, he collided with Flying Officer J.F. Drummond while attacking a Do 17. Williams was killed, his Spitfire crashing near Brighton; he was twenty years old.

sergeant. Thick black smoke belched from the wreckage as an ambulance arrived and conveyed the badly injured pilot to Barnsley Hall Military Hospital near Bromsgrove.

Sergeant Pattison was a married man from Nottingham, his wife, Joan, rushing to hospital only to see her husband linger in great pain until he passed away two days later. A VR pilot, Ken Pattison never met his daughter, Jean, who was born seven months after his tragic death. Pilot Officer Roger Boulding: 'It is astonishing, upon reflection, how many new pilots failed to return from their first engagement. To see was to live, but your 'eyes' only grew with experience.' Pilot Officer Denis Adams:

Sergeant Pattison would have been better off making a wheels up forced landing, his intention was no doubt to save his aeroplane, a valuable new Spitfire Mk II. I blame the CO and his Flight Commander for not briefing the new boy that his training was worth more than a Spitfire. In those days it was estimated that the cost of training a pilot to operational standard was £40,000, the cost of a Spitfire was £8,000.

Pilot Officer Peter Olver:

The mention of him dying in Bromsgrove Hospital grabbed me rather strongly as I was at Bromsgrove School and once visited a sick friend in the hospital. The thought of Sergeant Pattison also being there I find very sad, not implying any criticism of the hospital but rather that at such a young age I was unduly impressionable. At that period I was strongly under the impression that the war would be won before I could get there, so I applied for a posting straight from OTU to a squadron in the south of England. Fortunately for me, however, I was actually sent to 611 Squadron at Digby, a 'B' unit, on September 30th, with whom I remained for 16 days and received 18 hours of flying, some of it operational, until my posting came through to 603 Squadron, an 'A' unit, at Hornchurch. On my first subsequent operational trip, on October 25th, I was shot down by an Me 109.

Saturday 12 October Once more the *jabos* and fighters came in waves, there being seven attacks in total, five of which reached London.

Squadron Leader Bob Stanford Tuck, CO of North Weald's 257 Squadron, was at Biggin Hill visiting his old squadron, 92 Squadron, when the latter was scrambled. Jumping into a 92 Squadron Spitfire in preference to his own Hurricane, over Ashford 'Lucky Tuck' shot down an Me 109 of *Stab* II/JG 54, the pilot of which, *Leutnant* Malischewski, was captured. Sergeant Reg Nutter:

I found Tuck to be a very charismatic leader and this, combined with his exceptional combat record, immediately gave one a good deal of confidence in him. His style of leadership contrasted greatly with that of his predecessor, Squadron Leader Harkness. Tuck would make suggestions to the Controller as to how we would be better placed to make an interception, but Harkness would follow all instructions without question.

There is no doubt that before Tuck's arrival, squadron moral had sunk to a very low ebb; under his leadership there was a tremendous improvement. In many ways he was an individualist but he would go out of his way to give sound advice to other pilots.

On this day, *Generalfeldmarschall* Wilhelm Kietel announced the OKW's decision that the proposed invasion of England was to be postponed until the spring or early summer of 1941, and that in the meantime efforts would be made to 'improve the military conditions for a later invasion'.

Sunday 13 October More *jabo* attacks were made on London. Among the intercepting RAF fighters were the Spitfires of 66 Squadron, up from Gravesend. Corporal Bob Morris:

I remember Pilot Officer 'Bogle' Bodie coming back with his port mainplane knocked about by a cannon shell, and I had to rip part of the aileron off for him which he proudly took as a souvenir. I always remember a Spitfire coming in and making a horrible whistling noise – it had a bullet hole right through a propeller blade! As we didn't have a new propeller we smoothed the hole out and drilled corresponding holes in the other two blades – it then flew for another fortnight with that same airscrew! We had to drill the other holes because when a propeller is assembled it is very finely balanced to prevent vibration.

Monday 14 October Jabos caused damage to London's railroad network, and once more the fighters of both sides fought it out over south-east England. By now, in fact, due to their high flying tactics, aerial superiority was now swinging in favour of the Luftwaffe, which was winning the war of attrition. As ever, Fighter Command suffered not from a shortage of aircraft but battle-hardened pilots: on this day, another experienced pilot was among the dead, Flying Officer Ralph Hope of 605 Squadron who, while chasing an enemy aircraft, collided with a balloon cable. The loss of such men Air Chief Marshal Dowding could ill afford.

At night there was a massive raid on London, by the end of which 500 more Londoners were dead. Pilot Officer George Pushman:

We of 23 Squadron were based at Wittering, but flew mostly from Ford during the Battle of Britain, which was a very busy period. We used to have 10 days on duty followed by two days off. Flying at night in our Blenheims, we prowled around the east coast, but I never even caught a glimpse of a German aircraft.

Tuesday 15 October More disruption to the capital's railway network was caused by *jabos*, and in the resulting combats Fighter Command's losses were horrendous: eleven aircraft were lost, with five pilots killed. 46 Squadron's Hurricanes were among the RAF fighters in action that day, as the ORB describes:

The Battle of Britain was not just fought by Spitfires and Hurricanes, but by Defiants and Blenheims too. The happy groom is Pilot Officer Philip Ensor, a Blenheim night-fighter pilot of Wittering's 23 Squadron. Awarded the DFC, just ten days after his wedding, Ensor was killed in action on 8 September 1941.

Commencing at 1230 hours, a patrol was carried out by the Squadron over Seven Oaks and Gravesend. While flying at a height of over 20,000 feet, they were vectored east and attacked from the sun by a flight of Me 109s, three of our aircraft were shot down. P/O Reid attacked and destroyed one of the enemy but the others made a successful escape. It is recorded with regret that P/O P.S. Gunning was killed when his aircraft crashed near Little Thurroch, Essex. F/Sgt E.E. Williams was missing from this patrol, but it was later confirmed that his machine had crashed near Gravesend and his death had occurred. Sgt Gooderham escaped from his aircraft by parachute. He was suffering from burns but was not detained in hospital.

On this day, Major Galland led JG 26 on three escort missions to *Jabos* attacking London. During the morning sortie, *Unteroffizier* Scheldt destroyed a Spitfire of 92 Squadron over Maidstone, and during the afternoon I and II/JG 26 clashed with Hurricanes over the Thames Estuary; four were destroyed without loss. One of those Hurricanes was undoubtedly flown by Flight Sergeant Eric Williams, whose machine crashed through the roof of Barton's Timber Wharf at Albion Parade, Gravesend. So deep did the aircraft go in, that it defied all attempts at recovery, although a flight sergeant's crown was discovered together with other evidence identifying the aircraft as 46 Squadron's missing Hurricane. Indeed, Flight Sergeant Williams remains buried with his aircraft to this day, a recovery attempt by the authorities in 2006, following pressure from both enthusiasts and the developer building flats on the Albion Parade site, also being unsuccessful. Nearby, however, a memorial exists commemorating the missing airman, and the accommodation beneath which he lies entombed was appropriately named Williams Court.

Wednesday 16 October Fog ensured that flying, and fighting was minimal on this day. Pilot Officer Wallace 'Jock' Cunningham:

> Some six of the Czechs in our Duxford Sector had gained a working knowledge of English, although what they learned was influenced by their squadron associates. I remember one of them, Sergeant Plzak, sitting writing to his girlfriend in Cambridge and asking me 'Jock, what is difference between beautiful and bloody fool?' It was not long afterwards that we received a telephone call from that girlfriend but had to tell her that Plzak was dead.

Corporal Bob Morris:

> It was at about this time that we started seeing DFM and DFC ribbons on certain of our pilots' tunics, well deserved every one, we were all very proud.
>
> Once I watched some dogfights over Biggin Hill. We were in an aircraft bay and saw a German aircraft on fire. Four parachutes came out, two of which were on fire. We saw these two German aircrew falling faster and faster, until their parachutes were completely burnt away and they fell to their deaths.
>
> We rarely got to see shot down enemy aircraft because MUs took them away, but once I had the chance to look over an Me 109 which was on the Station and virtually complete. I looked in the cockpit and by our standards it was nowhere near up to the Spitfire's instrumental standards, it was very bleak.

Thursday 17 October The same pattern of raids continued. Sergeant Geoffrey Stevens:

> We of 213 Squadron were scrambled late in the afternoon, getting on for 1700 hours, and as we climbed away from Tangmere I remember thinking that I wished Flight Lieutenant Jackie Sing, the commander of 'A' Flight, was leading us as in my opinion he was the best. Neither did we have a Tail End Charlie, for reasons that escaped me.
>
> We climbed to about 17,000 feet when I noticed anti-aircraft shells bursting ahead and below. I reported this and at about the same time we had a course correction starboard. As we turned I saw strikes on Red Two, just ahead of me. We were flying the stupid close formation 'vic' of three aircraft in line astern (I was Yellow Two). Simultaneously I was hit in the engine by three or four cannon shells. The rev counter went off the clock and smoke and flames enveloped the outside. The standard practice if hit was to get out of

the action as quickly as one could. I therefore shoved the stick over and went into a spiral dive. Flames, smoke and glycol fumes were everywhere, and I went down switching off everything I could think of.

I entered cloud at about 10,000 feet, coming out at 5,000 feet whilst preparing to bale out. The flames appeared to have stopped. I lifted up my goggles to have a look round and saw that I was over a town. I knew that if I baled out my aircraft would cause some severe damage, possibly loss of life. A field containing an AA gun was within gliding distance and so I opted for a forced-landing.

I did not appear to be in any immediate danger at this stage and so settled into a straight glide towards the field. Having sorted everything out in my mind, knowing exactly what I was going to do, I was dismayed to see what I have since described as electric light bulbs, but what were in fact tracer shells, going past my cockpit. Looking in my rear view mirror I saw a yellow nosed Me 109 on my tail. Without power, evasive action is limited, especially with so little height to play with. I used rudder to skid out of the German's sights, and am told that fortunately he'd been chased off by another Hurricane. I had lost height, however.

The effect of this on my carefully planned approach was disastrous. I opened the hood and blinded myself with glycol fumes. I put my goggles on again, but by this time I was very low, about 100 feet, travelling much too fast and in the wrong position for an approach to the field. Everything was wrong! I did a steep left-handed turn towards the field and slammed the Hurricane onto the ground, it was all I could do. It was unfortunate that I had been forced to choose the one approach that ended up with my wing root against a four feet thick tree stump. The aircraft shot into the air and over onto its back, into a sort of marsh. With all that had gone on leading up to this, I had omitted to lock the sliding cockpit hood open, and my harness back. The hood consequently slammed shut and I was propelled forward upon impact with some force, cutting my head on the reflector gunsight.

I was now hanging upside down with blood running down my face. I could smell the petrol leaking out everywhere and hear the hissing of the cooling engine in the wet marsh. Otherwise everything seemed dead quiet. I tried to open the hood but it was useless. I was expecting the aircraft to go up in flames at any time and seemed powerless to effect an escape. I carefully released my straps and let myself down so that I lay on my back on top of the cockpit hood. I think that this was more to do *something* than continue hanging upside down doing nowt!

Although it seemed like an age, assistance actually came very quickly. People seemed to come from no where, including the Army. One helpful farmer got himself a corner post with a pointed metal end and rammed it through the perspex hood. Had I still been hanging upside down it would have gone straight through my head, as it was it went just past my nose! To cut a long story short, one wing was lifted enough to allow the hood to slide back. The small clearance from the ground was sufficient for me, I was out of the wrecked Hurricane like a bullet from a gun! I'd never moved so fast in my life!

When I got out I could not stand up because the stick had come back and whacked my knee and I was somewhat shaken. However, with two men supporting me on each arm

Sergeant E.E. Shepperd of 152 Squadron, pictured at Warmwell with the Squadron mascot, 'Pilot Officer Pooch'. On 18 October 1940, Shepperd was killed when his Spitfire inexplicably crashed near Dorchester.

we made it to HQ and I remember being amazed at the number of people there. As we walked up the field it was a crescent of people all looking to the centre. I only mention this because shaken though I was it left a clear impression that I can remember to this day.

They took me to Ashford Hospital, and later the soldiers returned and invited me to join them for a drink that night. Although I was willing the doctor was having none of it!

213 Squadron had clashed with the Me 109s of JG 77, flying out of Marquise, which were engaged on a *freie hunt*. It is possible that Geoffrey Stevens was shot down by *Gefreiter* Karl Raising of 3/JG 77.

Friday 18 October Dense fog prevented operations on this day.

Saturday 19 October Again there was very little fighting, Fighter only combat successes being a couple of Ju 88s damaged off the 10 Group coastline, and one destroyed by 11 Group. A 92 Squadron Spitfire was destroyed by Me 109s, however, the pilot being killed.

Sunday 20 October Improved weather saw a resumption of the massed fighter and *jabo* formations heading for London. 41 Squadron engaged 5/JG 52 over Kent, Pilot Officer Peter 'Sneezy' Brown destroying an Me 109 which crashed near West Malling. The enemy pilot, *Feldwebel* Bielmaier, baled out and was visited while in custody by his victor, who 'liberated' the vanquished pilot's *schwimmveste* and pilot's qualification badge. Such souvenirs were, of course, highly prized, and the Luftwaffe life jacket was far superior to the Mae West. 'Sneezy' wore his *schwimmveste* on operations, no doubt with great pride.

Monday 21 October Poor weather over south-east England prevented operations, but 10 Group's fighters destroyed a Ju 88 engaged on a *störflug*.

Tuesday 22 October Fog over south-east England once more prevented operations, although Convoy FRUIT was bombed at 16.00 hours.

Wednesday 23 October Again adverse weather prevented daylight operations.

Thursday 24 October Slightly improved weather conditions saw occasional fighter sweeps, but Fighter Command suffered no losses to combat. 421 Flight's Sergeant Don McKay, flying a Hurricane, claimed an Me 109 damaged over Ashford. This machine, of 8/JG 27, limped back across the Channel until crashing in the sea off Cap Gris Nez; the pilot, *Unteroffizier* Ulrich Linke, was reported *vermisst*.

Friday 25 October Improving weather saw the fighters of both sides once more embroiled over south-east England. 603 Squadron lost three Spitfires to III/JG 26, but 66 Squadron jumped 5/JG 26, shooting down *Oberleutnant* Kurt Eichstädt whose Me 109 broke up in mid-air; although thrown clear, the pilot's parachute failed.

Pilot Officer Ludwik Martel: 'Having escaped from Poland, during the Battle of Britain I flew with 603 Squadron from Hornchurch. On that day I was flying

Pilot Officer Ludwik Martel, a Pole serving with 603 Squadron at Hornchurch. Martel destroyed an Me 109 on 5 October 1940, and later scored over the Middle East with the infamous 'Skalski's Flying Circus'.

Spitfire Mk IIA P7350, which was damaged. That aircraft is still flying today, in fact, with the Battle of Britain Memorial Flight!'

Saturday 26 October Another day of high flying incursions. A total of ten enemy aircraft were lost on operations, against Fighter Command's eight.

Sunday 27 October The usual pattern of raids ensued, the airfields being the main target. Four British fighters were lost, including two 229 Squadron Hurricanes caught by Me 109s attacking an He 59 seaplane off the French coast.

Monday 28 October By now it was clear that the unpredictable and generally poor weather was going to increasingly impede offensive air operations over England by day. In the morning, the usual reconnaissance bombers were active. Pilot Officer Franek Surma:

> I was Red Two of the leading section of 257 'Burma' Squadron. We were following 249 Squadron when we were ordered to look for an enemy bomber. While searching in the Ashford area I lost the Squadron in the clouds. When I came out of the cloud I saw seven aircraft of either 257 or 249 Squadron, which I intended to follow, then I saw a twin engined aircraft flying in their direction and below them. I went to investigate and saw the crosses on the wings when I dived down on him, but could not attack head on as it was too late. I zoomed up and made an astern attack. When I was about three hundred yards behind the enemy aircraft, an He 111, the rear gunner opened up from below me. I gave a short burst to un-nerve them. When I was 150–200 yards behind the enemy aircraft's tail, on the port side, I gave a three–four second burst at the cockpit. Passing over him I fired at the starboard engine from about 80 yards. He continued to fly on level and I gave him another burst of about four seconds from about 100 yards at the starboard engine. Seeing no result I followed up the attack with another burst at the starboard engine. I noticed a small explosion from the engine and saw grey smoke pouring out. At this time the aircraft lurched to the right and, as I passed him, a piece of the aircraft flew by my Hurricane, almost hitting it.
>
> We went into cloud at about 4,500 feet. I levelled out, came out of the layer and searched above and below. As I came below cloud I saw that I was directly above the coastline, I looked for the enemy aircraft but did not find it.

The He 111 was credited as 'probably destroyed'. That afternoon the Squadron was in action again and Squadron Leader Stanford Tuck probably destroyed two more Me 109s, the ninth and tenth German aircraft he had claimed as either destroyed, probably destroyed or damaged since taking over command of 257 Squadron. Four Me 109s failed to return from operations over south-east England, but Fighter Command suffered no losses.

Tuesday 29 October The first raid penetrated to London, where bombs were dropped near Charing Cross station. The second threat, however, was met by four RAF fighter squadrons, which attacked in concert, destroying eleven Me 109s. Portsmouth was attacked by twelve Ju 88s of I/LG 1, and the Italian

Regia Aeronautica put in an appearance when fifteen BR 20s, escorted by CR 42 biplanes, bombed Ramsgate. In the afternoon, North Weald was attacked by the *jabos* of II/LG 2, which executed a precision dive-bombing attack, killing nineteen personnel and wounding forty-two. Flight Lieutenant Peter Brothers: 'I was having tea in the Officers' Mess when the raiders struck. We all dived under the table! My car, an open 3-litre Bentley, was parked outside and I was livid to find that a near-miss bomb had filled it with soil, which took forever to clean out.' 257 Squadron Combat Report:

Twelve Hurricanes left North Weald at 1640 hours on 29.10.40 to intercept raiders. Just as the squadron was taking off, the aerodrome was bombed by about 12 Me 109s, which were flying at about 3 to 5,000 feet from the south-east. Another 12 enemy aircraft attacked the aerodrome from the north side.

Just after Yellow Two, Sergeant Girdwood, had left the ground, a bomb exploded by him and threw his aircraft into the air, hitting it with splinters. The Hurricane crashed in flames just outside the north-west perimeter of the aerodrome; Sergeant Girdwood was burned to death.

Red One, Flight Lieutenant Blatchford, chased after an Me 109 which had just bombed the aerodrome. He got behind cloud, hoping to catch the enemy aircraft, but was there too soon. The Me 109 fired at him head on with cannon, making a big hole in the fuselage, piercing the oil tank and damaging the tail unit of his Hurricane. Green Four, Sergeant Nutter, went below the cloud and made a short beam attack on the Me 109 but did not observe results. Red One continued the fight with the other Me 109s.

Red Two, Pilot Officer Surma, saw the bombs falling as he was taxying over the aerodrome. A bomb exploded on his left hand side as his aircraft was running up. The explosion jerked him, but he took off satisfactorily. He noticed four of the enemy aircraft flying over the hangar between 4 and 5,000 feet. He also saw many planes on his right which he took to be Hurricanes.

When he had climbed to about 3,000 feet, he heard an explosion in his cockpit, which filled with white smoke. His plane went into a spiral dive, and he felt that he no longer had control of the steering gear. He opened the perspex. After a moment the Hurricane appeared to come out of its dive and level out, however it soon began to dive again to starboard. After trying to bring it out of the dive for a second time, without result, he attempted to bale out. By this time he had lost height to 1,500 feet. After struggling to get out of the cockpit, he baled out at about 1,000 feet and made a successful parachute descent, landing in a tree top near an inn at Matching. After quickly convincing a Home Guard that he was a Pole and not a German, he was given two whiskies and driven back to the aerodrome. He had lost both of his flying boots on jumping out of the plane, received a black eye but was otherwise unharmed.

Pilot Officer Surma had been shot down by an *experte*, *Hauptmann* Gerhard Schöpfel, *Kommandeur* of III/JG 26. Squadron Leader Bob Stanford Tuck:

Of course I knew Franek Surma very well and there are many stories I could tell you of him. He was a wonderful little chap – but wild! He was also a loyal and thoroughly trusty wingman. Franek and myself were born on the same day – July 1st 1916. On the occasion he was shot down near North Weald, he was wearing a German leather flying jacket, which he had taken from a German bomber shot down in Poland. This did not assist positive identification and a group of Free French soldiers decided that he was an enemy airman and prepared to lynch him on the spot! Fortunately I arrived on the scene in time to stop this nonsense, the French then insisting that we have a drink with them.

The bombing of North Weald, however, could and should have been prevented. Squadron Leader Bader was up with the Duxford Wing, but the 11 Group Controller was unable to communicate with the legless leader because of constant chatter of the R/T between Squadron Leader Bader and Wing Commander Woodhall. Pilot Officer Denis Crowley-Milling: 'Douglas always kept up an incessant stream of chit chat over the R/T, as if he hadn't a care in the world, organising squash and golf games and so on. It was inspiring.'

'Inspiring' young and impressionable pilots like the 'Crow' may have found it, but this behaviour by Bader and Woodhall was totally unprofessional and, on this occasion, had dire consequences. Moreover, had the Duxford Wing been patrolling the north bank of the Thames – where it should have been – the 12 Group fighters would have been perfectly positioned to intercept the raiders and thus prevent North Weald being bombed.

Although the Duxford Wing had not engaged, over Essex, some members of 19 Squadron reported seeing seven Me 109s above; back at Fowlmere, Squadron Leader Lane's pilots waited in vain for the return of Sub-Lieutenant 'Admiral' Blake, who was acting as a weaver behind the Squadron. It was therefore assumed that he had been picked off by the enemy fighters. 19 Squadron ORB: 'He was found near Chelmsford. It is a great loss to the Squadron as he was very well liked by us all as well as a pilot of exceptional ability.'

In all probability, Blake had been shot down by *Leutnant* Hubert Huppertz of III/JG 51. He was the last pilot of the controversial Duxford Wing to die during the Battle of Britain. Pilot Officer Wallace 'Jock' Cunningham:

I recall the 'Admiral' particularly well as he was very popular. I recall that up until he was killed he was Messing Officer at Fowlmere, running his personal account and the Mess account together. I don't think the resulting confusion had been resolved when I was shot down over Holland and captured a year later!

Wednesday 30 October Activity was again reduced. In the morning, 41 and 222 Squadrons bounced III/JG 26 over Kent. *Unteroffizier* Kurt Töpfer's 109 was hit and exploded in mid-air. In the afternoon JG 26 avenged this loss when on a *freie hunt*, Major Galland shooting down 41 Squadron's Sergeant I.A. Garvey, who

After the Battle: pilots of 501 Squadron at Colerne, Wiltshire, in 1941; from left: one of Fighter Command's top scorers in 1940, James 'Ginger' Lacey, a sergeant in 1940 who received the DFM and Bar; Pilot Officer Ken MacKenzie DFC, another ace; Pilot Officers Tony Whitehouse, Bob Dafforn and Vic Ekins. Only Dafforn did not survive the war, being killed in a flying accident in 1943.

was killed. In what was the final day of fighting, the Luftwaffe lost four fighters over England, while Fighter Command lost six.

Thursday 31 October Ironically, on this day of depressingly gloomy and wet weather, which saw no action over south-east England, officialdom decided that the Battle of Britain was over. The selection of this date, however, as with the start date of 10 July, is difficult to understand. The enemy's stated aim was to achieve aerial supremacy as a prelude to a seaborne invasion. On 12 October, the OKW announced that the proposed landings had been postponed, at least until the spring or summer of 1941. That date, therefore, represents a more appropriate date for the defenders to claim their victory. Moreover, the combats between the opposing fighter forces did not stop abruptly on 1 November; far from it, they carried on until February 1941, when winter weather brought the 'season' to a close. Indeed, German historians argue that the Battle for Britain did not conclude until May 1941, which saw both the zenith and end of the night blitz. Shortly afterwards, on 22 June 1941, Hitler invaded the Soviet Union, thereby abandoning plans for an invasion of England. Whichever interpretation is correct, the fact remains that the Battle of Britain was officially fought between 10 July–31 October 1940. Victory, however, was not decisive, as the Luftwaffe

After the battle came the medals: three stalwarts of 609 Squadron arrive at Buckingham Palace to collect their DFCs; from left: Pilot Officer John Curchin (Australian), who destroyed nine enemy aircraft in the Battle of Britain; Flight Lieutenant Frank Howell, seven and another shared, and Pilot Officer David Crook, four destroyed, two shared and two probables. Curchin was killed in action in 1941, Crook in a flying accident in 1944, and Howell in a post war runway accident.

remained very much an effective fighting force, but Fighter Command had staved off the threat of invasion. This meant that Britain remained a base from which the war against Nazi Germany could be prosecuted, and from where ultimately, with essential American help, the liberation of Europe could be launched in 1944. Without the survival of Fighter Command during the Battle of Britain, there would have been no other battles, however, and on this point let there be no mistake.

Altogether, 2,927 aircrew qualified for the coveted Battle of Britain Clasp to the 1939–45 Star. Of that number, 544 lost their lives during those sixteen weeks of high drama in 1940; many others would perish before the war was over. Churchill, as ever, ably captured the spirit and gratitude of the nation in his tribute to the young pilots of Fighter Command: 'Never in the field of human conflict has so much been owed by so many to so Few'.

And so it was that those 2,927 aircrew became known collectively as the Few, their august deeds passing into history and becoming legendary.

EPILOGUE

It is a sad fact that the two real architects of victory in the Battle of Britain, Air Chief Marshal Sir Hugh Dowding and Air Vice-Marshal Keith Park, were shabbily treated afterwards. Air Vice-Marshals Douglas and Leigh-Mallory had gathered top level support for their Big Wing theories, leading to a meeting at the Air Ministry on 17 October 1940, at which our two heroes were called to account for their tactical handling of the Battle of Britain, and to whom it soon appeared obvious that the conference's purpose was to push through the use of wing formations as standard operating procedure. Cutting a long story short, on 25 November, Air Chief Marshal Dowding was replaced as Commander-in-Chief of Fighter Command by Sholto Douglas. Against his wishes, 'Stuffy' was temporarily sent to America on a mission for which he was unsuited. Air Vice-Marshal Park was replaced as commander of 11 Group by Air Vice-Marshal Leigh-Mallory, and sidelined to become head of 23 Group Flying *Training* Command. Pilot Officer Wallace 'Jock' Cunningham:

> Dowding's is the big success story – a strong man who had resisted political pressure to throw away a lot more fighters in France for a battle already lost. He was preserving Fighter Command for the battle to come. Clearly his was the credit for the strategy. He listened, said little, but acted decisively. So treasure the memory of 'Stuffy' Dowding – do not sell him short. His was the victory in directing and sustaining his 'Twelve Legions of Angels'.

On 29 January 1941, Air Vice-Marshal Leigh-Mallory conducted a paper exercise using the circumstances of an actual attack on the Sector Stations of both Kenley and Biggin Hill occurring on 6 September 1940. The new commander of 11 Group completely mismanaged this exercise which had been orchestrated to conclusively prove the great worth of massed fighter formations. The enemy 'raid' was not intercepted while inbound and bombed both target airfields before Leigh-Mallory's fighters were airborne. Further comment on the so-called 'Big Wing Controversy' would be superfluous. Flight Sergeant George 'Grumpy' Unwin:

> At the time I felt that we of Fighter Command had done nothing out of the ordinary. I had been trained for the job and luckily had a lot of experience. I was always most disappointed if the Squadron got into a scrap when I was off duty, and this applied to all the pilots I knew. It was only after the event that I realised how serious defeat would have been, but then, without being big-headed, we never even considered being beaten, it was just not possible in our eyes, this simply was our outlook. As we lost pilots and aircraft, replacements were forthcoming. We were never at much below full strength. Of course the new pilots were inexperienced, but so were the German replacements, and it was clear by the end of 1940 that these pilots had not the stomach for a scrap with a Spitfire.

Pilot Officer Johnnie Johnson: 'The following year we expected the Germans to resume their aerial offensive, but by then we had 20mm cannon and most of our squadrons were equipped with Spitfires. We said, "Let 'em come!" As it was, Hitler attacked Russia, so it was our turn to reach out, go on the offensive, taking the war to the enemy in occupied France.' But that, as they say, is another story.

Today, the survivors are now in their nineties, and many friends whose accounts have been included in this book are sadly now deceased. Annually, on the closest weekend to Battle of Britain Day, 15 September, those survivors still fit and able to travel hold their reunion, followed by a commemorative service at Westminster Abbey. Around these heroes a cult has grown over the last twenty years or so, enthusiasts and aficionados avidly collecting the Few's signatures at air shows and other signings. To them, the Few remain revered. Notably excepting Duxford, now home to the Imperial War Museum's working airfield, the majority of other airfields that the Few once flew from have long since disappeared, either returned to the plough or built over. Today, historians debate the Battle of Britain, historiography revolving around whether Britain's survival really was at stake, or is this merely a myth? Whatever the truth may be, the fact remains, as evidenced by this book, that in 1940 Fighter Command rose to the challenge, and, in Churchill's words, was 'undaunted by insuperable odds'. The spirit and courage of the Few, locked in mortal combat, is not debated, and that fact alone means that the aircrew of Fighter Command who fought – and won – the Battle of Britain will always both command and deserve our respect and gratitude.

It is fitting, I think, to give the last line to one of the Few, Pilot Officer William Walker: 'They were the most exhilarating days, but one lost so many friends who were all so young. It is sad that the best pilots seemed to get killed, whilst the 'hams' like me survived.'

ACKNOWLEDGEMENTS

Over the years I have been privileged to meet or correspond with many of the Few, those connections having largely been facilitated through the late Wing Commander Pat Hancock, formerly secretary of the Battle of Britain Fighter Association and to whom I will always owe an enormous debt. Those whose memories have been included in this book are as follows:

Pilots:
Squadron Leader D.A. Adams
Wing Commander H.R. Allen DFC
Flight Lieutenant M.J. Appleby
Flight Lieutenant L.G. Batt
Wing Commander R.P. Beamont CBE DSO DFC
Squadron Leader R. Beardsley DFC
Squadron Leader V. Bergman DFC
Squadron Leader C.N. Birch AFC
Group Captain J.D. Bisdee OBE DFC
Wing Commander F. Blackadder DSO OBE
Wing Commander G.D.M. Blackwood
Wing Commander R.J.E. Boulding
Wing Commander F.N. Brinsden
Air Commodore P.M. Brothers DSO DFC
Flight Lieutenant B.M. Bush DFC
Squadron Leader L.H. Casson AFC
Flight Lieutenant A.R. Covington
Air Commodore J.B. Coward AFC
Wing Commander D.G.S.R. Cox DFC
Air Marshal Sir Denis Crowley-Milling CBE KCB DSO DFC
Flight Lieutenant W. Cunningham DFC
Air Vice-Marshal R. Deacon-Elliott CB OBE DFC

Group Captain G.L. Denholm DFC
Group Captain P.K. Devitt
Wing Commander R.F.T. Doe DSO DFC
Air Commodore E.M. Donaldson CB CBE DSO
Group Captain Sir Hugh S.L. Dundas CBE DSO DFC DL
Group Captain G.R. Edge DFC OBE
Wing Commander J.F.D. Elkington
Air Commodore H.A. Fenton CBE DSO DFC
Warrant Officer P.H. Fox
Group Captain D. Gillam DSO DFC DL
Squadron Leader E.D. Glaser DFC
Group Captain E. Graham
Flight Lieutenant J.P.B. Greenwood
Flight Lieutenant R.M.D. Hall DFC
Wing Commander N.P.W. Hancock DFC OBE
Wing Commander F.W. Higginson OBE DFC DFM
Group Captain J.H. Hill CBE
Air Vice-Marshal H.A.V. Hogan CB DFC
Squadron Leader J.I. Hutchinson
Wing Commander B.J. Jennings AFC DFM
Air Vice-Marshal J.E. Johnson CBE DSO DFC DL
Flight Lieutenant R.B. Johnson
Flight Lieutenant R.L. Jones
Flight Lieutenant K. Lawrence DFC
Squadron Leader K.N.T. Lee DFC
Group Captain D.S.W. MacDonald DSO DFC
Group Captain G.A.L. Manton DSO DFC
Warrant Officer A.L. Markiewicz
Squadron Leader L.A. Martel VM
Air Commodore E.W. Mermagen CB CBE AFC
Flight Lieutenant D.H. Nichols
Flight Lieutenant R.G. Nutter DFC
Squadron Leader A.K. Ogilvie DFC
Wing Commander P. Olver DFC
Mr J.K. Quill OBE AFC FRAeS
Flight Lieutenant T.G. Pickering
Group Captain H.M. Pinfold
Squadron Leader G.R. Pushman DFC
Flight Lieutenant N.H.D. Ramsay DFC
Air Vice-Marshal F.D.S. Scott-Malden CB DSO DFC
Squadron Leader B.G. Stapleton DFC
Flight Lieutenant G. Stevens
Wing Commander Sir Kenneth Stoddart KCVO KStJ JP LLD

Squadron Leader J. Stokoe DFC
Wing Commander G.L. Sinclair DFC
Wing Commander R.S. Tuck DSO DFC
Wing Commander H.M. Stephen DSO DFC
Wing Commander J.A. Thomson
Group Captain P.T. Townsend CVO DSO DFC
Wing Commander G.C. Unwin DSO DFM
Flight Lieutenant W.L.B. Walker
Flight Lieutenant K.A. Wilkinson
Flight Lieutenant G.H.E. Welford
Squadron Leader G.H.A. Wellum DFC
Air Commodore E.M. Wootten CBE DFC AFC
Group Captain A.R. Wright DFC

Support Staff:
Mr W. Ellams
Mr G. Gwillam
Mr R. Johnson
Mr W. Kirk
Mr J. Milne
Mr R. Morris
Mrs J. Nielsen (née Pepper)
Flight Lieutenant H.E. Morton
Mr F. Roberts

I would also like to thank Lady Bader for writing the foreword, and Keith Delderfield of the Douglas Bader Foundation for arranging it, and Jonathan Reeve, Senior Publisher at Amberley for suggesting that I write this book and for constant encouragement throughout; Dr Alfred Price, an old friend, also has my gratitude for sponsoring my election as a Fellow of the Royal Historical Society. My wife, Karen, together with my son, James, and stepson, George, provided tremendous support and the happy domestic environment necessary to produce such a work in between university semesters!

BIBLIOGRAPHY

Primary unpublished sources:
Correspondence and interviews with the Few, Dilip Sarkar Archive
Taped interview of Group Captain Sir D.R.S. Bader by Dr Alfred Price
Soldier, Sailor, Airman Too, the unpublished memoirs of Group Captain A.B.
   Woodhall.

Pilots' flying log books:
Group Captain Sir D.R.S. Bader (RAF Museum)
Flight Lieutenant D.M. Crook (National Archive)
Air Marshal Sir Denis Crowley-Milling
Wing Commander B.J. Jennings
Squadron Leader B.J.E. Lane (National Archive)
Squadron Leader W.J. Lawson (National Archive)
Sergeant K. Pattison
Squadron Leader P.C. Pinkham
Flight Lieutenant A.F. Vokes
Wing Commander G.C. Unwin

Operations Record Books (all in AIR 27 at the National Archive, Kew):
Fighter squadrons: Nos 1, 17, 19, 56, 74, 151, 213, 222, 238, 242, 257, 266,
   302, 303, 310, 501, 603, 607, 609, 611 & 616.
The Combat Reports for the fighter squadrons listed above were invaluable, all
   in AIR 50 at the National Archive.
Also at the National Archive, the official narratives concerning the Air Defence
   of Great Britain and the Daily Summaries of Air Operations, and reports to
   the War Office, all provided essential factual information.

Published sources:

The Battle of Britain's bibliography is enormous, so the following is selective but represents essential further reading for the interested reader.

Bekker, Cajus, *The Luftwaffe War Diaries*, MacDonald & Co Ltd, 1966

Caldwell, D., *The JG 26 War Diaries: 1939–42*, Grub Street, 1996

Crook, Flt Lt D.M., *Spitfire Pilot*, Faber, 1942

Dunn, B.N., *Big Wing: The Biography of ACM Sir T Leigh-Mallory*, Airlife, 1992

Ellan, Sqn Ldr B.J.E., *Spitfire! The Experiences of a Fighter Pilot*, 1942

Foreman, J., *RAF Fighter Command Victory Claims of World War Two, Part One: 1939–40*, Red Kite, 2003

Franks, N., *RAF Fighter Command Losses of the Second World War, Volume One, Operational Losses: Aircraft & Crews, 1939–41*, Midland Publishing 1997

Jefford, Wg Cdr A., *RAF Squadrons*, Airlife, 1988

Mason, F.K., *Battle Over Britain*, Aston Publications, 1990

Orange, Dr V., *Sir Keith Park*, Methuen, 1984

Overy, R., *The Battle*, Penguin, 2000

Price, Dr A., *The Hardest Day*, MacDonald & Jane's, 1979

Price, Dr A., *Battle of Britain Day: 15 September 1940*, Sidgwick & Jackson, 1990

Probert, Air Cdre H., *High Commanders of the RAF*, HMSO, 1991

Ramsey, W. (ed), *The Battle of Britain: Then & Now, Mk V*, Battle of Britain Prints International, 1989

Ramsey, W. (ed), *The Blitz Then & Now, Volume One*, Battle of Britain Prints International Ltd, 1987

Ramsey, W. (ed), *The Blitz Then & Now, volume two*, Battle of Britain Prints International Ltd, 1988

Sarkar, D., *Spitfire Squadron: No 19 Squadron at War, 1939–41*, Air Research Publications, 1990

Sarkar, D., *The Invisible Thread: A Spitfire's Tale*, Ramrod, 1992

Sarkar, D., *Through Peril to the Stars: RAF Fighter Pilots Who Failed to Return 1939–45*, Ramrod 1993

Sarkar, D., *Angriff Westland: Three Battle of Britain Air Raids Through the Looking Glass*, Ramrod, 1994

Sarkar, D., *A Few of the Many: Air War 1939–45, a Kaleidoscope of Memories*, Ramrod, 1995

Sarkar, D., *Bader's Duxford Fighters: The Big Wing Controversy*, Ramrod, 1997

Sarkar, D., *Missing in Action: Resting in Peace?*, Ramrod, 1998

Sarkar, D., *Spitfire! Courage & Sacrifice*, Victory Books, 2006

Shores, C., & Williams, C., *Aces High*, Grubb Street, 1994

Wakefield, K., *Luftwaffe Encore*, William Kimber & Co Ltd, 1979

Wright, R., *Dowding & the Battle of Britain*, Corgi, 1970

Wynn, K.G., *Men of the Battle of Britain*, Gliddon Books, 1989

INDEX

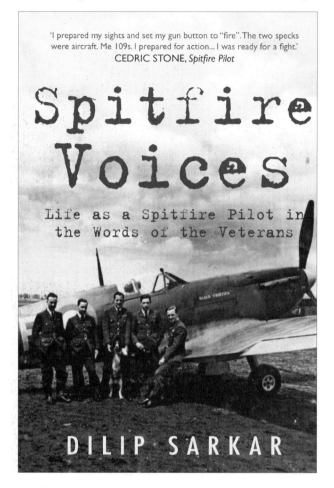

'I prepared my sights and set my gun button to "fire". The two specks
were aircraft. Me 109s. I prepared for action... I was ready for a fight.'
CEDRIC STONE, *Spitfire Pilot*

Spitfire Voices

Life as a Spitfire Pilot in the Words of the Veterans

DILIP SARKAR

*Spitfire fighter pilots tell their extraordinary stories of combat
during the Second World War*

'I prepared my sights and set my gun button to "fire". The two specks were aircraft. Me 109s. I prepared
for action… I was ready for a fight.' CEDRIC STONE, Spitfire Pilot

'There is nothing glamorous in being a fighter pilot. There is nothing glamorous in killing and being
killed. Exciting, very exciting, sometimes too exciting, but definitely not glamorous, not even in a
Spitfire.' MAURICE MACEY, Spitfire Pilot

£20 Hardback
169 Photographs
360 pages
978-1-4456-0042-0

Also available from Amberley Publishing

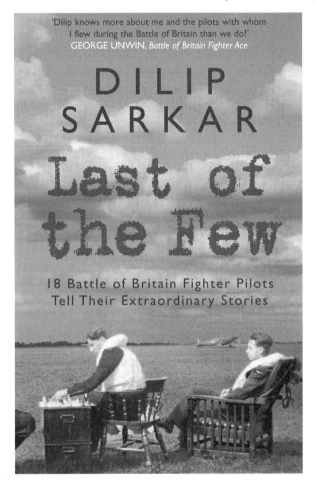

18 Spitfire and Hurricane fighter pilots recount their experiences of combat during the Battle of Britain

'Dilip knows more about me and the pilots with whom I flew during the Battle of Britain than we do! If anyone ever needs to know anything about the RAF during the summer of 1940, don't ask the Few, ask him!' GEORGE 'GRUMPY' UNWIN, Battle of Britain fighter ace

£20 Hardback
60 illustrations
240 pages
978-1-84868-435-5

Available from all good bookshops or to order direct
Please call **01285-760-030**
www.amberley-books.com

Also available from Amberley Publishing

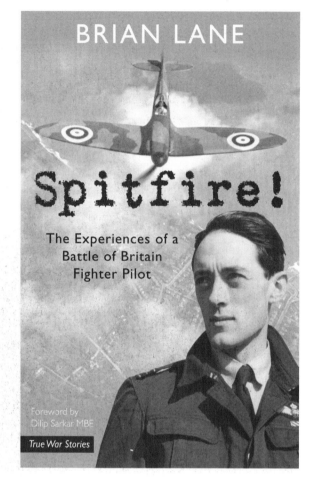

The remarkable Battle of Britain experiences of Spitfire pilot Brian Lane, DFC

'A very fine and vivid account' MAX ARTHUR

Brian Lane was only 23 when he when he wrote his dramatic account of life as a Spitfire pilot during the Battle of Britain in the summer of 1940. Lane was an 'ace' with six enemy 'kills' to his credit and was awarded the DFC for bravery in combat. The text is honest and vibrant, and has the immediacy of a book written close the event, untouched, therefore, by the doubts and debates of later years.

£9.99 Paperback
44 illustrations
192 pages
978-1-84868-354-9

Available from all good bookshops or to order direct
Please call **01285-760-030**
www.amberleybooks.com

Also available from Amberley Publishing

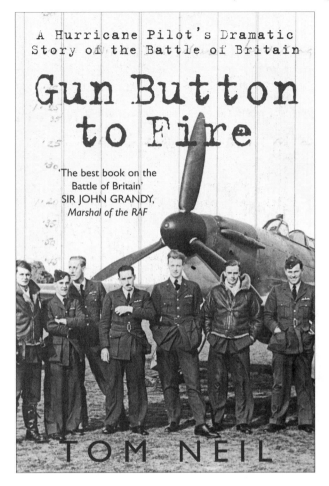

The amazing story of one of the 'Few', fighter ace Tom Neil who shot down 13 enemy aircraft during the Battle of Britain

'A thrilling new book... Tom Neil is one of the last surviving heroes who fought the Luftwaffe'
THE DAILY EXPRESS

'The best book on the Battle of Britain' SIR JOHN GRANDY, Marshal of the RAF

This is a fighter pilot's story of eight memorable months from May to December 1940. By the end of the year he had shot down 13 enemy aircraft, seen many of his friends killed, injured or burned, and was himself a wary and accomplished fighter pilot.

£20 Hardback
120 Photographs (20 colour)
320 pages
978-1-84868-848-3

Available from all good bookshops or to order direct
Please call **01285–760–030**
www.amberleybooks.com

Available from February 2010 from Amberley Publishing

How to fly the legendary fighter plane in combat using the manuals and instructions supplied by the RAF during the Second World War

An amazing array of leaflets, books and manuals were issued by the War Office during the Second World War to aid pilots in flying the Supermarine Spitfire, here for the first time they are collated into a single book with the original 1940s setting. An introduction is supplied by expert aviation historian Dilip Sarkar. Other sections include aircraft recognition, how to act as an RAF officer, bailing out etc.

£9.99 Paperback
40 illustrations
264 pages
978-1-84868-436-2

Available from all good bookshops or to order direct
Please call **01285-760-030**
www.amberleybooks.com